THE SPLENDID RISK

THE SPLENDID RISK

An Existential Approach
to Christian Fulfillment

*

BERNARD I. MULLAHY
of the Congregation of Holy Cross

UNIVERSITY OF NOTRE DAME
NOTRE DAME, INDIANA

The prayer by Michel Quoist on pp. 232-234 is re-printed by permission of Andrews and McMeel, Inc. (Sheed and Ward).

Library of Congress Cataloging in Publication Data

Mullahy, Bernard I.
  The splendid risk.

  1. Spiritual life—Catholic authors.   2. Perfection (Catholic)   3. Catholic Church—Doctrinal and con-troversial works—Catholic authors.   I. Title.
  BX2350.2.M82   248.4   81-40445
  ISBN 0-268-01705-0   AACR2

Manufactured in the United States of America

TO

Theodore M. Hesburgh, C.S.C.
President of the University of Notre Dame

*Without whose initiative and constant encouragement
this book would never have come to be.*

CONTENTS

FOREWORD

I HAVE KNOWN the author of this book, Father Bernard Mullahy, for a long time. We first met at a small house of studies in Rome, when I arrived there in early October of 1937. I was beginning the study of philosophy. He had studied philosophy at Notre Dame and had repeated an additional three years at the Gregorian University in Rome, plus his first two years of theology. That made him five years my senior in the pipeline of preparation for the priesthood in the Congregation of Holy Cross. Over the next two years, when we lived in close companionship in a house of a dozen students, I came to admire him greatly and still do to this day. He had a clear mind and a facility of expression. He was also an exemplary religious who took his profession seriously, but also with good humor and grace. He had the granite of his New England background about him, but plenty of sunshine, too.

I can recall the happy day of his ordination to the priesthood on December 17, 1938. Each morning after that, we left the house together in the chill wintry dawn and walked up Via Sistina where I served his first Masses in a convent of cloistered nuns.

The blitzkrieg of World War II ended my Roman days, and I went to Washington to complete theology. He had finished his course in Rome the previous year and was teaching philosophy at the University of Notre Dame.

Our paths crossed again as we taught together at Notre Dame, but then he was elected to be the Assistant Superior General of the Congregation, which meant returning to Rome. There, curiously, as years passed I began to see him fairly often again, since I was organizing an Ecumenical Institute of Advanced Theological Studies, to be located in Jerusalem at the request of Pope Paul VI. At each of the planning meetings in Rome, at one time eight in a single year, Father Bernie would meet me at the airport and see that I was back there on time for the returning flight. Given the odd hours of arrival and departure, and the mob scene at Da Vinci Airport, that was friendship over, above, and beyond the call of duty. Maybe he was lonely for an American face, but, for my part, I was always glad to see him waiting in that milling crowd at the exit gate.

Throughout those years, we used to discuss classes in spiritual theology he was teaching women religious at Regina Mundi in Rome. I sensed his enthusiasm for the subject and his willingness to readjust his ideas which, like my own, needed a good deal of adjustment during and after Vatican Council II. I welcomed the change and so did he, but it took some doing, given our Roman education which was structured quite differently.

As the years passed by, he eventually returned to South Bend to take up parish and hospital work. It occurred to me one day that he had something quite special to say.

One of the casualties in the new theological development and programs, even in the seminaries, was what we used to call spirituality or the theology of the spiritual life. It, too, needed updating and a new look, but in many seminaries it was simply no longer taught and where it was, there was no bridging the old and the new, the traditional and the modern. I thought of those long conversations we had enjoyed on this theme, the classes he had taught on the subject, both during and after the Council. One day I just asked him, why don't you take time out to write this book? He demurred at first, but then finally agreed.

What he tried to do is not easy. He would be the last to claim complete success, but then few others have even tried. In these times when environmentalists and ecologists are challenging our thinking about the quality and even the survival of human life on our planet, Father Mullahy raises some interesting questions about the task of spiritual ecology to analyze our contemporary spiritual climate—a climate recognized and affirmed by the Second Vatican Council—and to diagnose the style of spirituality it calls for.

He argues that whereas the spiritual climate of former times was dominated by Greek and Roman thought, our contemporary climate has been deeply influenced by other schools of thought, notably existentialism and personalism, and he seeks to see how spirituality can best be understood in the light of the basic attitudes and insights these have to offer. He believes that there is an affinity between many of these basic attitudes and insights and those characteristic of the biblical person, and that this affinity points the way to a spirituality that is at once contemporary and profoundly biblical.

Father Mullahy holds that a paramount characteristic of this spirituality is a holism which refuses both to create dichotomies within the human person and to abstract him from his environment which is a part of him as he is a part of it. By analyzing some of the spiritual implications of the three major components of the human environment—the material universe, the human community, and their historical and temporal existence—he maintains that, like the Hebrews, the people of the modern world can best understand their spiritual life in terms of a communal pilgrimage through time and history toward a future which God has promised. A holistic spirituality, he feels, calls for a holistic fulfillment: the environment of the human person, which is one with him through his pilgrimage, is destined to be one with him in his final transfiguration in the risen Lord. Thus Father Mullahy's interpretation of the spiritual life ends with the Teilhardian vision of all of humankind and all of creation reaching toward the "Omega point," toward "the fullness of Him who fills all in all" (Eph 1:23).

This theme is quite unlike the thin and superficial spiritual pap that fills so many books of spirituality today. It is not pap theology, nor is it the latest fad. For me, it is the rich result of a life of deep reflection and faithful living of the Word. I know Father Bernie well enough, after all these years, to be assured that if only a handful of dedicated Christians come to know and share his vision of the new life in Christ, he will feel amply rewarded for those long years of reflecting and writing, and I, too, will rejoice in having nudged him gently towards the completion of this needed book.

Epiphany, 1981

Rev. Theodore M. Hesburgh, C.S.C.
President, University of Notre Dame

PREFACE

THIS BOOK IS NOT INTENDED for professional theologians and scholars but for educated Christians who wish to deepen their knowledge and appreciation of the Christian life and to respond to the call to Christian fulfillment. It has a modest scope: its aim is not to provide a systematic treatment of even the major questions of spiritual theology but to give to the spiritual life in general, and to the search for Christian fulfillment in particular, a contemporary orientation and perspective.

Many persons have contributed, either directly or indirectly, to the making of this book. I wish to express my appreciation, first of all, for the inspiration and encouragement I received from my former students in spiritual theology, the Sisters at the Pontifical Theological Institute Regina Mundi in Rome and the Sisters of Charity of Mother Teresa of Calcutta at their novitiate at Tor Fiscale on the outskirts of Rome. I am deeply indebted to Father Edward O'Connor, C.S.C., Father Robert Nogosek, C.S.C., Mrs. Joseph Brennan, and Miss Mary Virginia Rosenfeld, who read the manuscript and offered many valuable suggestions. I wish to express my indebtedness also to Miss Claire Nantel, O.M.M.I. for her exceptionally devoted and competent secretarial assistance, as well as to Janet Wright of the Notre Dame University Faculty Steno Pool and to Mrs. Pat Molinaro for their generosity in typing the manuscript.

Biblical references are given in parentheses within the text. With very few exceptions, they refer to the *Jerusalem Bible*, ed. Alexander Jones (Garden City, New York: Doubleday, 1966). In a few instances, when a more literal translation seems desirable, the *Revised Standard Version* (New York: Collins, 1973) is used; these references are noted in parentheses in the text.

References to the Second Vatican Council are also given in parentheses within the text. For the sake of brevity, this Council is often referred to as "the Council," and the titles of some of the documents are often shortened, e.g., the *Church Constitution* for the *Dogmatic Constitution on the Church*, and the *Pastoral Constitution* for the *Pastoral Constitution on the Church in the Modern World*. The articles into which chapters of the documents are divided are indicated by Arabic numerals. Paragraphs within the articles are identified by small letters. When it is evident from the context which document is being referred to, the numerals and letters stand alone; when this is not evident, the documents are identified by the following abbreviations:

C ....*Dogmatic Constitution on the Church*
CL ....*Constitution on the Sacred Liturgy*
CW ....*Pastoral Constitution on the Church in the Modern World*
DR ....*Decree on the Appropriate Renewal of the Religious Life*
E ....*Decree on Ecumenism*
L ....*Decree on the Apostolate of the Laity*
M ....*Decree on the Church's Missionary Activity*
R ....*Dogmatic Constitution on Divine Revelation*
NCR........*Declaration on the Relationship of the Church to Non-Christian Religions*
B ....*Decree on the Bishop's Pastoral Office*
RF ....*Declaration on Religious Freedom*
CE ....*Declaration on Christian Education*

All quotations from the Council documents are from *The Document of Vatican II*, ed. Walter Abbott (New York: Guild Press, 1966).

Part I

SPIRITUAL ECOLOGY

CHAPTER ONE

THE NEW PENTECOST

THE CHRISTIAN LIFE is what the Greeks called "a splendid risk."[1] Faith is not a leap in the dark, but in many ways it is more of a risk than if it were. Faith is a leap into the fullness of light whose incandescence is so blinding that no created intelligence can grasp fully its meaning, much less demonstrate its truth. To live by faith is to live by a strange kind of logic: Christians find life by losing it (Jn 12:24-26; Mt 16:25); get by giving away (Mt 19:27-29); acquire strength through weakness (2 Co 12:9-10); ascend by descending and vice-versa (Lk 14:11; 18:14); achieve wisdom by becoming fools (1 Co 1:17-25); become great by becoming the least of all (Lk 9:48); learn to rule by becoming the servants of all (Mt 20:24-28). Faith proposes a strange set of values; it tells Christians that the most blessed are the poor, the persecuted, and those who mourn (Mt 5:3-10), and it calls them to conform their lives to this belief. Christian discipleship is costly (cf. Lk 9:23; Mt 10:17-18; 24:9), for although all grace is utterly gratuitous, there is no such thing as cheap grace.[2]

The Christian life is a risk because it consists essentially in love, and no love makes a person so vulnerable as does Christian love; the wounds of Christ on the Cross are there to prove it. Christian love calls for a totally altruistic giving of self, not just to a few friends, but to everyone. The Christian is one who cannot ever not love anyone, even the most despicable, even enemies and persecutors (Mt 5:43-44). The Christian commitment is a decision to risk all in love with the hope of gaining all in an unseen and undemonstrable future (cf. Rm 8:24-25).

Both faith and love are risks, but they are splendid risks, for the first is already the beginning of the future beatifying vision of the luminosity of God; and the other is already the beginning of the eternal ecstatic possession of the love that is God. Hope, too, is a splendid thing, for it is "rich with immortality" (Ws 3:4);

and "this hope is not deceptive, because the love of God has been poured into our hearts by the Holy Spirit which has been given us (Rm 5:5).

The Christian life is a risk for many other reasons, one of which is that the people of God are not a sedentary but a pilgrim people whose pilgrimage has traditionally had as its model the long, arduous journey across the desert which brought the first people of God to the promised land. For desert pilgrims, every day, almost every hour is a risk, since there are no clearly defined roads, no familiar signposts along the way. They must live a rootless life, constantly letting go of things discovered along the way. All the supports which provide a sense of security must be left behind. Such a risk is a splendid thing, not only because it eventually leads to a land "flowing with milk and honey" (cf. e.g., Ex 3:8,17), but also because all along the way it calls for great faith and hope in the promises, and even more in the unseen presence of the Lord, who must be the pilgrims' only support and security.

During the years prior to the Second Vatican Council, the idea of risk as something important and even essential in the Christian life had been lost sight of by many. Things had been relatively quiet in the Church for some time. Members of the Church had come to assume that lack of major change should be considered an essential characteristic of a religion based on immutable truths. The traditional principle that the Church must always be in a process of reform and renewal, *ecclesia semper reformanda*, had been almost universally forgotten. Reform was a risky business; the Reformation had made this abundantly clear.

The classical notion of the virtue of prudence had always involved some degree of risk, since, unlike speculative truth, the right way in the concrete, contingent circumstances of human affairs can never be strictly demonstrated. Perfectly prudent decisions can at times lead to tragedy. Yet the classical notion of prudence insists that the prudent person does not hesitate, delay, or postpone decisions unduly, but rather acts with dispatch once just enough (not too much) time has been spent in sizing up and judging the situation.[3] The classical notion of prudence calls the Christian to live in a constant state of mental hospitality for new ideas and new ways of doing things, as befits one who in baptism has been called "to walk in newness of life" (Rm 6:4, R.S.V.). Thus, prudence often demands that Christians be daring and innovative; at times it calls them to take chances, even when the chances involve their own lives.

For many, caution, which is only one of several elements in the traditional concept of prudence, had become almost a substitute for prudence itself.[4] It was all-important to remain "safe." Nothing risked nothing lost. This frame of mind was not universal, of course; but it was all too common, as the strong resistance to change during and after Vatican II and the anguish caused in the lives of so many by the changes of the Council testify.

The traditional notion of the Christian life as essentially a pilgrimage was often pushed far into the background. Christian existence was seen by many as a sedentary life to be lived as if this world were a waiting room for heaven.

The work of the Council may be described in many ways. One way is by saying that it focused attention on "the splendid risk" that is of the essence of the Christian life. John XXIII stated at the beginning that the Council would be a new Pentecost. On the first Pentecost, the coming of the Spirit smashed the locked-door security of the upper room and inspired the apostles to undertake what was probably the greatest risk in all history: twelve quite ordinary men took on the whole world, with all the corruption of paganism, all the power of the Roman Empire, and all the brutal capacity of the world to persecute, torture, and kill. The new Pentecost also smashed a great deal of locked-door security, often not by being innovative, but by being more traditional than the traditionalists who resisted change. Among other things, it revived the traditional notion of the people of God as a pilgrim people, a people called to sacrifice all the seductions of a sedentary life, with its familiar, comforting, and supporting surroundings, and to strike out on an uncharted road where the constant feeling of rootlessness would not be a sign of being lost but of being truly a pilgrim.

The substance of this book has been distilled from lectures in spiritual theology given during the Council and the years immediately following at the Pontifical Institute Regina Mundi in Rome, a school of theology for religious Sisters from virtually all parts of the world. Rome was an exciting place during the Council years. Besides the daily debates in the Council Aula, there were innumerable lectures and discussions going on in various parts of the city, in which many of the most eminent theologians of the world participated, including a number of theologians of other faiths. There was a yeasty feeling in the air. One had the sense of actually experiencing the new Pentecost which John XXIII had predicted. It became increasingly clear that a new climate was in the process of coming to birth in the Church, a climate which would call for a new style of spirituality. It was already possible to delineate the main features of this new style.

Many, if not most of the serious tensions that developed in the Council debates were basically conflicts between "essentialists," who viewed the Church largely in terms of an ideal unchanging essence, an abstract idea, and a juridical structure, and "existentialists," whose vision was that of a concrete community of living persons with evolving social dimensions, existing in time and therefore subject to all its flux and change, moving towards its fulfillment, but in the meantime imperfect and therefore always in need of being renewed and reformed. Actually, the Observers at the Council expressed a hope that its documents would reflect an existential theology, and in his allocation to them on October 17, 1963, Paul VI stated: "Your hope that 'a theology' will be developed 'that is both concrete and historical, centered on salvation history', is one which we gladly support. We believe that this suggestion deserves to be studied in depth." Generally speaking, in the major debates in the Council, the "existentialists" won the day. Clearly, the style of spirituality of the future would be one which would show the influence of an existential theology.

The times called for courses in spiritual theology which would construct a bridge that would help the students cross over from the old to a new style of spiritual life, but in such a way that they would not be tempted to burn the bridge behind them, in the sense of cutting themselves off from the great spiritual heritage of the past. Crossing that bridge would be a risk, but surely a splendid one.

Notes

1. The expression, "splendid risk," has its origin in Plato's *Phaedo*, 114, D. 5.

2. See Dietrich Bonhoeffer, *The Cost of Discipleship*, trans. R. H. Fuller (New York: Macmillan, 1963), especially pt. 1.

3. In "Prudence," *The Four Cardinal Virtues*, trans. Richard and Clara Winston (Notre Dame, In.: University of Notre Dame Press, 1966), Josef Pieper, after showing that the traditional concept of prudence has to a large extent been lost sight of in our times even by ethicists and moralists, gives an excellent analysis of the classical notion of this virtue.

4. See Karl Rahner, *The Dynamic Element in the Church*, trans. W. J. O'Hara (New York: Herder and Herder, 1964), p. 38.

CHAPTER TWO

ENVIRONMENT

Is THERE SUCH A THING as spiritual ecology? We have Christ's word for it. He rebuked his contemporaries because, though astute in matters concerning their physical climate, they were blind to the fact that his coming had created a new spiritual environment. They could read the face of the sky: redness in the evening was a sign of fine weather, redness in the morning a sign of bad weather; a west wind coming in from the Mediterranean meant rainy weather, while a sirocco blowing across the desert from the south meant a wilting heat wave. But they could not read "the signs of the times" (Mt 16:3; Lk 12:54-56). Spiritual ecology is the study of the signs of the times in so far as they relate to the spiritual life.

As a plant that flourishes in one climate will wither in another, so styles of spirituality that flourish in one cultural, social, and theological environment may lose their viability if this environment undergoes notable alteration. The history of spirituality is not just a history of holy men and women, of their writings, of the ideas and models of the spiritual life they have passed on to posterity, of the movements they have inspired and the schools of spirituality they have founded. It is not just a record of the evolution of theological reflection on the Christian life. It is also a history of various styles of spiritual life as they have existed in different times and places, styles that have evolved and dissolved as cultural, social, and theological environments have changed. It is, moreover, a history of spiritual movements and groups, including some religious orders, that have passed out of existence because they did not adapt to a changing spiritual climate.

The spiritual life is an existential reality. Precisely because it is a life, it cannot be contained within abstract doctrine. It is a personal existence, a lived experience that takes place in a changing world and in the process of time and history, as well as in a great variety of cultures. For example, how much chance would the spiritual style characteristic of nineteenth century France have of surviving in our present spiritual climate? In point of fact, it has not survived, even though in its time it produced many holy men and women, several canonized saints, and a remarkable number of founders and foundresses of religious congregations.

Vatican II created a difficult problem for religious institutes: it directed them, on the one hand, to return to the original charism of their founders or foundresses, and, on the other, to adapt to the changed conditions of the times (DR 2). This calls for a delicate discernment between charism and style.

Spiritual theology must take spiritual ecology into account. This is especially true in our times when a radically new spiritual climate has evolved and is still in the process of evolving.

I am taking "style" here in the sense in which we commonly speak of a "lifestyle." I am not suggesting that all spiritual lifestyles in a particular spiritual environment are homogenous. A person's life of love with God is too personal; saints are too original; and the workings of the Spirit are too surprising. But, generally speaking, the spiritual lifestyles in a particular spiritual climate manifest certain specific characteristics. Spiritual ecology must try to account for these characteristics by reading the signs of the times accurately and interpreting them with discernment, and, at the same time, by identifying and analyzing the manifold influences, cultural, historical, theological, and sociological, from whose confluence the spiritual environment has emerged. Spiritual ecology must also look beyond these influences to something deeper. It must realize that although "physical environment" is usually taken merely as an analogue of "spiritual environment," at their deepest levels the two are actually very closely related.

The factors entering into our physical environment are manifold, but they can all be reduced to three major components. First, the influence of the physical world around us goes far deeper than the question of whether water and air are polluted or clean, whether natural resources are being squandered or conserved, or whether the climate is tropical or nordic. We are body-persons; our material bodies are a part of our very essence. At the same time, the human body is also a part of the physical universe. The material world is not completely external to us; we ourselves are part of it, and in many profound and subtle ways we are caught up in its very being. For this reason the physical universe has more profound and far-reaching influences on our lives than polluted air or frigid temperatures.

Second, we live upon a peopled earth; we are members of the human family. Other human lives are constantly entering into ours and leaving an impact upon us. Other human beings weave a gigantic web of interrelationships in which we are inextricably caught. All this has a profound influence on our lives, quite apart from such problems as a population explosion or nuclear proliferation.

Third, we are beings in history. The whole universe, and we with it, are caught up in a ceaseless flow of time. We are constantly being hurtled forward into the future, and our fleeting existence makes us continually subject to growth and decline, to change and to chance. Our time-conditioned universe has more profound and all-pervasive influences upon our very existence than the fact that the cyclic movement of time brings a variety of seasons into our lives: times of warmth and times of chill, times of monsoon and times of drought. Thus thé three most basic components of our physical environment are other persons, the material world, and time.

These same components are also, though in quite a different way, the fundamental determinants of our spiritual environment. The human person is a being-with-others. The Christian person is called to be a being-for-others. That no man is an island, that it is impossible to be an authentic human person without a community plays an essential role in determining a spiritual climate. How we relate to others, how we succeed or fail in developing warm, close interpersonal relationships, and what kind of posture we have with regard to community will determine more than anything else our spiritual style. Psychologists tell us that this is the major factor in the development of the human personality. It is also the major factor in the development of the Christian person, for Christ made relations with others the distinguishing sign by which his followers were to be recognized (Jn 13:35).

The human person is essentially a being-in-the-world. Spiritual style is determined by how we relate to our own bodies and to the physical universe, by whether we try to live an angelic or an incarnational spiritual life, by whether we realize that we cannot hope to live an authentic other-worldly life except by living a this-worldly life, that we cannot be truly spiritual except by recognizing the essential role that matter plays in Christian spirituality.

Because the human person is also a being-in-history, time has a profound role to play in our spiritual climate. The spiritual style of one who, like a gnostic, tries to withdraw from time into some kind of static, timeless world will be vastly different from that of one who realizes that time and history play an essential part in the spiritual life, both because human life and the world are essentially time-conditioned and because Christ became incarnate, not only in the three dimensions of our flesh, but also in the fourth dimension of our time.

The thesis of this book is that we are going through one of the most profound cultural revolutions in history, that from this deep cultural change a new spiritual climate is emerging, and that the new spiritual styles this climate calls for are determined basically by the way in which other persons, the material world, and time enter into the spiritual life. Making the human environment an essential part of the spiritual life is a risk. A long tradition of spiritual literature has emphasized how great a risk it is and has warned against its dangers. Many spiritual writers have insisted on the seductiveness of the world, on the necessity of "flight from the world," *fuga mundi*, in order to strive for perfection, and on the impossibility of being a true Christian as long as one is "worldly." They have called attention to the fact that time is fleeting, that all the things of time are ephemeral and therefore of little value in comparison with the things of eternity. They have, of course, stressed the importance of love of neighbor and of charity for all; at the same time, they have warned against the dangers of human friendship, and have pointed out how easily involvement with others can rob one of the solitude necessary for growth in prayer and union with God. The aim of this book is not to make light of this risk, but to show how splendid a risk it is and why it must be taken in order to achieve a genuine Christian life.

*   *   *

When questions about changes in spiritual climate are raised today one spontaneously thinks of the Council, which is rather generally assumed to be the watershed from which has come all that is new and renewed in the Church and the spiritual life. In many ways it is indeed such a watershed; but it could be argued that the Council was more an effect than a cause in the evolution of the new spiritual environment in which we now live.

The Council was not as innovative as many suppose; for, apart from the fact that much of what seemed new and even startling was in reality a return to older and more authentic traditions of the Church, the Council was, for the most part, responding to the demands of a new spiritual climate that was already present. Without the presence of this new environment, Vatican II would never have been possible.

The Council was responding first of all to a number of vigorous movements that had begun to stir within the Church about thirty or forty years before: the liturgical movement; the new ferment in theological studies after a long period of stagnation; the Catholic Action movement, which was intimately associated with the growing consciousness of the importance of the role of the laity in the Church and of the independence and inherent value of secular realities; the new interest and the new approaches in biblical studies; the growing awareness of the social dimensions of the Christian life, and many others. But to an even greater degree the Council was responding to influences outside the Church; and here, far from being innovative, the work of the Council might more accurately be described as an almost-too-late attempt to catch up with a culture, a society, and a world that had long since declared their independence from the tutelage of the Church, and in going their own free way were in the process of passing the Church by. The last traces of what was once Christendom had vanished, except in the memories of a handful of churchmen who looked back wistfully to what was once the power and the glory of the Church. Secularization, probably the central and most significant element, along with the developments of science and technology, in the new emerging culture, had been running at high tide for a long time. The process of change in every area of human life had been continually gathering greater momentum and had already given clear indications that one of the few constants in the new culture would be constant change. The world was continually becoming more hominized, even though not always more humanized. Bonhoeffer had already declared that at long last man and his world had come of age. People were talking a strange language about "the death of God" and "religionless Christianity," about "worldly holiness" and "secular worship," and even about "Christian atheism." Christians were living in a post-religious era, in a state of diaspora, and in a society which was constantly becoming more pluralistic because there was no longer any common ground of a generally accepted metaphysic. Given all of these developments, the Church would probably have risked becoming an increasingly irrelevant subculture, had it not directed its attention toward the modern world.

The Council was indeed innovative if we compare its documents with previous Church documents. Much of its innovation resulted from the inspired suggestion of Cardinal Suenens, later adopted by the Council, that the Church be studied from two different perspectives: *ad intra* and *ad extra*. The first meant a reflection upon the Church in its own inner mystery, and this eventually resulted in the *Dogmatic Constitution on the Church*. The second meant a study of the Church in relation to the world around it, or, in other words, in relation to its environment, and this study eventually produced the *Pastoral Constitution on the Church in the Modern World*. This latter document turned out to be the most innovative of all the Council documents; indeed, the very attempt to study the Church in relation to its environment was something strikingly new in the history of ecclesiology.

This study made it evident that the Church exists in a world that is going through such a profound cultural revolution "that we can speak of a new age in human history" (54a; cf. 58a), an age in which "the human race has passed from a rather static concept of reality to a more dynamic, evolutionary one" (5d). This revolution "has repercussions on man's religious life" (4b).

In attempting to come to grips with the environment of the Church, the Council enunciated a principle which is one of the most significant statements in all the Council documents; it might even be argued that, from a certain point of view, it was the most momentous statement of the Council: "the Church has always had the duty of scrutinizing the signs of the times and of interpreting them in the light of the gospel" (4a; cf. 11). The "signs of the times" was a rich and significant biblical theme, but it had not been a clearly articulated and operative principle in theology or in the Church before the time of John XXIII. It was first expressed in *Humanae Salutis*, the bull of convocation of the Council, promulgated on December 21, 1961; but the preparatory commissions, still dominated by the abstract, timeless, and juridical theology of the post-Tridentine era, rather than the theology of a pilgrim Church conscious of its historicity, did not seem to attach any special importance to it. It was used again by John in his encyclical, *Pacem in Terris*, published on April 11, 1963, and was taken over by Pope Paul in his first encyclical, *Ecclesiam Suam*, promulgated on August 6, 1964.

The principle enunciated by the Council regarding the signs of the times has many important implications for theology in general, and for spiritual theology in particular.[1] It introduces something relatively new in theological methodology. It suggests that theology can use with profit an inductive method, and that it should use this method whenever it is reflecting on the incarnation, the Church, or the human person and the world. In a sense, this principle has made our concrete, worldly, societal, temporal, and historical existence a theological source, along with Scripture and Tradition, though not, of course, on the same level as they. Theology must scrutinize historical events, not merely to find facts which illustrate its doctrine, but as the object of theological reflection.

* * *

In the *Pastoral Constitution*, the longest conciliar document by far, the Council examines the nature of culture in general, the salient characteristics of the culture of our times, and many of its most significant problems. In studying this document, it is not difficult to discern three major themes around which cluster, either directly or indirectly, most of the problems discussed. They deal with the three most fundamental components of our environment, which, as I have suggested, determine more than anything else our spiritual climate.

In the Preface to the *Constitution*, the Council unites these three themes into one:

> The Council focuses its attention on the world of men, the whole *human family* along with the sum of those realities in the midst of which that family lives. It gazes upon that *world* which is the theater of man's *history*, and carries the marks of his energies, his tragedies, and his triumphs . . . . (2b)[2]

At the same time, this *Constitution* leaves no doubt that the most important of the three components of our environment is the human family. The document begins by stating that "the joys and the hopes, the griefs and the anxieties of the men of this age, especially those who are poor or in any way afflicted, these too are the joys and hopes, the griefs and anxieties of the followers of Christ," and that "nothing genuinely human fails to raise an echo in their hearts." Because the community of believers is a "community composed of men," it "realizes that it is truly and intimately linked with mankind and its history" (1).

The *Church Constitution*, at the beginning of its second chapter which deals with the Church as the people of God, enunciates a principle of great significance: "It has pleased God . . . to make men holy and save them not merely as individuals without any mutual bonds, but by making them into a single people . . ." (9a;

cf. also e.g., 1b; 4c; 7a; 13a,b). The Council considered this principle so important that it reiterated it twice in other documents.
It is repeated in the *Decree on the Missionary Activity of the
Church* (2c). The *Pastoral Constitution* reiterated it again ver-
batim, adding to it the following statement: "God did not create
man for life in isolation, but for the formation of social unity.
. . . So from the beginning of salvation history he has chosen
men not just as individuals but as members of a certain community" (32a). The entire second chapter is devoted to a discussion of
"The Community of Mankind" (cf. e.g., 1; 2b; 23a; 24a,c; 26a;
42c,d).

Clearly, the Council looked upon the human person, the Christian, and indeed the whole Church as a being-with-others, and a
being-for-others. Union with others was seen not simply in terms
of the communion which is the Church, but also as the reaching
out of that communion to other Christians, to non-Christians, and
to the whole of humanity. The Church declared itself ready to
enter into dialogue with all persons, even atheists, and willing to
learn from them; it expressed its ardent desire to be united with
all persons, and to serve them humbly, whatever their religious
persuasion might be (cf. e.g., C 15-16; CW 21g; 43i; 92a,c,d; E 1;
NCR 1; M 22a,c).

This open posture of the Church vis-a-vis the world is something relatively new in its history. As Joseph Ratzinger has pointed out, there had previously been only two kinds of doctrinal pro-
nouncements: "the creed of obligation and the anathema of negation." The *Pastoral Constitution* was a new kind of doctrinal pro-
nouncement which showed that the Church was moving away
from a posture of authoritative imperatives and returning to a
missionary posture.[3] Edward Schillebeeckx says much the same
thing when he points out that the Church of the Middle Ages was
a Church of monologue; it continually talked to the world, without listening to what the world and history might have to say.
During the Reformation and the Counter-Reformation there were
two monologues going on. Now the Church showed that it was
willing to listen and anxious to enter into a dialogue. "What is
new," writes Schillebeeckx, "is that the Church as a whole, including the Church as a hierarchy, has accepted dialogue as a
principle and as a *basic attitude*."[4]

Thus, the Council called earnestly for, and in a measure
brought about, an open Church. In an open Church the spiritual
life must necessarily be open. The Church has put itself in the
position of loving, listening, and learning. Contemporary spiri-

tuality must do the same. It must be willing to be enriched, and also, when necessary, to be corrected by other branches of Christianity, by other great religions, and by other cultures.

We have learned, for example, that other Christian denominations have, over the years, succeeded better than Catholics in keeping alive among their members a knowledge and love of Holy Scripture (cf. E 21a-b). We have also discovered that some Protestant denominations, as well as the Oriental Churches, have often given to the Holy Spirit a greater role in the Christian life than we have. Some Eastern religions have rightly criticized our prayer life as being too cerebral. The Eastern religions have, among other things, emphasized for us the wholeness of the spiritual person by stressing the role of the body in prayer. Whereas the disincarnate quality of much of our spirituality has tended to dull our senses, some of the Eastern religions are teaching us something that the biblical person already knew: the importance of sensitized perception to pick up and listen to the messages of God's revelation and love in the sensible realities around us. The *Decree on the Missionary Activity of the Church* speaks of the Church, and especially the young local Churches, taking "to themselves in wonderful exchange all the riches of the nations which were given to Christ as an inheritance (cf. Ps 2:8)." After warning against "every appearance of syncretism and of false particularism," the *Decree* states that "the Christian life can be accommodated to the genius and dispositions of each culture" (22a,c).

An open spirituality necessarily leads to a pluralistic spirituality. The time of spiritual colonianism, like every form of colonianism, has passed away. The time is past when the missionaries of the West could impose upon the peoples of Asia and Africa their own particular style of spirituality. Christian spirituality is, of course, fundamentally one; but, as I have already suggested, it can be lived and expressed in a variety of styles. This is true particularly of liturgy and prayer in general. The *Constitution on the Sacred Liturgy* explicitly recognized this fact and provided flexible norms for adapting the liturgy to various cultures (37-40).

*   *   *

In the Council the Church also became more fully conscious of itself as a being-in-the-world. The *Church Constitution* states that "the faithful . . . must learn the deepest meaning and value of all creation, and how to relate it to the praise of God" (36c). It calls attention to the duty of Christian laborers to "prepare the field of the world for the seed of the Word of God" (36e), to "raise all of society and even creation itself to a better mode of existence" (41h), and to show by "their earthly activities the love with which God has loved the world" (41j). It points to the destiny of the human body to share in the riches of the divine life (48g) and to the Christian destiny of the world to share in the freedom of the children of God by being transfigured in the glory of the resurrection (9d; 48a,c,d).

The *Pastoral Constitution* develops more fully and stresses more decisively the oneness of the human person with what we call the world (cf. e.g., 3b; 14a,b). The first section of chapter 4 of the first part of this document (40) explores the ways in which the Church and the world are mutually related. It states "that the earthly and the heavenly city penetrate each other" (d); it expresses the conviction of the Church that "she can contribute greatly toward making the family of man and its history more human" (e) and "that she can be abundantly and variously helped by the world in the matter of preparing the ground for the gospel" (f); and it proposes to set forth the "principles for the proper fostering of the mutual exchange and assistance in concerns which are in some way common to the Church and the world" (f). The document then proceeds to develop these principles at some length (41-45).

The *Pastoral Constitution* lays particular stress on the importance of human labor in the transformation of the physical universe, especially by means of science and technology (cf. e.g., 34c; 38c; 43a-c; 53). It looks forward ardently to the new earth and the new heaven when we shall find again "all the good fruits of our nature and enterprise . . . freed of stain, burnished and transfigured," when "Christ hands over to the Father a kingdom eternal and universal" (39e). Clearly, in the Council the Church opened itself wide to all that is positive in the world.

It is generally recognized that the writings of Teilhard de Chardin had an important influence on the *Pastoral Constitution on the Church in the ModernWorld* (cf. e.g., 39; 43; 57; 91).[5] And it is a measure of the profound change that had occurred in the Church that Teilhard, who died just seven years before the opening of the Council, and who had been forbidden by Rome to publish any of his writings during his lifetime, could have exercized this influence in the Council. The Church finally realized the importance of what Teilhard had been doing all his life: carrying on a continual dialogue with the world.

One might say that after seeing its task over the centuries as a mission to convert the world to the Church, the Church now suddenly recognized that in a sense, a very real sense, it needed to be converted to the world in order to be true to its own nature. This called for a profound act of humility. It openly and decisively declared that it had much to learn from the world and historical events, in spite of the impassioned oratory in the Council Aula insisting that it was below the dignity of the Church to get down on its knees before the world. The age of triumphalism had ended— at least in principle.

The Council also recognized that we by our very nature, and in a very special way the Church by its nature, are profoundly related to time and history. Without this profound relationship, all that the *Church Constitution* teaches about the church as a pilgrim people and about its eschatological nature would make no sense at all. The *Pastoral Constitution*, after pointing out the essential role played by time and history in contemporary culture (cf. 5d; 53c,d; 54a; 55a), had much to say about their role in the life of the Church. Christ "entered the world's history as a perfect man, taking the history up into Himself and summarizing it" (38a). In him "can be found the key . . . the goal of all human history" (10g), "the focal point of the longings of history and of civilization, the center of the human race, the joy of every heart, and the answer to all its yearnings" (45b; cf. e.g., 4a; M 8c; 9b).

*   *   *

If, as I have suggested, the Council was more a response to, than the source of the environment in which the spiritual life of our times must live and grow, the question spontaneously arises about identifying the real source of this environment. It would be an extremely complex and difficult task to try to analyze all the historical, philosophical, sociological, theological, and cultural aspects of the spiritual climate in which we now live and work and reach out for God. But perhaps a few pertinent things can be said.

Western civilization, and hence the original spiritual culture of the Church, emerged to a large extent from the confluence of Roman and Greek cultures. Greek thought made it possible for the Church to achieve a highly developed Christian theology and philosophy. At the same time, the Church was able to base its culture solidly upon the Roman tradition of law and institution. The positive contributions of both of these sources over the centuries have been enormous. But there developed, especially in the post-Tridentine era, a decadent kind of scholastic philosophy and theology which seemed in many ways to lose touch with concrete reality. During this same era the classical Roman concept of law and institution tended at times to degenerate into an excessive juridicism, the kind of juridicism which evoked strong reaction in the Council.

It is ironical that law and institution which, in the classical Roman tradition, was first developed to promote the human person, should in the course of time come to stand for something which, even when it did not sacrifice human personal values, not infrequently failed to take them sufficiently into account. Like juridicism, decadent scholasticism was in many ways a caricature of its primary sources, such as Aristotle, who was not only a philosopher but also a natural scientist, intensely interested in all the concrete phenomena of nature, and Thomas Aquinas, who strongly emphasized the importance of experiential knowledge. Our present culture in general, and our spiritual culture in particular, give low priority to the legal and the institutional and high priority to the human and the personal; their interest is concentrated not on the abstract but on the concrete, not on the disincarnate, the static, and the timeless but on the dynamic; they view reality not so much in terms of dichotomies and categories as in terms of relations and wholeness.

One way of trying to understand our contemporary spiritual climate is by reflecting on the several philosophical and theological schools which have a marked affinity with the temper of our times, and which have, in a variety of ways, influenced its development. The most important of these is existentialism, which has been defined by John Macquarrie as "the type of philosophy which concerns itself with human existence and which tries to understand this existence out of the concrete experience, which, as existents, we all have."[6] Existentialism views reality and especially human beings in their concrete, holistic existence, rather than in terms of abstract essences or categories. Its central problem is: how does a person exist as a fully authentic human being? It views people in both their intrinsic and their extrinsic wholeness. By intrinsic wholeness I mean the oneness of body and soul. Here as elsewhere the existentialist is interested in the oneness of concrete realities and not in the dichotomies of abstract thought, and rejects the exaggerated dualism of body and soul which in the past often strongly influenced Christian spirituality.

The extrinsic wholeness of human beings consists in their oneness with their environment. We do not live in a vacuum; we live in a concrete environment of which we are a part, as it is a part of us. Existentialists insist that the person is no longer real if abstracted from or lifted out of the whole matrix that goes to make up the totality of human life. The real person is all of a piece with a fabric that is made up of tightly interwoven relationships. In particular, existentialism emphasizes seeing people in terms of the three relations that are a part of their very being: relatedness to other persons, to the concrete world, and to the time in which they live and the historical evolutionary process in which they grow and become. Though I have used the term "extrinsic wholeness" to distinguish it from the intrinsic wholeness which excludes any exaggerated dualism, in reality these relationships are not extrinsic to us; they are a part of our very being. To abstract ourselves from them is like taking a statement out of the context from which it gets its true and full meaning. To emphasize the fact that these relations are a part of our inner being, existentialists have "hyphenated" the person with other persons in community, with the world, and with history and time. We are beings-with-others, or beings-in-community; beings-in-the-world; beings-in-time and beings-in-history.

The climate of our times has also been influenced by the philosophy of personalism, which developed as a reaction to philosophies, such as materialism and idealism, that did not take the reality and the value of the human person sufficiently into account. Its special focus is the dignity and the liberty we all share as persons, and it is opposed to any kind of juridicism which is willing to sacrifice the person at the altar of law and institution.

As Emmanuel Mounier has pointed out, personalism must be considered an offshoot of existentialism, and actually a number of philosophers, like Mounier himself, Gabriel Marcel, and Martin Buber, are included in both schools. One reason why existentialism and personalism are intimately related and in many ways overlap is that for the existentialists only persons really exist; things, as Heidegger puts it, simply are.

In their *Concise Theological Dictionary*, Rahner and Vorgrimler, before discussing the traditional scholastic definition of person, give an existential definition, and point out that this type of definition is of great importance in contemporary theology: "Man as such, of course, is a personal being who can only act in a concrete body, in history here and now, in dialogue with another Thou, constantly exposed with his fellows to painful experience of the world through his own deeds."[7] It is clear that in this contemporary notion the triple existential hyphenation with the environment enters into the very definition of the human person.

Another philosophical and theological school which has a certain affinity with the spiritual climate of our times is known as "process thought." Like personalism and existentialism, it covers a rather wide spectrum of philosophical and theological tendencies, and in some cases overlaps the other two. Its basic principle is that reality and life are not fixed and static, but fluid, and therefore in a constant process of becoming. The human person is seen as a part of a vast evolutionary process, of a world that is constantly moving, changing, and developing. It views reality not so much in terms of things as in terms of events. All reality, in its innermost being, is dynamism and novelty. Process thought stresses the historicity of the human person and of the human community in which every moment is the past-come-alive-in-the present. Some theologians consider process thought to be typical of the biblical person, for whom history and pilgrimage played such an important role. In this book I am interested in process thought, not so much in the strict sense, in which it is limited to the thought of Alfred North Whitehead and the movement that has derived from him, but in the broad sense, which includes other thinkers, and especially Pierre Teilhard de Chardin, who have stressed the fact that cosmic reality is in a constant state of process, that the universe and the human beings in it are caught up in the mobility of time and history, and that pilgrimage is essential to the human person and to the human community, especially the Christian person and the Christian community.

It should perhaps be made clear here that my purpose is not to write a book of spiritual theology such as might be composed by a professional existentialist, personalist, or process theologian. Rather, it is to try to cull from these schools of thought certain insights and orientations which I believe throw light on the spiritual climate of our times, and to try to develop them in such a way that some of the more important features of the spiritual style which this climate calls for will be brought into clearer focus.

In the next chapter I shall be speaking of "the existential Christian," "the contemporary spiritual person." Such a person does not exist. He is the personification of a combination of some of the major cultural influences and trends in contemporary spirituality. Though he may often appear in a favorable light, there is no intention to suggest that anyone who does not possess the same combination of spiritual qualities (and this means all of us in some degree) is necessarily less holy.

The phenomenological description of some of the predominant characteristics of contemporary spirituality will serve several purposes. It will provide a concrete image and model of what I have in mind in speaking of spiritual style, and in particular of the kind of spiritual style that is responsive to the signs of our times. But more importantly, it will, I hope, prove a stimulus for the reader in the sense of raising many more questions and issues than it answers—questions and issues which will be addressed in subsequent chapters.

When I suggest that the contemporary spiritual person is an existentialist, a personalist, and a process thinker, I do not mean that he is any of these in the sense of his being, in any formal or conscious way, a philosopher or a theologian, but simply that his habitual way of thinking and his attitudes are similar to those of the representatives of these schools of thought. One of the main reasons why existentialism has had a pervasive influence in our times is that it expresses itself not only in formal philosophical writings but also in a great number and variety of literary works, in novels, plays, short stories, journals, and autobiographical essays. One thinks of the immensely popular works of writers such as Sartre, Camus, Kafka, Dostoevsky, Hemingway, and a host of others. In one way or another, directly or indirectly, they have influenced the thinking of the contemporary spiritual person. What the Council says about negative influences applies equally to positive influences: "In numerous places these views are voiced not only in the teachings of philosophers, but on every side they influence literature, the arts, the interpretation of the humanities and of history . . ." (CW 7d).

In maintaining that the spiritual life is conditioned by the cultural climate in which it exists, I have no intention of laying down a rigid law to which God is forced to conform. God conforms only to the law of his utterly gratuitous love. He can touch those whom he loves in ways that do not fit in with their cultural environment. Indeed, he can make sport of human conditions and human expectations by giving those who open themselves to him personal contact and union with himself regardless of environment and background.

In every new spiritual culture there is the temptation, sometimes subconscious, to look with some degree of disdain on the culture of the past. This is particularly true in our rapidly changing, future-oriented times, when the past seems synonymous with the obsolete. We would be well advised to resist such a temptation and to be modest in appraising our own styles of spirituality. From a certain point of view, the old spirituality was more experiential (and in this sense more existential) than the new. The old spiritual culture produced many great saints; and they in turn, to a very significant degree, produced the old spiritual culture through the multiple influences they had on it by the example of their lives, by their teachings and writings, by the movements they initiated, and in a great variety of other indefinable ways. The new spirituality is too new to have produced a great harvest of saints and to have been both enriched and authenticated by their lives. A test of the authenticity of a spiritual *aggiornamento* is its capacity to assimilate and to integrate in the new all that is best in the heritage of Christian wisdom in the spirituality of the past. Every new spiritual culture must have a radical continuity and a living relation with the past, along with the discontinuity that makes it new. It will remain shallow and rootless unless it can make its own the most authentic spiritual riches of the past.

Notes

1. M.-D. Chenu has written two articles which analyze and assess the theological implications of this principle: "Les signes des temps—réflexion théologique," *L'Église dans le monde de ce temps* (Paris: Les Éditions du Cerf, 1967), LXV, tome 2, 205-225; and "Les signes des temps," *Nouvelle revue théologique,* LXXXVII (January 1965), 29-39. See also Peter Hebblethwaite's "The Signs of the Times," *The Way Supplement,* no. 13 (Summer 1971), 26-35; and an article with the same title by M. C. Vanhengel and J. Peters, *Concilium XXV, Understanding the Signs of the Times,* ed. Franz Böckle (New York: Paulist Press, 1967), 143-152.

2. Italics mine.

3. *Theological Highlights of Vatican II,* trans. Werner Barzel (New York: Paulist Press, 1966), pp. 156-157.

4. *God the Future of Man,* trans. N. D. Smith (New York: Sheed and Ward, 1968), p. 120; see also pp. 65-66.

5. George Lindbeck, a Lutheran Observer at the Council, writing about the theological discussions that went on in Rome while the Council was in session, states: "It is symptomatic that in these no recent thinker was discussed more frequently and more favorably than Teilhard de Chardin." *The Future of Roman Catholic Theology* (Philadelphia: Fortress Press, 1970), pp. 11-12.

6. *Studies in Christian Existentialism* (London: SCM Press, 1965), pp. 115-116.

7. Ed. Cornelius Ernst, trans. Richard Strachan (New York: Herder and Herder, 1965), p. 351.

Bibliography

The primary sources for this chapter are the documents of the Council, particularly the *Constitution on the Church* and the *Pastoral Constitution on the Church in the Modern World.* Among the many commentaries on these documents, two works seem to me to be by far the best. The first is the *Commentary on the Documents of Vatican II*, ed. Herbert Vorgrimler, 5 vols. (New York: Herder and Herder). Volume 1 (1967) contains studies of various aspects of the *Church Constitution* by highly qualified scholars. The whole of volume 5 (1969) is made up of excellent articles on the *Pastoral Constitution*. The other commentary, in many ways an even more impressive work, is a part of the *Unam Sanctam* series of theological studies (Paris: Les Éditions du Cerf). Of the 77 volumes now in print, volume 51 and all the volumes from 60 on are studies of the work of the Council. Volume 51 (ed. G. Baraúna, 1966) is devoted to the *Church Constitution*, and volume 69 (eds. Yves Congar and M. Peuchmaurdo, 1967) is a study of the *Pastoral Constitution*. Each of these volumes is made up of three tomes, with the first containing the document itself, and the other two comprising commentaries and reflections by a number of highly competent scholars, many of whom participated in the Council as experts. George Lindbeck's *The Future of Roman Catholic Theology* (Philadelphia: Fortress Press, 1970) is an excellent analysis and evaluation of some of the most significant achievements of the Council by a Lutheran Observer.

The literature on existentialism is extremely vast. The best sources, needless to say, are the writings, both philosophical and literary, of the existentialists themselves. The best anthology of these writings I have come across is *The Fabric of Existentialism* (Englewood Cliffs, N.J.: Prentice-Hall, 1973). The editors, Richard Gill and Ernest Sherman, quite rightly remark in their introduction: "Of the making of books on existentialism there appears to be no end . . ." (p. v). An excellent overview of existentialism is found in John Macquarrie's *Existentialism* (Baltimore: Penguin Books, 1973). Among other writings of Macquarrie on this subject, I recommend his *Studies in Christian Existentialism* (London: SCM Press, 1965). The best presentation and assessment of existentialism from the Christian point of view I have found is *The Christian Philosophy of Existence*, trans. Lilian Soiron (Dublin: Gill and Son, 1965) by Ignace Lepp. A helpful Christian perspective is also found in Bernard Haering's *The Christian Existentialist* (New York: New York University Press, 1968). For an acquaintance with the philosophy of personalism I recommend *Personalism*, trans. Philip Mairet (Notre Dame, In.: University of Notre Dame Press, 1952) by Emmanuel Mounier, who is acknowledged to be one of the most outstanding exponents of this school. Perhaps the best introduction to process theology is the work edited by Ewert H. Cousins, *Process Theology* (New York: Newman Press, 1971), which is what it describes itself to be: the "basic writings by the key thinkers of a major modern movement."

CHAPTER THREE

EXISTENTIAL CHRISTIANS

BECAUSE EXISTENTIAL CHRISTIANS are personalists, they rejoice in the belief that the Christian God is supremely personal, that he is not just one person but a community of persons whose very personhood consists in interpersonal relationships of love; they rejoice that in the incarnation this God entered into human flesh, the physical world, and the flow of time, into all the concrete situational experiences that make up the fabric of human life, and, above all, into intimate interpersonal relationships with people. They are convinced that, since God is supremely personal, he will be found especially in the personal dimensions of human life. They agree with the statement of Blaise Pascal, who is considered a forerunner of contemporary existentialism, that the God of the Bible is not the God of the philosophers and the sages, but the God of Abraham, Isaac and Jacob—the God of persons. They relate most easily to the kind of God revealed in St. John, the God who is love (1 Jn 4:16).

If they take the statement of Pascal to mean that the God of revelation goes infinitely beyond anything that the metaphysicians have been able to conceive, no one will argue. But they could mean more than this. For they easily become victims of the antimetaphysical bias that is one of the negative signs of our times. They frequently have little interest in the First Cause and the Unmoved Mover, and show little inclination to spend time "paying metaphysical compliments to God," to use the expression of Whitehead. In this case, though their position is presently a popular one, they will have many to argue with them, including many saints who were metaphysicians and whose intense personal and existential union with the living God did not in any way diminish their esteem for the value of metaphysical knowledge. For anyone deeply in love, every avenue which leads to a deeper and fuller knowledge of the beloved is precious.

As personalists and existentialists, Christians of our times feel strongly that the subject of the spiritual life is not the human spirit, not the soul, but the whole person. They reject the exaggerated dualism of body and soul that at times has had a baneful influence on the spiritual life. They are interested in saving and sanctifying, not souls, but human persons. They have little patience for the opinion of those who in any way hold the human body in contempt or consider it a handicap for the spiritual life. They will not accept a sprirituality that does violence to their wholeness and integrity as human persons.

They want a spirituality that promotes the fullness of personal existence and that nourishes the maturation of the person. They believe that authentic spirituality should have something significant to say about what constitutes real human existence in our contemporary world; it should be a spirituality of human values, a spirituality that is able to speak to modern life and its problems, a spirituality that can be lived realistically in everyday life. They believe that the spiritual life has much to learn from modern developments in psychology and from the philosophies of personalism regarding the importance of the dynamics of personality development. They are convinced that in the mystery of the incarnation is the implication that God communicates himself to us in and through the processes of human development and that the gratuitous gift of divine life is normally given in and through the natural growth of the human person. They ascribe wholeheartedly to the frequently quoted phrase of St. Irenaeus: "The glory of God is man fully alive." They find it hard to believe that the spiritual life must mean a renunciation of the desire to be fully alive and fully human in this life, and that all this must be postponed to a future life.

Their spirituality constantly seeks for both God and self-fulfillment. They see no conflict in these two goals; in fact, they find it difficult to conceive of one without the other. They believe that only by being fully alive can one share in the fullness of God's life. They seek a spirituality that involves in depth their total human personality. Though being fully human and being holy may not in themselves be the same thing, they see no reason why they cannot coincide, in such a way that there is no gap between the holy and the human.

If they propose the integration between the holy and the fully human as an ideal to be striven for, they are surely on solid ground. But they can easily be tempted to become too absolute, to make the laws of God's gratuitous love dependent upon the laws and norms of modern psychologists, in such a way that only a person who is, humanly speaking, perfectly normal can become a saint; they can be led to believe that any kind of neurosis necessarily precludes sanctity. The lives of many saints do not justify such a conclusion, and, in any case, it is always presumptuous to make laws for God's gratuitous love. For he seems to take delight in manifesting his love and power through human infirmities: "I am quite content with my weaknesses.... For it is when I am weak that I am strong" (2 Co 12:10).

Contemporary spirituality is not opposed to asceticism, though it would probably prefer a more positive term—one which would relate asceticism to the paschal mystery. What it is opposed to is any kind of asceticism that goes counter to the normal and full growth of the human person, or an asceticism that springs from a hatred or a fear of the flesh and the world. It rejects any kind of asceticism that is an end in itself, or that does not have any deeper spiritual meaning than the training of a spiritual athlete. The only asceticism it is interested in is the one that is a living of the paschal mystery of the death and resurrection of the Lord, and that draws its inspiration and strength from the paschal sacraments, especially the celebration of the paschal mystery in the eucharist.

Existential Christians would tend to agree with Karl Rahner that asceticism in our present affluent consumer society should consist in a moderate use of the world's goods.[1] Prefabricated, highly contrived, and artificial forms of penance make them uncomfortable. They prefer what is often called functional asceticism, or what Douglas Rhymes calls "situational asceticism," which consists in a life of love and concern, and of openness to the world. They favor an asceticism that is more a matter of love than of law, an asceticism that knows how to identify with all who suffer and is eager to help them carry their cross. They prefer to pay the cost inevitably demanded by trying to live in loving service to others, by laboring for social reform and for the building of a better and more human world. Indeed, they would maintain that the effort to become fully alive, to become holistic in the sense of becoming a balanced human person, is a very costly enterprise.

It would be difficult to disagree with any of these principles; yet contemporary spiritual persons would be well advised not to arbitrarily limit the direction of the Holy Spirit completely to functional and situational asceticism. The Spirit does not seem to have limited himself to functional and situational asceticism in the lives of the saints; there is no assurance that he is inclined to do so in the lives of the saints of our times.

In their prayer, existential Christians look for some kind of personal, direct, concrete, and immediate experience of God. This is one reason why the Charismatic Renewal movement has had such a phenomenal growth. Not only do the Charismatic prayer meetings provide for personal involvement, spontaneity, and creativity, they also create an atmosphere in which one has the feeling of experiencing directly the presence and activity of the Spirit of the risen Jesus. This is also one of many reasons why millions of Americans in recent years have been turning to Eastern forms of religion and prayer. Here they often succeed in finding teachers whose methods and techniques seem to introduce them almost immediately into a personal and direct experience of God. Karl Rahner has even gone so far as to say that "the devout Christian of the future will either be a 'mystic', one who has 'experienced' something, or he will cease to be anything at all."[2] A caution is called for here, however: saints and masters of the spiritual life have insisted too much on "the cloud of unknowing" and on "the dark nights" inseparable from growth in prayer for us to be naive about any facile form of mysticism.

*   *   *

As existentalists, contemporary spiritual persons have a holistic view of the spiritual life. They would gladly accept as the summary of their spirituality the title of Josef Goldbrunner's book, *Holiness is Wholeness*,[3] but they would carry the meaning of wholeness much further than Goldbrunner. They believe that the Word did not become incarnate in man living in a vacuum, but in the existential man in the totality of his wholeness. He became incarnate in a human community, in our world, and in time and history. And the human person was redeemed in his wholeness: the human community, the world, and human history were a part of the redemption.

Since three kinds of interrelatedness constitute the matrix in which the human person lives, grows, and achieves fulfillment, and since God's love and life generally work within the laws and forces of personality development, it is in terms of these three relations that we must see the operation of the risen Jesus working in us through the Spirit, who is on mission in the world to draw us to that fullness of maturation which is our ultimate glorification. Hence there are three pivotal points in the mission of the

Holy Spirit: (1) interpersonal relationships in a communion of love; (2) a communion in love open to and bound up with secular reality; and (3) a communion of love in a state of pilgrimage through time and history.

Of these three basic existential relationships, relatedness to others is by far the most important.[4] "Person" is not to be identified with "individual." The person is essentially related to others; the individual is opposed to others. Individualism claims autonomy and independence with regard to others and to a human community. On the contrary, personalists and a number of existentialists insist that the essence of human life consists in what happens between persons in community, that we cannot become and continue to exist as real persons except in intersubjective communion with others. Encounter with others awakens ever deeper insights into self. Self-giving and self-commitment to other persons in a community of love is necessary for the discovery and fulfillment of personhood. There is no "I" by itself alone; there is only the "I" of the "I-Thou" relationship. The "We" that emerges from existential communion is a wholly new existential reality vastly richer than the "I" and the "Thou," which thus enriches the individual personalities.

Some personalists and existentialists define the human person in terms of generosity. Persons as persons are characterized by giving, and especially by self-giving. To be a person essentially means to be open to others. Individuals can be grouped into collectivities; they can go to make up states. Only authentic persons can create true communities. If people withdraw from others or try to isolate themselves, or if they develop the habit of relating to others only as objects, they remain locked within themselves; their deepest being remains unfulfilled, and they never grow into mature persons. Contemporary spirituality emphasises very strongly the importance of friendships.

At the same time, personalists and psychologists insist on the need of solitude for a full and balanced personality development. Without a capacity for solitude, there can be no great depth, no great interiority, and, as a consequence, participation in community, as well as contribution to the needs of others, will be at best superficial. True solitude is not narcissistic; it is something quite different from loneliness. Indeed, it is indispensable for the development of a capacity for self-giving. Those who do not experience solitude before God do not really possess themselves; hence they cannot truly give themselves away.

The other-centeredness of existentialist and personalist spirituality inevitably provides many positive and functional kinds of asceticism. A true "I-Thou" relationship preserves the "Thou" in his or her otherness; indeed, the closer the "I-Thou" relationship, the more does the other become other. But this can be achieved only at the cost of constant vigilance and of constant sacrifice of every tendency towards possessiveness. The "Thou" can never become a means to something beyond himself or herself; true love can never allow itself to degenerate into an "I-It" relationship. It is impossible to open oneself to love without becoming vulnerable. Other-centeredness will call for constant loving service of others, a sharing in the problems, the sufferings, and the pain of others; it will demand putting others' interests and concerns ahead of one's own, and a constant sacrificing of one's own preferences for the common good of the community. All this is very real asceticism.

*   *   *

Other-relatedness cannot be realized simply by interpersonal relations existing in an existential vacuum. People are also beings-in-the-world, rooted in this universe as flowers in soil. Communion with others, including communion with God, takes place in and through the world. It expresses itself in cosmic language, and sometimes this cosmic language takes the form of sacraments. As Karl Rahner has pointed out, "man cannot fulfill his spiritual or indeed his supernatural life without embodying this fulfillment in material reality."[5]

Human persons are cosmic beings through and through. Their life and their very personhood are not only related to, but are intimately bound up and made one with the universe in which they live and move and have their being. Conscious of this, existential Christians believe that, since the world is the very matrix of their being, they should not be expected to try to go to God in a way that implies they are pure spirits. They look upon this world as their natural environment. It is their natural abode, not only because they were destined to live in it, but also because they themselves through science and technology have transformed it and continue to do so more and more. The universe is not just a place in which people are destined to live for a certain time in preparation for eternity (though it is also that, of course); it is the natural environment which makes it possible for them to become fully themselves. The contemporary spiritual person sees the world as neither an accidental nor an incidental background to the spiritual life, but as a source from which the "new creation" is being built: "Now I am making the whole of creation new" (Rv 21:5; cf. 2 Co 5:17). He prefers to view his future, not as independent of the future evolution of the world, but as bound up with it.

In the incarnation, the Word did not draw human beings to himself and redeem them in isolation from the world; he did not pull people out by the roots from the world. Rather, he drew them to himself in his hyphenation with the world, and both people and world remain in his embrace forever. Thus, contemporary spirituality is incarnational. It believes that holiness consists in prolonging the incarnation of Christ in the world throughout history. In the incarnation, Christ entered into the mainstream of life; the spiritual person of these times considers this a standing invitation to do likewise, for if Christ came to establish his kingdom in this world, we must in some sense have a worldly spirituality.

Existential Christians desire to praise God for his world, as many of the psalms do; they want to rejoice in its secularity, to have faith in the potentialities of secular realities, and to have hope in the progress of humanity and the world. They seek a sense of God's presense and action in every aspect of human life in the world and in history.

However, contemporary Christians who look upon this world as their natural abode and who feel at home in it will encounter in Scripture a number of texts which refer to life on earth as an exile, and which speak of their true homeland in a future world (cf. e.g., Ph 3:20; Heb 11:10, 13-16). Moreover, in their enthusiasm about the existential and personalistic approach of the Council to the Church as a pilgrim people, they are faced with the conclusion that the people of God are constantly in a process of pilgrimage through the world to the promised land that lies beyond. But they would not interpret this in the way in which it is usually understood; they would not look upon this pilgrimage as something that leaves the world behind, as if the pilgrim people were straining toward an entirely different world. They believe that in redeeming mankind Christ redeemed the world as well (cf. Rm 8:19-25) and that in consequence the world is destined to be eternally transfigured and to remain intimately hyphenated to the glorified Christian forever (cf. 2 P 3:13). They are convinced that it is their earthly duty to help prepare the world for this destiny.

They will argue that St. Paul does not say that the world itself is passing away, but the world *in its present form*, the world as we know it (cf. 1 Co 7:31). They are convinced that they are called, not to leave the world in its present form with all its present limitations, with all the effects that sin has had on it, but to do what they can to free it from its present form, to transform it into a Christian world. They see their pilgrimage, not as something that leaves the world completely behind, but as a constant effort to carry forward all that is truly best in the world to its final destiny.

Many existentialists have emphasized the limitations of the human condition as we now know it. Running through their writings is a profound preoccupation with human finitude; with nothingness, as shown especially by the ultimate defeat of death; with the tragic and the ambiguous aspects of life; with contradictions and miseries; with the experiences of guilt, dread, alienation, absurdity, anxiety, anguish, boredom, malaise and even nausea that seem inseparable from human life. The human person is defined as an existent for death.[6]

Although Christians should be fundamentally optimistic because of the resurrection and God's self-gift to them in love, they will be very superficial, naive, and nonexistential if they do not share some of this anguish. It comes from a realistic understanding of the meaning of sin, of one's own sinfulness and the sinfulness of humanity; from sharing with St. Paul the experience of the unending battle between the flesh and the spirit; from consciousness of the precarious fragility of all human existence; from the constant disregard for justice in the world, especially the lack of just distribution of the world's goods; and from the depersonalization of the human person in our bourgeois society. In some ways the existential anguish of Christians should be even more intense than that of the atheistic existentialists, for Christians know that if anyone is hungry or suffering in the world, if anyone anywhere is the victim of war, oppression, or persecution, this must mean for them that Christ is suffering. Christian anguish should caution spiritual persons against any kind of naive optimism with regard to the world. It should move them, if they are truly and deeply spiritual, to make the most of the potentialities and possibilities latent in the world for the good of humanity, to work for justice and peace and for the elimination of all that is not authentic in human life and in our culture; it should inspire them to wage a continual war against sin, not only personal but also social. It is of interest to note here that Mounier tried to combine his existential anguish with the Good News by calling himself a "tragic optimist."

Existentialists hold that even though human beings are indeed beings-in-the-world, they are at the same time above and apart from it. Everything else in the world is only a thing, while they are persons; everything else is an instrument, while they are agents; everything else is only an object, while they are subjects; everything else is only an "it," while each person is an "I." The word "existence" comes from the Latin verb *ex-sistere*, which means "to stand out from." Hence the being of things, such as stones, trees, and animals is not true existence. Only people truly "exist," for they alone "stand out from" this world of things. Existence in its most authentic meaning implies interiority, self-awareness, intimacy and freedom, and these are found only in persons.

We are related to the world by bonds of great depth; but the same world which makes it possible for us to exist as persons also continually threatens to rob us of our transcendence, and therefore of our specific existence as persons. While seeking always to develop all that is positive in our interrelatedness with the world, we must practice constant asceticism to save ourselves from this fate. There is something here which has at least a remote relation to the Christian formula of being in the world but not of it. Existential Christians would agree that when the "I" becomes a "We" with Christ there is an infinitely greater reason why the human person should not fall into subjection to the world (Jn 17:14-15). But they would add that this can and must be brought about without rejection of the world. Worldly spirituality is indeed a risk, for the world is seductive. How splendid this risk is will be seen when we come to consider the Christic character of the universe.

We may look to Dietrich Bonhoeffer as the one who first articulated the importance of worldly spirituality:

Later I discovered and am still discovering up to this very moment that it is only by living completely in this world that one learns to believe. . . . This is what I mean by worldliness—taking life in one's stride, with all its duties and problems, its successes and failures, its experiences and helplessness. It is in such a life that we throw ourselves utterly in the arms of God and participate in his sufferings in the world and watch with Christ in Gethsemane. That is faith, that is *metanoia*, and that is what makes a Christian (cf. Jeremiah 45). How can success make us arrogant or failure lead us astray when we participate in the sufferings of God by living in this world?[7]

World-related spirituality has its own built-in asceticism. Striving to prolong Christ's incarnation in the world of our time will inevitably lead to Gethsemane, as the original incarnation did.

* * *

By the fact that people are beings-in-the-world, they are also beings-in-time.[8] Existential Christians will not accept the traditional opposition between the spiritual and the temporal. In fact, they will insist that human spirituality is essentially conditioned by temporality, not merely in the sense that human life in this world is destined to come to an end, but in the sense that human spirituality is caught up in the flow of time.

Thus human beings are four-dimensional, extended not only in the three dimensions of space, but also in the fourth dimension of time. They are incarnated in a world that is in constant motion—evolving, changing, and developing. They cannot withdraw from this concrete existential world into some kind of ideal world of fixed and timeless essences. Their very existence is a process; in a sense they must keep running continually in order to remain in existence.

By the very fact that people are involved in history, they are never fixed and finished; they are continually in the process of becoming. Hence, at no given moment of their lives do they possess their own existence fully. The present moment is an emergence from the total past and already the beginning of the future. Thus they are a part of the flow of time and cannot be understood apart from it.

To be a person is to be constantly in the process of becoming a person. A realization and an acceptance of this is important for personal growth. Persons who cut themselves off from the times in which they live and try to live some kind of static existence that prescinds from time and their times become thwarted and stunted. In a word, human persons are essentially pilgrims who must move forward in time toward a historical goal.

Just as the hyphenation of the human person with others and with the world provides its own built-in functional asceticism, so also does the hyphenation with time and history. While taking to themselves the particular forms, patterns, and structures in which the Christian life expresses itself in each period of history, Christians must remain detached from them in order to be ready to welcome the appropriate forms and structures which a new historical period may bring. This detachment springs from the realization that no changing historical patterns can ever express definitively the Mystery of Christ.

Through the triple hyphenation with others, with the world, and with time, spiritual persons will discover God in their environment and enter into an ever fuller and deeper communion with him. They will discover God in terrestrial realities, which were created in, through, and for the Word (cf. Col 1:15-17), who became incarnate in them so that they could all become "words" by which he might continue to carry on a continual dialogue with those he loves. The modern Christian believes that the word of God is truly found not only in Scripture, though it is present there in a very special sense, but also in the human environment. God speaks powerfully, sometimes dramatically to those who have learned to listen, through all the things that go to make up the world; through the events of time, because history for those with faith is always a history of salvation and sanctification; and especially through others, particularly those with whom one is related in special and providential ways. Existential Christians know that they must spend their lives in a constant state of attentive and sensitive listening to what God is saying to them through the world, history, and personal relationships. And they will discover that there is often a reciprocity between the two ways in which the Lord speaks: the more attentive they are in listening to God's word coming to them from secular realities, history, and their fellows, the more clearly and forcefully will the revelation in Scripture come through to them; conversely, the more intently they listen to God's word in Scripture, the more powerful and meaningful will the word of the Lord be as it comes to them from their environment.[9]

*   *   *

For centuries the spiritual life has often been called "the interior" or "the inner life." Because of their deep conviction that the subject of the spiritual life is the person in his or her wholeness and that this wholeness includes all the links and bonds which the person has with the universe, contemporary Christians may be inclined to consider these phrases inappropriate and to judge that they reflect a type of "angelic" spirituality that views the spiritual life as something found only within the inner enclave of the spirit. Yet, St. Paul speaks of the "hidden self" growing strong through the Spirit (Ep 3:16), and of a life "hidden with Christ in God" (Col 3:3). The interiority of which St.

Paul speaks here, and of which St. Augustine and many saints have spoken over the centuries, is not only something of immeasurably greater depth than the introspection and the interiority spoken of by psychologists and the inner world of the philosopher and the poet; it is something of an entirely different order, since it is a share in the interiority of God's inner life. It has nothing to do with "angelism" or introversion, nor does it in any way separate the human person from his environment. Indeed, it calls for a holy exteriority, the kind of exteriority which even the inner life of God himself achieved in the incarnation.

The liturgy is the best witness to the fact that there is such a thing as a holy exteriority and a blessed materiality, and that both exteriority and materiality belong to the essence of our spiritual life. In the incarnation the inner depth of God's own life drew to itself the exteriority and the materiality of human flesh, and indeed of the whole of human life. Shining through this materiality and exteriority was the luminosity of the Word of God. For this reason Christ has been called the primordial Sacrament. The liturgy consists essentially in sacramentality, a sacramentality which is a kind of prolongation across time and space of the Sacramentality of the Word made flesh. "Our Redeemer's visible presence," says St. Leo the Great in an Easter homily, "has passed into the sacraments."

No other aspect of contemporary spirituality responds quite so fully to the spiritual climate characteristic of our times than the liturgy. Nothing is so profoundly bound up with the integrity and the wholeness of the human person. For this reason there is no clearer, no more noteworthy sign of our times than liturgical spirituality. It is significant that the first document promulgated by the Council was the *Constitution on the Sacred Liturgy*. It was the spearhead in the Council's efforts to respond to the signs of our times. Existential Christians are enthusiastic about the renewal of the liturgy and seek to steep their spiritual life ever more fully in it.

The Council stressed the intimate union between the liturgy of the Church on earth and the liturgy of the society of the blessed in heaven (CL 8a; C 50f). Yet there is a profound difference between the two. The worship of the angels and saints does not have the exteriority and the materiality that are essential to the liturgy on earth. Our liturgy is not the liturgy of pure spirits or of separated souls; it depends essentially upon the human body, upon its natural sacramentality, upon its capacity for being supernaturally sacramentalized, upon both its verbal and non-verbal language in prayer, and upon its power both to call into being and to mediate the spiritual movements of the soul.

Not only does the liturgy call for a union of soul and body, it also calls for an intimate union between human beings and their environment. Liturgical worship is essentially communal; individualism has no part in it. There is no more profound or intimate hyphenation of person with community than in the Body of Christ, which is his Church. Generally speaking, the liturgy is carried on in the assembly of the faithful, and at no time or place is the Church more Church than in the liturgical assembly. Here hyphenation means being made one with others by being one with the Lord Jesus.

In the liturgy we are brought into intimate union with the cosmos, for the sacraments are composed of cosmic stuff, such as water, wine, bread, and oil. The liturgy is always reaching out for an involvement with as much of the material world as possible. The ritual contains blessings for many of the material things that enter into human life: food, homes, water, wine, bread, beer, butter, cakes, cheese, eggs, seeds, fields, fruit, the harvest, herds of cattle, trains, airplanes, mountain meadows, printing presses, ships, schools, vineyards, fire, bridal chambers, sheep, blast furnaces—the list is almost endless. In a sense, the liturgy reintroduces us to the world with a new dimension which we do not ordinarily encounter in it. Even the Mass draws into its supreme act of worship, not only the human body and the material elements of bread and wine, but the gold of the chalice, the bronze of the candlesticks, the silk of the vestments, the marble of the altar, the wax of the candles, and the linen of the altar-cloths. No wonder Romano Guardini can define the official and public prayer life of the Church as "creation redeemed and at prayer."

The liturgy also keeps us continually involved in time, for it is made up of ordinary time and extraordinary times, of the cycle of seasons and of the constant celebration of historical events. In the new *Sacramentary* published after the Council, the cycles of liturgical time have been computed up to the beginning of the twenty-first century. They will continue after that, century after century, until the Parousia, when all time will finally stop running. Throughout its cycles, the liturgy makes sacramentally present in our lives the great mysteries of Christ's life; and since these mysteries recapitulated and brought to fulfillment all the great saving acts of God in the Old Testa-

ment, the liturgy makes it possible for us to relive continually in
our own lives the whole of salvation history. And while making
the whole past of saving history present to us, it makes the future
present as well. According to St. Paul, whenever we share in the
eucharistic banquet we are anticipating the Lord's coming again
(1 Co 11:26). The liturgy of the Mass tells us that every time we
celebrate we do so "as we wait in joyful hope for the coming of
our Savior, Jesus Christ."

The human body shares so intimately and so profoundly in the
spiritual life and especially in the liturgy that it is destined on
the day of the resurrection to be totally spiritualized and glorified and thus be able to participate for all eternity in the liturgy
of heaven. The liturgy is a preparation for, and already an anticipation of, this destiny. Moreover, the oneness of the Christian
with his or her environment is so profound, so powerful, and so
enduring that the resurrection of the human person necessarily
involves the resurrection of his or her environment as well. The
community of persons with which the Christian has been intimately united on earth will become the society of the blessed
in glory. The ecclesial Body of Christ will finally come to its
own fulfillment when all its members will themselves be glorified and become one forever with the glorified body of their
Lord (cf. Ph 3:21). And the resurrection of the human body will
draw along with it the resurrection of the physical universe (cf 2
P 3:13).

As the spiritual person is caught up more completely in the liturgy and in contemplative prayer, the interiority of God's inner
life, communicated to the sacraments of the liturgy, invades
ever more clearly and more fully the exteriority and the materiality of his or her life. This invasion begins at the moment when
the liturgy first touches the human person in baptism. From then
on, the Spirit of the risen Jesus continues to draw Christians
ever closer to their ultimate and total glorification by a gradual
process of spiritualization—a spiritualization not only of their
spirit but of their body too, and indeed of their whole environment. The luminous presence of the divine interiority in the
sacraments is somehow extended to Christians themselves and
to their world. Only the eyes of a deep faith can see it, but it
is there with increasing clarity as they respond ever more fully
to the Spirit of their risen Lord.

Spiritual persons discover in their own body not only the presence and activity of their own spirit, but also the active indwelling of the Spirit of Jesus. They find a sacramentality in the ma-

terial universe, which, because it is profoundly and intimately hyphenated, not only with the individual Christian, but with the whole Body of Christ living in the world, can in a sense be called the "body" of the Body of the Lord. They also discover a sacramentality in time and history because they see in the events of history the saving acts of God shining forth. They see history as time being gradually brought to fulfillment, the fulfillment of that eternal plan of the Father which Paul called the Mystery of Christ. Thus, to the eyes of faith the whole human person and the whole of his or her environment become luminous and diaphanous, and, as a consequence, a continual epiphany of the presence and action of the Lord and his Spirit.

At the end, the seven sacraments and the many sacramentals will disappear because they will have fulfilled their purpose; they will have brought people and their total environment to the fullness of sacramentality, to the radiant incandescence of their glorified state, in which they will be totally transfigured in Christ. "And we, with our unveiled faces reflecting like mirrors the brightness of the Lord, all grow brighter and brighter as we are turned into the image that we reflect; this is the work of the Lord who is Spirit" (2 Co 3:18). "It is the same God that said 'Let there be light shining out of darkness,' who has shone in our minds to radiate the light of the knowledge of God's glory, the glory on the face of Christ" (2 Co 4:6).

Notes

1. "Christian Living Formerly and Today," *Theological Investigations* VII, trans. David Bourke (New York: Herder and Herder, 1971), 19-24.

2. Ibid., p. 15.

3. Trans. Stanley Goodman (New York: Pantheon Press, 1955).

4. Relatedness with others is an important theme in the writings of existentialists, but there is a great disparity in their views. Some insist on the primacy of the individual in all his uniqueness to such an extent that their writings are haunted by feelings of isolation, alienation, and loneliness. This is particularly true of Jean-Paul Sartre, who is deeply concerned with the limitations placed upon self by others. See, for example, his discussion of "Concrete Relations with Others," in *Being and Nothingness*, trans. Hazel E. Barnes (New York: Citadel Press, 1966), pp. 361-430. Other existentialists take a very positive view of interpersonal relationships. The best known work on this question is Martin Buber's *I and Thou*, trans. Ronald Gregor Smith (New York: Charles Scribner's Sons, 1970). Gabriel Marcel also takes a very positive view of relations with others. This is a constantly recurring theme in his writings. He attaches great importance

to what he calls *coesse*, "being with"; for him "to be is to be with." See, for example, *The Philosophy of Existentialism*, trans. Manya Harari (New York: Citadel Press, 1956), p. 39; his first essay "The Ego and its Relation with Others," *Homo Viator*, trans. Emma Craufurd (New York: Harper and Row, 1962); and *Creative Fidelity*, trans. Robert Rosthal (New York: Farrar, Straus and Co., 1964), pp. 32-37, 147-174.

5. *The Christian Commitment*, trans. Cecily Hastings (New York: Sheed and Ward, 1963), p. 47. The concept of the human person as a being-in-the-world is a question of major interest for existentialism. See, for example, Martin Heidegger's *Being and Time*, trans. John Macquarrie and Edward Robinson (New York: Harper and Row, 1962), pp. 78-148.

6. Kierkegaard was a man who experienced a great deal of personal interior torment and melancholy. Because of this he took an extremely negative view of the human condition. In particular, he had a profound sense of the sinfulness of man. Sartre, too, has an extremely pessimistic view of human existence, though his pessimism stems from Nietzsche rather than from Kierkegaard. The pessimistic outlook of Kierkegaard based on man's sinfulness eventually turns into a kind of optimism when he views human life in the context of God's love and mercy coming in history. Nothing redeems or modifies Sartre's pessimism, which is caused, not by sin, but by the fact that there is no real meaning built into the world and human life. Sartre's philosophy is summed up in these statements: "Nothingness lies coiled in the heart of being—like a worm." "Human reality . . . is by nature an unhappy consciousness with no possibility of surpassing its unhappy state." *Being and Nothingness*, pp. 21, 90.

7. *Prisoner for God, Letters and Papers from Prison*, ed. Eberhard Bethge, trans. Reginald H. Fuller (New York: Macmillan, 1963), p. 169.

8. Several existentialists have given special attention to the temporal character of human existence. The most noteworthy work on this subject is Martin Heidegger's *Being and Time*. Cf. especially pp. 383-488. Sartre has also reflected on this question; see his discussion of temporality in *Being and Nothingness*, pp. 107-170.

9. See Karl Rahner, *The Christian Commitment*, p. 71.

Bibliography

Concilium, true to its original purpose, has, since Vatican II, kept abreast of the latest developments in spiritual theology, as well as in other branches of theology. It has published a number of worthwhile articles which treat the new aspects of spirituality either in general or in connection with special questions, such as the problem of secuarlization and the question of contemporary prayer. Among the articles which discuss contemporary spirituality in general, one of the most insightful is Albert Marie Besnard's "Tendencies of Contemporary Spirituality," IX, *Spirituality in Church and World*, ed. Christian Duquoc et al. (New York: Paulist Press, 1965), 25-44. Thomas Sartory provides a very perceptive discussion of the characteristics of the spirituality of our times in "Changes in Christian Spirituality," *Life in the Spirit,* ed. Hans Küng (New York: Sheed and Ward, 1968), pp. 55-105.

Karl Rahner has written extensively on various aspects of contemporary spirituality. Valuable insights into the implications of the fact that Christians in the modern world are living in a state of diaspora are found in "The Present Situation of Christians: A Theological Interpretation of the Position of Christians in the Modern World," which is the first chapter of *The Christian Commitment,* trans. Cecily Hastings (New York: Sheed and Ward, 1963). This work also appears as vol. 1 of *Mission and Grace,* published by Sheed and Ward in the same year. Special attention is called to two articles by Rahner in *Theological Investigations*: "The Man of Today," VI, trans. Karl-H. and Boniface Kruger (New York: Seabury Press, 1974), 3-20; and "Christian Living Formerly and Today," VII, trans. David Bourke (New York: Herder and Herder, 1971), 3-24.

The writings of Teilhard de Chardin have had a profound influence, either directly or indirectly, on the spiritual thinking and attitudes of our times. The best expression of his spirituality is found in *The Divine Milieu,* trans. Bernard Wall (New York: Harper and Brothers, 1960). Dietrich Bonhoeffer has also had a significant influence on contemporary spirituality. Along with his own writings, the widely read book of John A. T. Robinson, *Honest to God* (Philadelphia: Westminister Press, 1963) has done much to popularize his ideas.

Part II

BIBLICAL EXISTENTIALISM

CHAPTER FOUR

THE EXISTENTIALISM OF THE BIBLE

BEFORE REFLECTING MORE FULLY on the spiritual implications of the hyphenation of the human person with others in community, with the world, and with time and history, it will be helpful to search the Scriptures for a basis and a background for our reflections. This task seems all the more important because of the renewed interest in Scripture that is a salient characteristic of contemporary spirituality.

Contemporary spiritual persons have a great love for Scripture. They delight in reading it and in meditating on it. Their growing awareness of the primordial role it plays in the spiritual life is one of the most significant signs of our times. This growing awareness derives from many sources: the advances made in Scripture studies in recent years; the publication of a number of new versions of the Bible which reflect the findings of contemporary biblical scholarship; developments in theology, especially in the theology of the word; the growth of the liturgical movement, which could never have developed except in conjunction with a renewed interest in Sacred Scripture; the popularity of directed retreats, which call for meditation on God's living word in the Bible for several hours every day; and the extraordinary development of the Charismatic Renewal movement, which almost invariably stirs up a great love and hunger for reading and reflecting on Holy Scripture.

The Council provided a powerful impetus to this whole movement. In its directives for the reform of the liturgy, it placed particular stress on enriching the worship of the Church as fully as possibly with Scripture: "The treasures of the Bible are to be opened up more lavishly, so that richer fare be provided for the faithful at the table of God's Word" (CL 51 cf. 24; 35; 52). In the last chapter of the *Constitution on Revelation*, entitled "Sacred Scripture in the Life of the Church," the Council stressed the great importance of reading frequently God's holy word and of making it the wellspring of prayer (21-26 cf. DR 6b). One of the most inspired and inspiring statements of the Council regarding the meaning of Scripture for the liturgy and for the Christian life in general is the declaration that "Christ is present in his word . . ." (CL 7a). In reading Scripture, Christians truly encounter the Lord Jesus himself.

At the same time, they encounter the typical biblical person and become acquainted with that person's characteristic way of thinking and acting. And this is a matter of some significance. For several authors have pointed out that there is a close affinity between the biblical person's way of thinking and the thinking characteristic of our times. If this be true, and we think it is, it provides a precious key to open the door to the kind of spirituality that has the best chance of being viable in our times: a spirituality at once contemporary and profoundly biblical. But in order to possess and use this key, it is necessary to specify clearly in what this affinity consists.

Some writers feel that the bond between contemporary and biblical thought consists in existentialist, personalist, and process modes of thinking. This does not mean, of course, that the biblical person possessed an explicit philosophy of existentialism or personalism. It simply means that he or she habitually thought in terms of the existential and the personal, and in terms of process.

In *Studies in Christian Existentialism*, John Macquarrie writes: "Used with proper care, the term 'existentialism' could draw attention to an affinity between what the New Testament writers were doing and what modern philosophers of existence are doing."[1] There does not seem to be any reason to limit this statement to the New Testament. Bernard Haering sees a significant relationship between the "existentialism" of the biblical person and contemporary personalism: "The Bible, particularly the New Testament, makes a unique contribution to our knowledge of a personal mode of existence that is not found in any other philosophy or religion. It is a new understanding of existence concentrating on a new understanding of person. Today, biblical thought has a renewed impact on modern personalism."[2]

The Bible is a collection of existential and personalistic writings. It abounds in stories about specific and concrete persons, events, dramatic happenings, particular places and things. It is made up of a variety of literary genres: history (but its own special kind of history), poetry, drama, allegories and myths.

The sacred writers do not present abstract doctrine; they do not construct philosophical definitions or demonstrations. They simply present individual human beings in concrete, existential situations. In this, there is a striking similarity between a number of the books of the Bible and the literary writings of contemporary existentialists. One thinks spontaneously of the books of Job and Ecclesiastes, but many other parts of the Bible, such as a number of passages in the prophets, the psalms, and the wisdom literature, also reveal this similarity. Here we find questions raised about the nature of the human condition, its weaknesses, its anxieties, and even its absurdities. In this connection François Dreyfus writes:

> ...Job and Ecclesiastes are *questions* raised by the man who asks himself about evil and the precarious nature of human affairs. On this level of questioning, the cultural gap between us and the biblical authors is bridged at once; these questionings, these problems, touch man in his deepest being, his fundamental anxiety, his agony of discontent. Here we find a constant, a structure. To use the language familiarized by Heidegger and Bultmann, we should say that we are on the level of the existential.[3]

Parts of the Bible are real history; but the sacred authors did not write history as it is written today. They wrote it in the way that would best serve the religious purpose they had in mind, and hence they did not hesitate to introduce a great many subjective and personal elements. Generally speaking, the biblical writer did not simply aim at achieving factual accuracy; he saw himself as a witness to a concrete, personal, existential experience which had a religious significance and subjective implications.

*   *   *

When an attempt is made to describe the characteristics of the thinking of the biblical person, it is often done by drawing a contrast between Scriptural and Greek thought. This method is used for two reasons. One is that Hebrew and Greek thinking present such a striking antithesis that the salient features of the one are brought into clear and sharp relief against those of the other. But the more important reason is that, however unlikely bed-fellows these two might seem to be, they have been bedded down together since the dawn of Christianity. Indeed, Hellenistic influence on Hebrew thought actually began long before the coming of Christ.

The use of this contrast can be a helpful method of getting an insight into the characteristics of the thinking of the biblical person, provided we keep certain qualifications in mind. First of all, the contrast between Greek and Hebrew thought is, to a significant degree, simply the difference between a philosophical and a non-philosophical way of thinking. This point is often overlooked. Moreover, in depicting this contrast, writers usually have Platonic philosophy in mind, and often the impression is given that this represents Greek thought in general. The major Greek philosophers do have a number of things in common; but there are also noteworthy differences. The brief contrast presented here is particularly true of Platonic thought.

The Greek thinker tends to stand back from his environment and to take a detached view of things in order to observe them objectively, to classify them, and to abstract the common essence shared by the groups of things he observes and judges. He seeks to mirror the essences of things. His thought is logical and deductive; he seeks reasons behind appearances. He strives to put things together in harmony, and he has an instinctive distaste for anything that unexpectedly disturbs the order of things. Because the material world is not orderly but full of chance and unexpected events, the Greek thinker detaches himself in some measure from it in order to deal with universal abstract essences.

The Hebrew thinker has a different approach to reality. Far from feeling detached from his environment, the biblical person feels very much a part of it. He feels called to become actively involved with it, for it is a part of his very life and its meaning. It never occurs to him to try to stand back and achieve a detached view of the variety of sensible things in the world around him, so as to compare them and to order them. For the Greek, things have meaning only in so far as he can define them, and he withdraws in some degree from concrete, existential, material things because they cannot be defined but only described. The Hebrew thinker, on the contrary, is not interested in definitions but in descriptions of the existential realities. Only descriptions that try to grasp things in their wholeness can capture existential reality in its individuality and its concreteness. In this sense it may be said that the biblical person takes a phenomenological approach to reality. Unlike the Greek, his tendency is not to analyze but rather to relate; because he is not a dualist, he sees human beings not as divided within themselves, nor divided from other things, but as related. In a word, his thinking is holistic.

The Greek ideal in knowledge is impersonal objectivity and neutrality. Because the biblical person is an existentialist, he easily becomes subjectively involved. As I have already noted, this is true not only of ordinary reality but also of history, much to the distress of those who, having been brought up in the culture of the West, feel that history, as well as science and philosophy, must seek for impersonal objectivity. For the Greek thinker experience is only the starting point, and he begins to feel at home only when he has, through abstraction, entered into a world of ideas. He is therefore a conceptualist. The biblical person, on the other hand, values experiential knowledge in its own right and is content to rest in the experience of reality. In a sense, the Greek mind sees things from the outside because, in seeking for objectivity, it knows things precisely as objects. The biblical person, by being subjectively related to what he experiences, knows things from the inside, through the existential involvement of his whole being. His encounter with reality is not just a question of the intellect; it involves himself, everything in his makeup: his "heart," his senses, his feelings, and his instincts. His approach to things is something like that of an artist who in some sense identifies himself with nature. Because knowledge for the biblical person means a personal, intimate experience, he can, and often does, speak of sexual intercourse as a kind of knowledge (cf. e.g., Gn 4:1 R.S.V.).

The Greek thinker is uncomfortable with existential reality because its opaque density of matter seems intellectually impenetrable. He delights in the abstract universal, which seems luminous with intelligibility. For the Hebrew, sensible reality provides direct existential meaning—precisely the kind of existential meaning in which he is interested. Only particulars exist, and the biblical person is interested only in things as they actually exist.

Throughout salvation history Yahweh keeps choosing particular persons and events to bring about his designs and to teach through concrete existing reality. Nothing could be more existential than salvation history. It is narrated with the greatest attention to concrete detail, and it is usually told in terms of human drama. To use Shakespeare's phrase, everything has "a local habitation and a name." Whatever theology the Hebrews possessed was expressed in historical narrative, concrete allegories,

word pictures, "wise sayings" culled from concrete human existence, and detailed laws. All the difference in the world exists
between the concrete wisdom literature of the Hebrews and the
abstract wisdom of the Greeks. "Wisdom calls aloud in the streets
. . . she delivers her message at the city gates" (Pr 1:20-21).

The Hebrew term for "word" is *dabar*. It is a term that has
extremely active and dynamic connotations. It connotes something that is projected forth and that remains dynamic. *Dabar*
signifies not only "word" but also "thing," "deed," and "event."
The whole of reality was conceived by the biblical person as
having been brought from non-existence into existence by the
word of God. In the creation narrative the sacred author keeps
repeating "God said" in describing the coming into existence of
all the various parts of the universe. This same idea is often
repeated throughout Scripture. "By the word of Yahweh the
heavens were made, their whole array by the breath of his
mouth; . . . He spoke and it was created, he commanded and
there it stood (Ps 33:6,9). "He gives an order; his word flashes
to earth: to spread snow like a blanket, to strew hoarfrost like
ashes" (Ps 147:15-16). "Does not my word burn like fire . . . is
it not like a hammer shattering a rock?" (Jr 23:29).

The use of *dabar* for word-thing-event shows the Hebrew dynamic concept of reality. The biblical person was interested not
only in what sensible things might mean, but also in what they
did, what action was implicit in them, in what way they might
involve him. Sensible, tangible, bodily things were intelligible to
him because they were created by God's word. Each individual's
name, each man's individuality was unique. By the very fact of
creation by the word of God, the material, sensible world was a
language. It involved a dialogue. "So from the soil Yahweh God
fashioned all the wild beasts and all the birds of heaven. These he
brought to man to see what he should call them; each one was to
bear the name the man would give it" (Gn 2:19). Secular things,
deeds, and events of history spoke to the biblical person. In their
deepest meaning they were words. God could speak through
them and often did in most powerful ways. He spoke eloquently
to Jeremiah, for example, in the most commonplace things: a
boiling kettle (1:13-15), a linen loincloth (13:1-11), two baskets
of figs (24:1).

The biblical person's idea of knowledge is somewhat similar
to that found in poetry. In poetry there is a kind of implicit universal that is never abstracted, but concretized in imagery. The

biblical person is by nature poetic, and it was almost inevitable that his culture should give birth to the psalms. "We have a world which is poetic-throughout," writes Claude Tresmontant, "because it is significant-throughout. Poetry is no more the sole property of the magicians of language; poetry is henceforth the life of any man who lives in a universe where elements are words."[4]

There is a vast difference between Platonic contemplation and the contemplation of the biblical person. Platonic contemplation is disincarnate; it implies a flight from the body and from the world. The contemplation of the biblical person, on the contrary, is existential. It looks at things in somewhat the same way as a child does, not attempting to do anything to them. It discovers the word of God incarnated, so to speak, in the existential, sensible things it sees.

Something of the same difference is found in the love of the Platonist and the love of the biblical person. For the Platonist whatever beauty and goodness is found in individual things and individual persons is but a faint shadow of the fullness of beauty and goodness in the world of ideas. It is to the attainment of this fullness that he must constantly strive. The love of the biblical person, on the other hand, is existential. It is the love of particular things and especially of particular persons. Sometimes in the past charity has been presented, especially in religious communities, as though it were a kind of all-embracing universal love for others in general, and what were called "particular friendships" were to be avoided. True Christian love, which has its roots in biblical love, is existential; it loves the concrete, existential, particular person in all that makes him or her particular.

Jesus is, of course, the biblical person par excellence. He is also in a sense an existentialist par excellence. We find this in the way he loved, in the way he taught, and in the way he told parables. His teachings were a series of concrete word pictures. The parable of the good Samaritan is typical. The Hebrew lawyer asked Christ, not a Greek, but a Hebrew question: he did not say, "*What* is *a* neighbor?" but "*Who* is *my* neighbor?" And Jesus did not answer by giving a Greek definition: "A neighbor is one who...."; he answered in a typically Semitic way: "A man was once on his way down from Jerusalem to Jericho..." (Lk 10:29-30).

In *A Christian Philosophy of Existence*, Ignace Lepp has spoken eloquently of the existential character of Jesus and his Gospel:

Every religious truth which Jesus taught his disciples was incarnate
in his life and world, even before it was expressed in words. No
other philosopher or sage embodied to such a degree the direct expression of an authentic existential experience. In Christ existence
and existentialism are truly one.... Long before Bergson and the
modern existentialists, he used descriptions and images as more apt
than abstract definitions to convey adequately the most profound
teachings.... In the Gospel all is vibrant and concrete. One would
seek in vain for even a hint of a scholastic system or technique. It is
not necessary to be deeply learned to realize, as we read the Gospel,
that the men who recorded the teaching of Christ as shown in his
deeds and words, did not intend to write merely history, or even
theology. The chronology of the facts interested them but little, and
logical definitions even less. They are relating—often, from a strictly
literary point of view, very unskillfully—their own existential experience, their encounter with him whom they justly recognized as the
son of the living God.... As soon as a Christian goes back to the
very source of his faith, he becomes 'existential'.[5]

The notion of the word of God becoming "incarnate" in the
things-deeds-events of the world can be seen as the first stirring
of something that will eventually find an astounding realization in
the incarnation of the Word of God in an existential human being
in our world of things and deeds and events. In the incarnation the
person who, as the Word, is the fullness of truth, became concretized, so to speak, in a particular human being, became a part of
our existential world. He in whom "all the jewels of wisdom and
knowledge are hidden" (Col 2:3) was one whom "we have seen
with our own eyes ... and touched with our hands" (1 Jn 1:1).

We can likewise see in the ancient belief of the Hebrews that all
things were created by the word of God an anticipation of the full
revelation in St. Paul: "He is the image of the unseen God and the
first-born of all creation, for in him were created all things in
heaven and on earth: ... all things were created through him
and for him. Before anything was created, he existed, and he
holds all things in unity" (Col 1:15-17).

In this perspective we can appreciate more fully the inherent
sacramentality of creation and even sacramentality in its strict-
est sense. For, in the one term *dabar* we find expressed a word, a
concrete sensible thing, an event, and an action. In the sacraments we have a word and a concrete sensible thing, or action,
both of which together actually produce what they signify.

*   *   *

The contrast I have drawn between Greek and biblical thought seems so stark that it gives rise to many serious questions about the possibility or validity of trying to combine the two in developing a Christian theology. Indeed, the same questions arise with regard to other types of philosophical knowledge as well, since as I have already pointed out, the basic difference between Greek and biblical thought is, to a large extent, the difference between a philosophical and a non-philosophical approach to reality. I cannot attempt an adequate discussion of these questions here; but at least a few points need to be established clearly, so that there will be no ambiguity about the main thrust of this book.

Let it be understood, first of all, that I am not espousing any form of fideism which would limit the Christian mind to simply accepting on faith the concrete existential truths found in the Bible, and deny the legitimacy of any attempt to develop these truths in terms of an abstract metaphysical theology. I do not agree with Karl Barth that the only valid Christian theology is one which is drawn directly from the divine revelation of the Bible without the assistance of any human philosophy or speculation. Moreover, even though I have sought to establish an affinity between the existentialism of the Bible and contemporary existentialism, I do not share Bultmann's opinion that the only "right" philosophy for the development of a truly Christian theology is existentialism. Nor do I feel that the striking antithesis between Greek philosophical thinking and the existential thinking of the Bible automatically disqualifies the former from serving as a means to develop the latter into a valid and viable Christian theology. In point of fact, this is precisely the way in which the theology of the Church has developed over the centuries. I believe that the wedding of Greek and biblical thought has, on the whole, been an extremely fruitful one, even though from the beginning it was fraught with many dangers—dangers which were not always avoided.

At the same time, Greek and Roman cultures have lost their dominance in our contemporary culture. Because of this and because of the existentialism of the Bible, I feel that existentialism is saying many important and pertinent things, offering many fresh insights, and providing a number of significant correctives for the imbalances which entered into traditional spirituality over the centuries, especially through the influence of Platonic thought. Contemporary spirituality can be greatly enriched by these contributions.

In the last analysis, though the Church, the Christian life, and

Western culture in general have inherited much of great value from the abstract, speculative thinking of the Greeks, and though abstract doctrine plays an extremely important role in the life of the Church, it cannot of itself provide for the Christian an existential and personal encounter with the Lord. Such an encounter is to be found principally in the *dabar* of God's holy word and in the *dabar* of the sacraments. For the Council has told us that the Lord is truly present in his word and in his sacraments: "By His power He is present in the sacraments, so that when a man baptizes it is really Christ Himself who baptizes. He is present in his word, since it is He himself who speaks when the Holy Scriptures are read in the church" (CL 7a).

In both word and sacrament the Christian experiences a true, existential, personal encounter with Christ, who is himself the Sacrament of encounter with God. Encountering the Lord in the celebration of the sacraments, in which God's holy word always plays an important role, the Christian can say in the words of St. Ambrose: "You have shown yourself to me, Christ, face to face. It is in your sacraments that I meet you." Encountering Christ day by day in the words of Scripture, Christians will be led along their pilgrim way to the future where at last all words will be hushed in the presence of the one Word who expresses all truth in its absolute plenitude—the Word who now wears the form of a Man. The sacraments have as their inherent purpose to make themselves eventually superfluous by leading the Christian to transcend all signs and to encounter the ultimate Reality which they now signify here on earth. St. Athanasius tells us that we should read God's word until we become "wordified." When the "face to face" that St. Ambrose speaks of in relation to the sacraments becomes the actual face to face of the Beatific Vision, we shall then be fully and finally "Wordified."

Notes

1. (London: SCM Press, 1965), p. 116. See also Macquarrie's *An Existentialist Theology, a Comparison of Heidegger and Bultmann* (London: SCM Press, 1955), pp. 19, 21.

2. *The Christian Existentialist* (New York: New York University Press, 1968), p. 8.

3. "The Existential Value of the Old Testament," *Concilium* XXX, *How Does the Church Confront the Old Testament?*, ed. Pierre Benoit et al. (New York: Paulist Press, 1967), p. 35.

4. *A Study of Hebrew Thought,* trans. Michael F. Gibson (New York: Desclee Co., 1960), p. 177.

5. Trans. Lilian Soiron (Dublin: Gill and Son, 1965), pp. 72, 73-74, 77.

Bibliography

Among the works which deal with the existentialism of the Hebrews, the most informative and insightful by far is the work of Claude Tresmontant, *A Study of Hebrew Thought,* trans. Michael F. Gibson (New York: Desclee Co., 1960). Thorleif Boman's *Hebrew Thought Compared with Greek,* trans. Jules L. Moreau (New York: Norton & Co., 1970) provides less significant but still helpful reading. Among the many books which treat of the theological or cultural background of the Bible, I recommend the following: Gerhard von Rad's *Old Testament Theology,* trans. D. M. G. Stalker (New York: Harper and Row, vol. 1, 1962; vol. 2, 1965); Bernhard Anderson's *Understanding the Old Testament* (Englewood Cliffs, N.J.: Prentice-Hall, 1966); John L. McKenzie's *A Theology of the Old Testament* (Garden City, N.Y.: Doubleday, 1974); and Luke Grollenberg's *A New Look at an Old Book,* trans. Richard Rutherford (Paramus, N.J.: Newman Press, 1969). Among the many articles which discuss the characteristics of Hebrew thought, I recommend as particularly pertinent to the topic of this chapter an article by François Dreyfus, "The Existential Value of the Old Testament," *Concilium* XXX, *How Does the Church Confront the Old Testament?*, ed. Pierre Benoit et al. (New York: Paulist Press, 1967), pp. 33-44.

CHAPTER FIVE

THE BIBLICAL PERSON

A DRAMATIC CONFRONTATION between Hebrew and Greek thought occurred one day in Athens when St. Paul, in proclaiming the Good News to the Council of the Areopagus, spoke of the resurrection from the dead. "At this mention of rising from the dead, some of them burst out laughing" (Ac 17:32). Though the Athenians were noted for their interest in new ideas and their willingness to discuss them (cf. Ac 17:21), the doctrine of the resurrection was to them so absurd that it deserved only mocking laughter. If Paul had mentioned the immortality of the soul, the Athenians would have been willing to discuss the question. But the resurrection held for them something of the same "madness" which St. Paul on another occasion said they found in the doctrine of the crucifixion (1 Co 1:23).

It took a long time for the Hebrews to arrive at a notion of an afterlife. Only in the latter part of the Old Testament did it begin to emerge with any degree of clarity, and it was never universally accepted. But when the conviction of an afterlife finally came to the biblical person, it had to be in terms of a resurrection of the whole person, rather than in terms of a survival of a spiritual soul. The Greek discussions concerning the immortality of the soul would make no sense at all to the biblical person, just as faith in the resurrection of the total man was for the Greeks an absurdity.[1] The reason for this difference is that the Greek concept of the human person was dualistic, while the concept of biblical man was monistic.

For the Greeks, the human person was a composite of two elements. According to Plato the person was really the spiritual soul, which was incarnated, or, more exactly, incarcerated in a body that was alien to it. The body was a hindrance and a burden to the soul, and the person could find fulfillment only by achieving freedom from it. For Aristotle the human person was made up of two co-principles which together constituted his essence. But the person was not the soul, nor was the body alien to the soul. The person was the composite of the two intimately united into one. By contrast, the biblical person never thought of himself as a composite of two elements. His concept was holistic: he always viewed the person in terms of what I have called his intrinsic wholeness. This was all a part of the concrete, existential, non-analytic character of Semitic thinking.

Because the biblical person's view of human nature was holistic, his concept of an afterlife had to be in terms of the whole person. He could not conceive of it in terms of the immortality of a spiritual soul because he was not conscious of possessing a spiritual soul. There was no word in his vocabulary which corresponds to our term "soul."[2] The biblical person looked upon himself as a living body, and since his body was corruptible and perishable, the only way he could conceive of an afterlife was in terms of a restoration of life to the body by a resurrection which would render it imperishable. Speaking of the resurrection, Paul says that "our perishable nature must put on imperishability and this mortal nature must put on immortality" (1 Co 15:53).

What has just been said about the Bible's monistic concept of the human person might seem to be contradicted by a distinction frequently found in Scripture, and especially in St. Paul, between "flesh" and "spirit" (between *sarx* and *pneuma* in Greek). We often come across, not only a distinction, but a conflict between these two.* In several passages (e.g., Rm 7 and 8; Ga 5:16-25) St. Paul says that living the Christian life means living according to the spirit and not according to the flesh, and that the only way to live according to the spirit is to remove from our lives all the ways of the flesh. These texts seem to fit in perfectly with the Platonic teaching of a dualism of soul and body, and this is in fact the way they were generally interpreted for many centuries. Moreover, these texts seem to suggest that the person is really the spirit, and that the flesh is a kind of unhappy adjunct, a hindrance, an enemy.

---

*To understand the problem, the pertinent texts must be read in a version which translates literally the Greek term *sarx* as "flesh." Several recent versions have chosen to substitute other expressions which seek to interpret the real meaning this term had for the Hebrews. Thus, for example, the Knox version uses "nature," and the Jerusalem Bible employs the terms "unspiritual," and "self-indulgence."

Actually, what Paul means by spirit and flesh is not at all the same as what is meant by the Greek concepts of soul and body. Though these terms are used in Scripture in a variety of meanings, when they are used by St. Paul in opposition to each other, "flesh" does not mean just the body as distinguished from the soul, but the whole person or the whole of humanity, considered apart from any relation to the supernatural. Flesh is the ego-centered person in his or her purely human condition, bound up with material creation. Spirit refers to that same person, but now considered as God-centered, able to transcend the world and the limitations of his human condition and be united with God.

Hence, what Paul says of the flesh must not be taken as meaning exclusively, or even chiefly, something pertaining to the body in the Greek sense, as distinguished from the spiritual soul, but as signifying concrete human existence in this world, the historical human person in his earth-bound existentiality, with all his weaknesses, both of soul and body, his subjection to law, his perishability, his frailty, and his liability to temptation.

Several Pauline texts make it clear that flesh and spirit do not refer to an intrinsic dichotomy in the makeup of the human person. When, in writing to the Galatians, he distinguishes between the works of the flesh and the fruits of the spirit, most of the former are things pertaining to the soul, such as "idolatry, sorcery, enmity, strife, jealousy, anger, selfishness, dissension, party spirit" (5:20 R.S.V.). Similarly in his first letter to the Corinthians, Paul attributes jealousy and strife to the flesh (3:3 R.S.V.). It is clear in these and other texts that flesh means the human person considered in his distance from God, and that spirit refers to the human person as open to the Spirit and as animated by his influence and activity.

Sometimes the term "flesh" is used to signify the neutral character of earthly existence, without necessarily involving any opposition to the things of God. It is in this sense that St. John tells us that "the Word was made flesh" (Jn 1:14), meaning that the Son of God became man in all his concrete, limited, human condition. Yet, because this human condition is so weak and so liable to temptation and to the slavery of sin, St. Paul can say that God has sent his Son "in the likeness of sinful flesh" (Rm 8:3 R.S.V.). Because the pattern of human existence, whenever it is determined only by the flesh, is frail and vulnerable, it tends to become inimical to God. Hence, in many texts, when it is used in contrast to the spirit, there is an opposition to God, insofar as the human person resists or contradicts God's designs. But this opposition comes primarily and essentially from the human will, which is a power of the soul, as we understand the term. The basic Christian dualism is not an opposition between soul and body, but an opposition between the human and the divine wills. Though there is indeed a great need to discipline the body and to bring it under subjection, there is an even greater need to discipline the soul.

Christian existentialism calls for a holistic view of the human person, though not in the same sense as the Hebrew view. The Christian concept of person has issued from a union of Hebrew and Greek thought. This union provides a good illustration of how Greek philosophy played at one and the same time a positive and a negative role in the development of Christian theology and spirituality from their biblical roots. The Christian person must be viewed, not just as a living body, but as a composite of a material body and a spiritual soul. The two elements which make up this union are not to be considered two distinct essences only loosely united, but co-principles of one essence. Human beings are essentially psychosomatic, and the multiple relationships between the two co-principles which constitute their essence reach down to its very roots. Only by emphasizing this point can the intrinsic wholeness of the human person be understood. The Christian person is not a spiritual soul incarcerated in a body that is alien and hostile to it. Christian fulfillment does not consist in striving to liberate the soul from the trammels of the body. Indeed, the body is called to have a profound share in the ultimate destiny of the Christian. The leading Neoplatonist, Plotinus, is often quoted as saying that he was ashamed he had a body. This would make no sense at all to the biblical person. It should also be devoid of sense to Christians, who must love their bodies as a part of their very essence. The Christian life does not consist simply in saving and sanctifying souls; it is always the total person who is engaged before God.

The Christian concept of the afterlife has also issued from a union of biblical and Greek thought. Christians view the afterlife in terms of both the immortality of the soul and the resurrection from the dead. Because the soul is spiritual, it will survive separation from the body. But it will not be fully a human person in this separated state. Only when life is restored to the body and when what is by nature perishable is made imperishable will the afterlife be complete. Greek thought had a very positive influence in the development of the Christian view of the person as a composite of soul and body, and also upon the Christian view of the afterlife. In its Platonic form it also had an extremely negative influence on Christian spirituality, especially with respect to the role of the Christian body and the nature of Christian asceticism.

The duality of soul and body in the Christian view of the human person may seem to make this view less holistic than the Hebrew view. Actually, the intrinsic unity is far greater, especially when we view Christians in terms of the ultimate achievement of their vocation. For, in the Hebrew concept, the body had no higher spiritual principle like the soul to give it lasting unity and identity. Its natural destiny was total disintegration into the dust from which it was formed. Not only does the Christian body possess on the natural level the higher unity and identity given it by its spiritual soul, but it is called to be, along with the soul, the temple of the indwelling Spirit, who carries on in it a growing spiritualization which unites it ever more fully with the utter unity and simplicity of his own life. The Spirit gives to the perishable body an imperishable destiny in which it not only will be totally conformed to the imperishable unity of its soul, but will also be given a share in the unity and simplicity of the glorified Body of the risen Lord.

*　　*　　*

Existentialism and personalism have many implications for the Christian life. The first and most important is that the person in his or her wholeness is the subject of the spiritual life. The unity between the soul and the body is so intimate that the body enters even into the highest reaches of the functioning of the soul. It is impossible to have a thought without the body participating in the very act of thinking. The body is involved in our highest experience of prayer. It is true, of course, that human persons are capable of a spiritual life only because of that part of them which is spirit, for it is the soul which is the immediate and primary subject of grace. Moreover, all the material and external aspects of the spiritual life have their wellsprings in the depths of the spirit. Yet, in the last analysis, it is the human composite of matter and spirit who is sanctified; it is the whole human person who loves and prays and offers himself or herself in sacrifice.

When we use the term "the spiritual life" we are evidently speaking about the life of some spirit. If we think that this means primarily the spiritual soul, we have already become captives of

Plato, and from that point on all we think or say about the spiritual life will be tinged with "angelism." It is not primarily the human spirit we are talking about when we speak of the spiritual life, but the Holy Spirit, the Spirit of the risen Jesus who, in his gratuitous love, communicates his life and himself to the Body of Jesus which we call the Church, and to all its members. During the time-in-between Pentecost and Parousia, the Spirit of the risen Jesus is on mission not only in our souls but also in our bodies, and indeed in the material world itself. If we separate the soul and the body in our thinking about the spiritual life we run the risk of never coming into close contact with either God or the world. Like the biblical person, the spiritual person of our times wants to be totally involved in his spiritual life.

Subtle vestiges of Platonism still running in the bloodstream of many Christians, when combined with an Anglo-Saxon inheritance, make many feel that any manifestation of the emotions should be ruled out of one's spiritual life. Yet, they are a part of the total human experience and hence should not be seen as something alien to the spiritual life. Jesus himself was far from being an unemotional person: he wept on at least two occasions (Jn 11:36; Lk 19:41); his soul was troubled (Jn 12:27); "sadness came over him and great distress," and his soul was "sorrowful to the point of death" (Mt 26:37); he experienced anguish on the cross (Mt 27:46); he became angry (Jn 2:14-16); frequently his heart was moved with pity (Mt 9:36; 14:14); he knew what it meant to be filled with joy (Lk 10:21). In view of all this, it is difficult to understand how the Stoic and Gnostic *apatheia*, the complete stilling of all the emotions, could ever have become an ideal for Christians striving for holiness, as has actually happened on numerous occasions, especially among the anchorites in the early centuries of the Church. Virtue does not consist in fleeing from the powers of the body, the sense appetites, the human emotions and feelings, but in employing them in an appropriate manner.

Contemporary developments in medicine, psychology, and the philosophy of personalism are bringing out more and more clearly how much the somatic aspect of the human person influences and conditions the psychic aspect, and how deeply the organic side of a person's nature enters into the very makeup of his or her character. The health and equilibrium of the body influence the health and equilibrium of the mind; thus the way in which the divine life is able to compenetrate man's human life and take full possession of it will ordinarily depend upon his psychophysical condition. How often have not the spiritual lives of Christians been impeded, thwarted, and dwarfed by a lack of provision for proper psychophysical development, by an excessively negative and Jansenistic doctrine of self-denial and self-disparagement, by a lack of some of the basic requirements of physical and psychological hygiene, by lifestyles which impeded the full and normal development of the human personality, by regimes in religious houses which were culturally sterile and which prevented the development of a discriminating capacity for participating in the finest forms of human enjoyment, without which there cannot be full personality development?

To balance this we must, of course, add that though holiness is indeed wholeness, this wholeness must not be conceived too narrowly. To be Christian wholeness, it can be neither self-sufficient nor self-contained. It must not be confined to the limitations of mere human or natural wholeness. It must possess a capacity to transcend itself and even sacrifice important human values, as in the case of consecrated virginity. Christian self-fulfillment cannot mean a fulfillment brought about by self alone. It cannot mean a fulfillment that is direct and immediate, without passing through the purification of suffering. Nevertheless, those who make a sacrifice of such profound human values as in a life of consecrated virginity, a sacrifice which reaches so deeply into both the physical and the psychical aspects of the human person, must be aware that if the transcendental gifts of divine love, of union with God in prayer, of total availability to God and neighbor, are not continually sought after and achieved, then nature will have its revenge in the form of a limited, stunted, introverted, and egotistical personality. This is a part of the splendid risk which is the Christian life.

We usually find that those who have negative ideas, feelings, and attitudes toward the body tend to concentrate their negativity in a special way upon the body's sexuality. They fail to realize that in human sexuality we have a beautiful reflection of the generation and birth found in the inner life of the Trinity. It is significant that birth is present only at the two extremes of reality: in God and in the material world. In God the second person of the Trinity is born of the Father from all eternity as light from light. But in all the angelic hierarchies there is no birth. The angels are too imperfect to have the kind of birth that is of the essence of God's inner life and, because they are pure spirits, they cannot have the kind of birth that requires a body. While it is true that birth is found in bodily beings lower than human beings, only in human life does birth, while remaining a bodily function, also participate in the realm of the spirit. For human birth to be truly human, it must involve not only the body, but also the spirit. For it to be truly Christian, it must also involve the Holy Spirit, who is not a Platonist and who does not disdain to share intimately in human sexuality, and thus make of it a radiant reflection of the luminous relation between the Father and the Son in the Trinity. There was from the beginning a beautiful natural sacramentality in sexual union, long before Christ elevated marriage to the status of a sacrament in the full sense of the word.

Matter can never lose the worth and dignity given to it in the incarnation, which keeps telling us that we must become ever more fully and more authentically incarnate, more totally and more fully human as Jesus was. Throughout his public life, Jesus continually gave evidence in his miracles of his tender love for the human body. The healings of Jesus were not performed to provide us with apologetic arguments; they were motivated by the desire of Jesus to see the human body whole. When he sent his disciples out to carry on his mission, he did not give them a long list of detailed instructions; but one thing he always told them was to heal the sick.

Some spiritual writers give the impression that God must be some kind of Platonist who despises matter. Yet, not only is God the one who created it and pronounced it good, he is also the one who became incarnated in it. The real Platonist is Lucifer. Proud pure spirit that he is, he despises matter and material things. For matter was his undoing in the incarnation; it continues to be his undoing in that prolongation of the incarnation which is the sacramental life of the Church. A few drops of water in baptism, and the human person, the composite of matter and spirit, is given a share in the very inner life of God, in which he, Lucifer, can never participate. A few kernels of wheat and a grape or two mean for Christians an intimate, exquisite union of love with the Lord of the universe; and all this through the animal process of eating and drinking. The material body is destined to participate in the final glorification with a glory that Lucifer will never be able to attain or even understand, in spite of the brilliance of his intelligence.

The liturgy shows an extraordinary regard and tender love for the human body. In the sacraments and the sacramentals it is

continually caressing the body with a divine touch. In baptism it
bathes the body and anoints it twice with oil, the sign of healing,
the sign used for kings, prophets, and priests in the Bible. Again
in confirmation the body is anointed with the unction of the Holy
Spirit. Once again in the sacrament of the sick it is anointed with
the oil of salvation. The liturgy sacramentalizes the bodies of
those united in marriage. And the most stupendous thing of all is
that the liturgy nourishes the body with the body and blood of
Christ. How often do not the prayers in the celebration of the
eucharist ask that this banquet will bring health not only of mind,
but also of body? The sacraments are the main channels of divine life; and it is precisely through the body that this life comes
to the Christian.

From the moment of baptism the total person, body as well as
soul, becomes a member of the Body of the risen and glorified
Christ, who thereafter remains like a great magnet drawing the
total person to an ever fuller share in his risen and glorified life.
St. Paul tells us that in baptism we already begin to share in the
resurrection of Christ (Rm 6:4), and the power of his resurrection
continues to work in us, gradually spiritualizing our bodies more
and more. The unknown author of *The Cloud of Unknowing*
makes an interesting remark which is relevant here: "as a person matures in the work of love, he will discover that this love
governs his demeanor befittingly both within and without. When
grace draws a man to contemplation it seems to transfigure him
even physically so that, though he might be ill-favored by nature,
he now appears changed and lovely to behold."[3] Anyone who has
had opportunity to observe John XXIII closely or has known
Mother Teresa of Calcutta will understand.

The resurrection of the body is an article of faith; but it is one
which seems of only marginal interest to the average Christian,
who is concerned with saving his or her immortal soul at the hour
of death. But this truth was not at all marginal in the preaching of
the apostles. In its vital connection with the resurrection of Christ
it was a central truth in the Good News. The resurrection of the
body is an essential part of God's plan to bring about a whole new
creation. Moreover, redemption must not be seen in a purely individual perspective; it must be seen in both its social and its cosmic dimensions, in what Charles Davis has called "the framework of salvation as a cosmic history centered on Christ."[4]

St. Paul tells us that Christ, through his resurrection, is the first
fruits of the new creation (1 Co 15:20). John tells us that we are

already sons of God, but that what we shall be in the future has not yet revealed (1 Jn 3:2). In writing to the Romans, Paul gives us some idea of what the future holds for us: he speaks of Christ "who, in the order of the spirit, the spirit of holiness that was in him, was proclaimed Son of God in all his power through his resurrection from the dead" (Rm 1:4-5). Christ was already Son of God before his resurrection, but it was only after, and because of, his resurrection that he entered fully into the glory that was his as God's Son. So it will be with us: only after we have become fully glorified human persons through the resurrection of our bodies shall we finally enter into the fullness of our divine adoption. Paul tells us that our risen body will be a spiritual body (1 Co 15:44 R.S.V.). This means that it will be a real body, but at the same time a body which is a pure expression of the Spirit. Only after the resurrection of the body does the Spirit at last take full possession of us.

The problem arises about how our souls can be fully beatified in the time between death and the resurrection of the dead. Since the soul by itself is not a human person, will it not be living in an unnatural state? The separated soul will be beatified to the fullness of its capacity by being totally caught up in the vision and ecstasy of God's inner life. After death it will have an extremely vital, intimate, and intense union with the glorified body of Christ, who already has the fullness of risen and glorified life in his whole being, body and soul. Moreover, the separated soul's duration will not be measured by the time which measures our existence here on earth. In the spiritual world there is duration, but a duration that is not extended in time. To get an idea of what this means let us compare two persons watching a parade, one standing on the sidewalk, the other at a window on the twenty-fifth floor of a skyscraper. The person on the sidewalk sees only an extremely narrow segment of the parade at any one moment. What has already gone by him is past; what has not yet reached his point on the sidewalk is future. But the person on the twenty-fifth floor sees the whole parade simultaneously in one simple view. What is past and future for the person below is present for the person above. God lives in an eternal "now" in which there is no succession; the whole past, present, and future of the entire creation is always present to him, who sees all in one simple vision. The angels, it is believed, do not have that degree of simultaneity, but something which approaches it. The time between the hour of death and the Parousia may be billions of years, but they will not be billions of years for the separated soul as it awaits reunion with the body in order to become finally a glorified human person. The separated soul shares intimately and profoundly in the life of God himself, and because of this it will share to some degree in the simultaneity of God's eternal "now."

In this life the soul in many ways has to conform to the laws of the body. It becomes subject to the law of inertia. The highest intellectual and spiritual activities can cause great fatigue. But it is not the spiritual soul itself that gets fatigued, for spirits never tire; it is the fact that thinking and praying cause fatigue in our cerebral and nervous systems. But in the state of glorification the relationship between body and soul will be just the reverse; the spirit will not be conformed to the body, but the body, through that spiritualization of matter which is its glorification, will be perfectly conformed to the soul.

The Church prays for the deceased: "Eternal rest grant unto them, O Lord, and may perpetual light shine upon them." Will our eternity, then, be an eternity of rest? There may be times when, weary of all the stirring and trafficking that goes on in our lives, we might look forward with some relish to a prolonged rest. Yet we know from experience with illness or inactivity that nothing makes us more restless than prolonged rest, and the prospect of an eternity of rest seems like an eternity of complete boredom. Our eternity will indeed be an eternity of rest, but a rest that consists in the fullness of activity. The prayer of the Church suggests this when, after praying for eternal rest, it adds: "And may perpetual light shine upon them." Light is a powerful stimulant. That is why, when we want to rest, we turn out the lights and pull down the shades. But the consummation of our Christian life and its fulfillment will consist in being immersed in the infinite light which is God (1 Jn 1:5). All the powers and faculties of the glorified person will be stimulated to their fullest capacity and far beyond because of God's gift of the light of glory. All human potentialities will be superactualized. All human faculties will be set racing, and because the glorified person will no longer be subject to the law of inertia, they will race on forever. Process is finally ended: to be a person no longer means to be in the constant process of becoming a person, for the fullness of personhood is now achieved. Process is ended, but activity goes on forever with an intensity that is sheer ecstasy. All this because the glorified Christian shares profoundly and intimately in the inner life of God, who is, as St. Augustine has said, "always active and always at rest." This is Christian fulfillment.

Notes

1. See Oscar Cullman, *Immortality of the Soul or Resurrection of the Dead?* (London: The Epworth Press, 1958). Edward Schillebeeckx, in *Jesus, An Experiment in Christology*, trans. Hubert Haskins (New York: Seabury Press, 1979) questions the universality of the contrast between Hebrew resurrection and Greek immortality, and points to some indications of a belief on the part of some Jews at the time of Jesus of the existence of a spiritual principle which survives after death. *Cf.* pp. 518 ff. However, these exceptions are not typical of Hebrew thought, and they are, generally speaking, attributable to the influence of Hellenistic thought.

2. In English versions of the Bible, the word "soul" is often inaccurately used as a translation of the Hebrew *nephesh*, a term which has many nuances of meaning, but which, generally speaking, may be taken to signify, not a spiritual soul, but the concrete living self. Gerhard Kittell points out that in some Rabbinical schools there developed a dualistic concept of the human person as composed of spirit and body, but he attributes this development to a Hellenistic influence. *Cf. Theological Dictionary of the New Testament*, VI, trans. and ed. Geoffrey W. Bromiley (Grand Rapids, Michigan: Wm. B. Eerdmans Publishing Co., 1968), 377 ff.

3. Ed. William Johnston (Garden City, N.Y.: Doubleday Image Books, 1973, p. 117.

4. "The Resurrection of the Body," *Theology for Today* (New York: Sheed and Ward, 1962), p. 272.

Bibliography

The works mentioned in the bibliography of the last chapter which give an insight into the spiritual, cultural, and theological background of the Bible also serve this chapter. Two other books are especially pertinent to the topic of the present chapter. The first is the highly esteemed work of John A. T. Robinson, *The Body, a Study in Pauline Theology* (London: SCM Press, 1952). This slender volume seeks to correlate and synthesize all the texts of St. Paul which refer to the human body. The second is Dom Wulstan Mork's *The Biblical Meaning of Man* (Milwaukee: Bruce Publishing Co., 1967), which gives a lucid explanation of the intrinsic wholeness of the biblical person.

Much has been written about the problem of the resurrection. In a brief but scholarly work, Oscar Cullmann studies the contrast between the Greek concept of immortality and the Hebrew notion of the resurrection of the dead: *Immortality of the Soul or Resurrection of the Dead?* (London: The Epworth Press, 1958). Charles Davis has an exceptionally clear and concise treatment of the resurrection of the body in his book, *Theology for Today* (New York: Sheed and Ward, 1962), pp. 269-273. I also recommend Karl Rahner's article, "The Resurrection of the Body,"

Theological Investigations, II, trans. Karl-H. Kruger (Baltimore: Helicon Press, 1963), 203-216. Anyone wishing to explore this topic more fully will find a number of articles treating its various aspects in two volumes of *Concilium:* XLI, *The Problem of Eschatology,* eds. Edward Schillebeeckx and Boniface Willems (New York: Paulist Press, 1969), and LX, *Immortality and Resurrection,* eds. Pierre Benoit et al. (New York: Herder and Herder, 1970).

CHAPTER SIX

BIBLICAL ENVIRONMENT

THE BIBLICAL PERSON was an existentialist because he always saw the human person, not only in terms of intrinsic wholeness, but also in terms of what I have called, for want of a better word, extrinsic wholeness. He was no more a dualist with regard to the human person and his or her environment than he was with regard to the makeup of the individual person. He considered himself one with the environment around him; he felt that he was a part of this environment and that it was a part of him. The human person was inconceivable for him except in this perspective.

First of all, the biblical person considered himself to be one with his people, to be a person-with-others-in-community. More than anyone else Martin Buber has emphasized the fact that no one can be considered an authentic person except in relationship with others, that the human person is a person precisely in and through his hyphenation with community. Buber's writings call upon the rich heritage of his own people. Throughout history there has always been a bond, unique in strength and intimacy, between the Jew and his people. Nothing has been able to rupture this bond; it has survived every possible kind of historical stress. It has survived the diaspora, the dispersion of the Jewish people in various parts of the world. It has survived systematic persecution and torture, inflicted for the most part by Christians; it has survived the Nazi attempt at genocide. It has remained strong enough to inspire a heroic and successful struggle to regain the "promised land," and to bring about once again a localized nation. It has heroically defended this nation, and still continues to do so.

The biblical person found his identity and his importance in the fact that he was a Hebrew, a member of God's chosen people. He always felt a strong bond uniting him to his family, his clan, and his nation. He could not conceive of any other kind of human life except group life. In other words, a person was not a person except in relation to community. A greater misery could hardly be imagined than to be banished from community as Cain was.

For the biblical person the family was the model for every other community. The whole family, and by extension, the whole clan and the whole nation, were somehow present in the individual members and identified with all their blessings, sufferings, responsibilities, and destiny. Individual members did not act for themselves alone; the family, the clan, the tribe, the nation were deeply involved in all their actions. The oneness of the Hebrew people was something more than the clannishness found in other primitive cultures, for Yahweh had elected this people as his own and had given them a destiny in which all shared. Yahweh was God of the nation more than of the individual person, who was relatively unimportant in comparison with the whole people. The biblical person had the notion of God as a Father; but he saw God as Father of the whole people rather than of the individual person.

In all the great crises and turning points of its tortuous history, Israel is concretized in individual persons who act in the name of the entire people. Here again it is interesting to contrast Greek and Hebrew culture. In Greek literature there are many isolated, and one might even say "lonely" heroes. But all the heroes in biblical literature, such as Moses, Samuel, David, and Samson, have absolutely no meaning apart from the life and history of their people.

The Bible is replete with instances which illustrate what H. Wheeler Robinson has called "corporate personality," a phrase now widely accepted by Scripture scholars. Let us take just one example: the story of Achan as related in Joshua, chapter 7. At the seige of the city of Jericho, Achan disobeyed God's command that everything in the city be destroyed, and secretly kept some of the spoils. The next step in the campaign was the assault of the city of Ai, which by any military calculation should have fallen with the greatest ease. But the assault turned out to be a disaster for the Israelites, which made them realize that someone in their group must have disobeyed God. They cast lots to find out who the sinner was, and Achan turned out to be the guilty person. Because of the secret sin of this one individual, the whole nation was branded as a sinner and therefore had to undergo punishment at the hand of Yahweh. To appease "the burning anger of God" Joshua had not only Achan, but also all the members of his family, stoned to death, and his tent with all his possessions destroyed by fire (7:24-26). This story, for us so gruesome and so difficult to understand, points out that Achan was identified with his family and everything that belonged to him, and that this identity was so bound up with the whole nation that his personal sin injured the whole people. Achan was not just an isolated individual and the nation was not just a collection of individuals. The two were identified, and Achan could not be seen apart from his solidarity with his family and the entire nation. The biblical people saw themselves as one entity in a way that goes far beyond the concept of the wholeness of the human person proposed by any contemporary existentialist.

Basically, Israel was a "flesh" community. In the Hebrew mind, the unity of a people was a development of the fundamental unity found in marriage, in which "two become one flesh" (cf. Gn 2:24 R.S.V.; Ep 5:31), an expression which for the Hebrew meant one, concrete, human reality. The children were a further extension of this flesh. This extension continued to the entire family, the whole clan, the whole community, the whole people: they were all one flesh.

The corporate personality of Israel had both a horizontal, or spatial dimension, and a vertical, or time dimension. Horizontal solidarity meant that all the people of a given generation or a given time were one person. Vertical solidarity meant that the people of any given time were identified with all their ancestors, going all the way back through Moses to Abraham, and reaching forward to all future generations. Israel was a continuous reality, never interrupted or dispersed by time. All the great events of the past were somehow present to and actually affecting each generation which inherited the glory, the responsibilities, the blessings, and the punishments of its past history. The prophets could speak of the great events of the past as though the people of their generation were actually participating in them. Not even death broke the solidarity of persons with their people; individuals who died went to join their ancestors, and at the same time continued to live with their people through their progeny. This is one of the reasons why genealogies were so important for the Hebrews. You might say that while horizontal solidarity was an extension of the *pater familias*, vertical solidarity was the extension of the ancestors.

This group solidarity had two aspects: the group was made one in a single individual, and at the same time it was an extension of the individual. The person in whom the nation or group was personified was not looked upon merely as a representative of the group. It was something far more real than an "as if" situation. The two were considered to be one and the same single, concrete, physical reality. Adam was looked upon as being something more than just a representative of the whole human race. In a certain sense he was considered to be identified with the whole race, and in Scripture his name is frequently used to signify the whole race. This explains why in many passages in the Bible there is a continual oscillation between the group and the individual, between singular and plural pronouns. It is in this context that we must situate the notion of the sin of one person making sinners of the members of the whole group, the whole nation, and even the whole human race. It is also in this same perspective that we must see how the sufferings of one person can atone for the sins of a whole people (cf. Is 53:4-10; Rm 5:12-21).

Yahweh seemed to participate in the concept of corporate solidarity. In connection with horizontal solidarity I have already mentioned the story of Achan. Many other instances could be cited, like the destruction by pestilence of 70,000 people because of David's pride in calling for a census of his people (2 S 24:1-25), and the three years' famine for the whole of Israel because of Saul's slaughter of the Gibeonites (2 S 21:1-2). The same was true of vertical solidarity: "For I, Yahweh your God, am a jealous God and I punish the father's fault in the sons, grandsons, and the great-grandsons of those who hate me; but I show kindness to thousands of those who love me and keep my commandments." (Ex 20:6).

I have said that basically the corporate solidarity of the Hebrews was a "flesh" solidarity. This, however, is not completely true. Though all the Hebrews liked to pride themselves on having descended from the seed of Abraham, they were far from being an ethnically pure race. Over the centuries there had been a great deal of intermarriage with other people. Moreover, not only individual "outsiders," but at times even other tribes and nations threw in their lot with Israel and were incorporated into the chosen people. In the description in Exodus of the departure from Egypt we read: "The sons of Israel left Rameses for Succoth, about six hundred thousand on the march—all men—not counting their families. People of various sorts joined them in great numbers" (Ex 12:37-38). Actually, what we seem to have here are caravans of a rather motley crowd of Bedouin whose various ancestors had come originally to Egypt because of the fertility and abundance of the area. The origin of Israel as the chosen people of God came later under the leadership of Moses and through the gratuitous intervention of Yahweh. It was during their long pilgrimage in the desert, and, as we shall see presently, because of it, that this crowd of heterogeneous people came to discover Yahweh as the one and the only true God and became one people by entering into a covenant with him. Eventually Paul was to preach that not physical descent from Abraham but spiritual descent was the thing that mattered (Rm 4; Ga 3:27-29; cf. Jn 8:33-41).

Thus, Israel was not simply a "flesh" community; it was even more a "spirit" community. The gratuitous election of Yahweh and the Sinai Covenant fused a motley crowd into one people. It is interesting to note in this connection that the Hebrews thought, not so much in terms of blood relationship as we do, but in terms of flesh relationship. Yet the Covenant created a kind of consanguinity among them, for it was sealed by the blood of the holocausts offered by Moses: "Then Moses took the blood and cast it towards the people. 'This' he said, 'is the blood of the Covenant that Yahweh had made with you'" (Ex 24:8). The full significance of all this will become apparent when we come to consider the unity and wholeness of the new people of God.

God's chosen people had many distinctive characteristics. One of them calls for special attention here. The people of God were essentially a pilgrim people. They were an exodus people centuries before the historical event known as the exodus: they continued to be an exodus people long after that event. In fact, they never really lost this distinctive characteristic. They began to be an exodus people when Yahweh commanded their Father Abraham: "Leave your country, your family, and your father's house, for the land I will show you." And Abraham obeyed, leaving Haran, taking with him his wife Sarai, his nephew Lot, and all the possessions and peoples they had acquired (Gn 12:1-5). "He set out without knowing where he was going" (Heb 11:8). From then on his descendants were a nomadic people for centuries; mobility was a part of their very existence. Israel had some of its most privileged moments while on the road, especially during its wanderings of forty years through the Sinai peninsula. Even after it had settled down in the promised land and become a sedentary people its nomadic existence continued to be a part of its cherished traditions and indeed of its very life. Yahweh had instructed them: "Land must not be sold in perpetuity, for the land belongs to me, and to me you are only strangers and guests" (Lv 25:23).

David prayed to Yahweh: "For we are strangers before you, settlers only, as all our ancestors were" (1 Ch 29:15). Each year, on the solemn occasion of offering the first fruits to Yahweh, the ritual began with the repetition of the same phrase: "My father was a wandering Aramaean" (Dt 26:5). The Old Testament is filled with expressions and figures of speech relating to nomadic life.

It has often been pointed out that the Hebrews were unique among all other peoples in that they drew their concept of God from history rather than from nature, and that its religion was more a history of events than a body of doctrine. We can even say that it was from its continual wanderings that Israel was able to develop its notion of the one transcendent God, which was absolutely unique among all the gods of the pagan peoples. Yahweh was a wanderer's God, and in a sense a wandering God. He had to be a leader to guide his people from one place to the other. He was their Shepherd (Ps. 23). Hence, he could not be identified with any one place, any particular aspect of nature or any personified power of nature. Sedentary peoples had sedentary gods. These gods lived in permanently fixed temples. Sedentary people depended for their life on the fertility of the land around them. Hence they needed a god like Baal to assure them of this fertility. There were fixed and constant aspects of nature that easily in the course of time developed their own deities. But a wandering God, a God that could intervene at any time and at any place in the history of his people, transcended all aspects of nature and all places on the earth. Even if the Israelites were to go to the farthest point in the universe, Yahweh would be there guiding and sustaining them: "If I flew to the point of sunrise, or westward across the sea, your hand would still be guiding me, your right hand holding me" (Ps 139:9-10). From this concept of a God of history who transcended nature there was a relatively easy transition to a God who was eminently transcendent, so much so that, rather than being subjected to any aspect of nature, all aspects of nature were subjected to him. He so transcended them all that all nature must have come from him through creation. Thus the wandering God, the God of history, became the God of creation.

During the time of its sedentary life, Israel was constantly tempted to accept the sedentary gods of its neighbors. It often felt the seduction of Baal. There were times when many of God's people tried to substitute Baal for Yahweh or to serve both. They were punished by the Babylonian captivity when once again they

had to take to the roads. But their wandering God went with them
and eventually led them back home.

For many centuries Israel had no fixed temple. Yahweh had
the same kind of dwelling as all nomads, a tent, the meeting
place where he made his revelations to Moses. For long after
Israel had become sedentary and its kings had begun to live in
palaces, the meeting place of Yahweh was a tent. And when
David proposed to build a temple for him, Yahweh, through the
prophet Nathan, forbad him to do so, saying: "I have never
stayed in a house from the day I brought the Israelites out of
Egypt until today, but have always led a wanderer's life in a
tent" (2 S 7:6). Yahweh promised on that occasion that it would
be a son of David who would provide him with a temple. This
prophecy was not completely fulfilled until Yahweh found his
permanent temple in the body of his Son. Very fittingly, when
John, in the prologue to his Gospel, wrote that the Word was
made flesh and dwelled among us, the literal phrase he used
was: "He pitched his tent among us" (Jn 1:14).

*　　*　　*

The biblical person was deeply conscious of his hyphenation,
not only with his people, but also with the world around him; he
felt strongly that he was all of a piece with the rest of creation. He
was deeply rooted in the world; he was embedded, so to speak, in
his material environment. From it he had taken his origin:
"Yahweh God fashioned man of dust from the soil. Then he
breathed into his nostrils a breath of life, and thus man became a
living being" (Gn 2:7). Moreover, his destiny was to return to the
soil from which he had been taken (Gn 3:19). This notion of the
dust of the earth being the origin and final end of the human person is a constant theme, not only in Genesis but throughout the
Old Testament (cf. e.g., Ps 90:3; 146:4; Jb 4:19; Qo 3:20; 12:7; Ws
2:3; 7:1). The Church has continued this thought across the centuries in its Ash Wednesday liturgy. The etymological origin of the
name *Adam* is not certain, but many scholars believe that it came
from a word meaning red clay. The biblical person looked upon
himself almost like a plant which had emerged from the soil and
was continually being nourished by it because still rooted in it.
But not quite. Like some contemporary existentialists who see the
human person as not completely a part of the world like a thing,
and therefore as possessing a certain transcendence, so also the
biblical person recognized a certain transcendence in himself in

relation to the rest of creation, for he alone was created in the image of God himself (Gn 1:27). Moreover, he was created as the lord of the whole of creation (Gn 1:28).

The biblical person loved the world from which he had sprung and of which he was a part, and he was convinced that God loved it also: "For had you hated anything, you would not have formed it" (Ws 11:25). During the many centuries when he had no clear notion of any other world, this was his only world. His destiny was bound up with it. In order to appreciate how closely the biblical person identified himself with the material world around him, one has only to read the prayer of the three young men in the fiery furnace (Dn 3:52-90), traditionally known as the *Benedicite*, in which they call upon just about everything in material creation to join with them in praising the Lord. The same theme is found in a number of the Psalms (cf. e.g., Ps 148). This is in keeping with the character of the Psalms and of biblical prayer in general, which issues directly from the heart of concrete reality and historical experience.

*   *   *

The biblical person was also very conscious, though not in a speculative or reflective way, that time was an important, indeed an indispensable element of his environment, and that his life was deeply involved in it. In recent times, a number of Scripture scholars have taken a special interest in the biblical notion of time.[1] I shall dwell on this aspect of biblical environment at greater length than on the other aspects, not only because this will serve to bring out more fully the existentialism of the biblical person, but also because the Hebrew notion of time provides a rich and significant background for a future consideration of Christian time in general, and of liturgical time in particular.

In Hebrew thought, time implies the whole of reality. It implies a continuous development of new reality. There is, so to speak, an ongoing parturition of the world in history. This way of loking at the world is strikingly similar to the way the process theologians view reality.

For the biblical person, life was a continual process with a goal in mind, at least in the mind of God. The biblical person had a supreme reverence, which at times took the form of a profound fear, with regard to the transcendence of God, his absolute otherness. Indeed, Yahweh was known to him as "the Wholly Other." Yet, paradoxically, this "Wholly Other" entered continually and in extremely intimate ways into his life through the events of history. Yahweh communicated himself through historical events in such a way that history was made up of an onward movement of happenings which never turned back and never repeated themselves, for the acts of God are essentially irreversible and unrepeatable.

For the biblical person there was at the beginning of time, not a void, but the "I Am," Existence himself, the one who in Exodus (3:14) revealed his name (and therefore for the Hebrews his very essence) in terms of existence. Albright suggests that one of the ways of translating this obscure revelation of God's name might be: "He causes to be whatever comes into existence." At the beginning of time this "Existence" brought all things from non-existence into existence through creation. By contrast, for the Platonists, generally speaking, the genesis of sensible, material, and manifold reality is owing to some kind of downfall, decline, or degradation. The beginning is a fall, a descent, a dispersal of the One into multiple material things. For the biblical person, time begins with a positive creation, an ascent, and everything in creation is very good. (Gn 1:31).

History in Hebrew thought is not like a river of unrelated events that is continually flowing away, a light that is continually being dissipated in the darkness; rather it is a maturation, a growth, a continual evolution of something new. It is a movement towards an end. The prophet is one who has been inspired with a sense of history; he is able to grasp the direction in which events are moving. Time is a positive movement towards the fullness of time (cf. Mk 1:15).

All this is not to say that the biblical person had, as the Greeks did, an explicitly developed notion of time as the universal measure of motion. Time for him signified an order of the succession of historical events, each of which is destined to come at its appointed hour. The present moment in some sense both recapitulates the past and already contains the future.

The Hebrew notion of time is often contrasted to that of the Greeks by saying that whereas the former was linear, the latter was cyclic. Some of the Greek thinkers did have a cyclic idea of history, for a cyclic notion of time endows singular events with a certain kind of universality which for them was necessary for intelligibility. It is sometimes suggested that these contrasting notions of time and history are symbolized by the contrast between the story of Ulysses and the story of Abraham. Ulysses left his home in Ithaca, only to return later in life, after the battle of Troy and many wanderings, to Penelope and the home from which he started. On the contrary, the exodus of Abraham and his family from Haran was definitive; he never returned there again. The same might be said of Moses, and indeed of the whole Jewish people, who, having once initiated their exodus from Egypt, never returned to their starting point. For the biblical person the events of history, and especially those most important events which were the actions of Yahweh, could happen only once. They had a "once-and-for-all" quality that made it necessary for time to be linear and that stamped his people with a distinctive "exodus" quality which drew them continually forward toward a fulfillment that was always new. The biblical concept of history is in some ways similar to that of Marxists: history is a movement guided by an ineluctable process which leads toward a liberation that lies in the future. For the typical Greek, any concept of liberation, of the fullness of freedom, or of redemption, would have to consist in being set free from the enslavement of the circle of history and indeed from time itself. It would be difficult for him to conceive of freedom, salvation, and redemption as taking place in an historical event or a series of events in time.

One of the best known passages from the Old Testament is found in the opening lines of Ecclesiastes, where Qoheleth, the Preacher, writes:

> The sun rises, the sun sets; then to its place it speeds and there it rises. Southward goes the wind, then turns to the north; it turns and turns again; back then to its circling goes the wind.... What was will be again; what has been done will be done again; there is nothing new under the sun. Take anything of which it may be said, "Look now, this is new." Already, long before our time, it existed (Qo 1:5-6, 9-10).

Here Qoheleth seems to challenge what I have said about the biblical concept of time as linear. Actually, he is not presenting in this passage a typically biblical view. Some commentators see here a trace of the Hellenistic culture imposed throughout the Middle East by Alexander the Great and his successors. Others feel that it betrays the influence of the wisdom literature of some of the neighbors of Israel. It is well known that the wisdom literature of the Bible has much in common with the wisdom literature of other primitive peoples who lived in the areas surrounding Israel. It is also well known that many of the peoples of the Middle East held a circular view of time based on the recurring seasons of nature.

The Hebrew concept of time and history was linear, but not in the same sense in which the modern concept of time is linear. Time for us is an abstraction; it is divorced from the concrete events that take place in it, and is, therefore, completely neutral with respect to them. It is a homogeneous and empty duration extending from an endless future to an endless past. It is like an open, blank line waiting to be filled in with content as it continues its flow. It is thought of in terms of a purely quantitative and external measure of the cosmic process. It is something that can be accurately measured, in a purely objective and impersonal way, by clocks and calendars. In this concept the relativity of time and its transitory character are strongly emphasized.

Because the biblical mind was not inclined toward abstractions, it did not think of time in the abstract. In the Hebrew language there is no word which would convey the meaning of purely cosmic time. Biblical time is not simply quantitative, but essentially qualitative. It is not empty and neutral; rather it is specified by the content of events which take place in it. It is therefore "eventful." It is not simply objective and impersonal, but is judged in relation to how it affects the persons involved in it. This is one of the reasons why the Hebrews wrote history in such a subjective and personal way. Historical actions, particularly those by which Yahweh had fashioned his people, were viewed, not as relative and transitory, but as absolute and endowed with a certain kind of permanency.

In connection with the eventfulness characteristic of the biblical concept of time it is important to note that in biblical language there are two kinds of time, which are distinguished by the Greek words *chronos* and *kairos*. *Chronos* signifies the ordinary flow of time. *Kairos* refers to a time of special eventfulness, a time of opportunity and of special grace, a time particularly pregnant with possibilities. The most important *kairoi* were the times when Yahweh intervened in the history of his people, when the events of time were his acts of revelation and salvation.

Although the Israelites shared many things with the primitive peoples living around them, some of whom had a considerably more advanced culture than their own, they were unique in that they had a concept of history. The neighboring peoples (at least according to our present knowledge of them) had no realization that the events which made up their lives had any particular connection with each other or that they were moving in any particular direction. Nature went through an annual cycle which kept repeating itself. Their many gods did intervene in their lives but according to no plan. But the God of the Hebrews was in no way capricious; indeed, he was noted for his steadfast and enduring love (cf. e.g., Is 49:15; Jr 31:3; Ezk 16:60-63; Ho 11:1-9; Ps 136). He had a destiny for his chosen people, and his interventions in history kept them moving toward that destiny. It is significant that among all the religions that have appeared in the world only three are essentially historical: the Jewish religion, and the two which have developed from it, Christianity and Islam.

The religion of the Israelites was not, like all other religions around them, drawn from nature but from time and history (cf. Dt. 4:19-20). Israel was very conscious that its very existence came from a gratuitous intervention of Yahweh. It was history that gave God's chosen people its unique identity. God revealed himself to the Hebrews not so much through doctrine as through events and actions. That is one reason why the Old Testament books are so existential. They are either historical (not, however, completely in our sense, as I have already pointed out), or they have to do with concrete human life, as in the wisdom literature. History was not put into writing for the sheer sake of having a record of the past, but because the past was considered relevant for the present and somehow continued to live in the present. Like the wisdom literature, the historical books were written for pedagogical reasons.

Although biblical time was specified principally by the extraordinary interventions of Yahweh in history, it was also specified by the ordinary events of human life. Thus, for example, Scripture speaks of the time for bringing in the flocks (Gn 29:7), the time when women go down to draw water (Gn 24:11), the time when kings go campaigning (2 S 11:1), the time for the harvest (Mk 4:29). Qoheleth, in another famous passage, tells us that "there is a season for everything, a time for every occupation under the sun." He then proceeds to enumerate a series of fourteen antitheses which sum up the "times" of human life: "a time for giving birth, a time for dying; a time for planting, a time for uprooting what has been planted; a time for killing, a time for healing; ... a time for tears, a time for laughter; a time for mourning, a time for dancing .... a time for war, a time for peace" (Qo 3:1-8). For the biblical person various times are known and distinguished from each other, not primarily by the order in which they come in a temporal sequence, but rather by their content. And he attributes to God not only the extraordinary events in history but also the ordinary events of human life. Yahweh gives the land rain in season (Dt. 11:14); he provides food for all living beings (Ps. 104:27-28; 145:15). Thus, when the Psalmist prays: "My times are in thy hand" (Ps. 31:15 R.S.V.), he is thinking of the many events that go to make up a lifetime.

But biblical time and history were determined primarily by the extraordinary saving actions of Yahweh, which had fashioned them into a people peculiarly his own, and which continually guided them throughout their history. Basically, the history of Israel was a story linking promise with fulfillment, and therefore memory with hope. What God did to the forefathers he did for all coming after. In the life of both the individual and the nation what was done in the past was still alive and active in the present. Persons and events were much more closely identified for the biblical person than they usually are for us. Nor did he draw such a clear and sharp line between the now and the then as we do. The moments and events of the past were creative of what was present and would continue to determine the future.

When the great saving acts of Yahweh were celebrated in festival times, they were considered to be made present in such a way that the time of their ancestors became united with the time of those celebrating the festivals. For this reason the celebration of these festivals played an extremely important role in the biblical person's concept of time. They made him especially sensitive to the role played by Yahweh in the history of his people and therefore in his history. Festivals were the days the Lord had made. They identified the flow of time even more than the various seasons did for other primitive peoples (although some of the biblical festivals were also related to seasons of nature). These festive celebrations kept alive in the people the true meaning of time, a sense of history, and in particular the unique kind of history that was theirs. It made them deeply conscious of the fact that history determined their very existence as a people. When the community of Israel gathered to celebrate these festivals, the solemn proclamation of the encounter of their fathers with the God of history became, in a very real sense, their own personal encounter with Yahweh. Among the most venerable traditions of the Mishna is a command which is a part of the ritual of the Passover: "In every generation, it is the duty of every man to consider himself as having personally come out from Egypt." The corporate personality of Israel was extended to its unique history and became what has been called its "vertical corporate personality" (cf. Ex 13:8-10; Dt 6:23). One might say that the hyphenation of the biblical person with time was all bound up with his hyphenation with community. "The most distinctive feature of the Jewish people" writes Bernhard Anderson "is their sense of history . . . . Indeed, if historical memory were destroyed, the Jewish community would soon dissolve."[2] For this reason, the Hebrew was constantly being reminded to remember. Deuteronomy is replete with such reminders: "Think back on the days of old, think over the years, down the ages. Ask of your father, let him teach you; of your elders, let them enlighten you" (Dt 32:7; cf. 5:15; 7:18; 8:19; 16:3).

The extremely strong sense of vertical corporate personality made the participants in the festival liturgies feel that they were really contemporaneous with their ancestors who actually took part in the historical events being commemorated. It was not simply a question of commemoration, not simply a calling to mind, not just an attempt to capture again in memory what the flow of time had long since swept away, but the conviction that the event of the past entered into the present, that the time of the celebrant of the festival liturgy was somehow synchronized with the time of his forefathers in such a way that he was actually participating in the events of past history. In every succeeding generation the pregnant word "today" was spoken emphatically, and somehow throughout the centuries it was considered to be the same "today" (cf. e.g., Dt 5:2-3; 29:9).

James Mitchner, in his best-selling novel, *The Source*, brings out strikingly this orientation of the Jewish people to the past. One of the principal characters, a Jewish girl named Vered, speaks out in a moment of intense feeling:

> . . . it seems to me we Jews spend our lives remembering, and I've suddenly discovered that I'm sick and tired of living in a land of remembrance. My year in Jerusalem begins with Rosh Hashana when I remember Abraham, four thousand years ago. Then comes Yom Kippur, and we remember everything. The Feast of Booths and we remember the desert years. Like a great bronze bell tolling over the churches of Jerusalem, we tick off our days and remember our grief. Of course, there are a few happy days. Simhat Torah, Hanukkah, when we remember the victory of the Maccabees, Arbor Day for remembering trees. At Purim we remember Persia three thousand years ago, and at Passover we remember Egypt even longer ago. For years I dutifully remembered and thought it was natural to spend one's life weeping over the dead past, uttering lamentations for things that happened so terribly long ago. It was a burden, but it was our inescapable Jewish burden and I accepted it.[3]

In her moment of emotion Vered forgot that it had been typical of her people not only to look back to the past but also to look forward with expectation to the future. The constant recollection of past events, and particularly the annual celebration of the Exodus, were for the Israelites something that referred not only to the past but to the future as well. The deliverance of the past was in itself a promise and an assurance of an even greater deliverance in the future. The life of the Israelite was made up not only of recollection but also of expectation, not only of memory but also of hope. What God had done in the past was an earnest of what he would do in the future. Through hope the future was already present. And just as the biblical person's identity with the past was experienced as a member of a people, so also he could never conceive of historical evolution toward the future apart from his people. With his people he was called to live in eschatological expectation of the final saving action of Yahweh in the messianic era. Thus, time and history were viewed in terms of two aeons, the aeon of the present and the long-expected aeon of the future which would supercede the present age.

Mircea Eliade, in his many studies in comparative religion, professes to have discovered a characteristic of "sacred history" common to the various forms in which man's religious experience has expressed itself. This characteristic he calls the "Myth of the Eternal Return." He has explored this question not only in his work which bears this title,[4] but in other works as well, such as *Myth and Reality*[5] and *Myths, Dreams and Mysteries*.[6] His thesis is that religious people, in their rites and liturgies, return over and over again to their origins, to the great personages and events of the past, in the belief that recapturing the past affects the present and makes those who participate in the liturgy contemporaneous with the persons and events of the past. As a result, religious time is necessarily circular.

Eliade is too good a historian and scholar not to recognize the essential difference between the Hebrew and Christian view of time as linear and the view of circular time common to mythological religions. He admits that in the Judaeo-Christian tradition, time and history are viewed as linear and irreversible. At the same time, he holds that *"by the very fact that it is a religion,* Christianity had to keep at least one mythical aspect—liturgical Time, that is, the periodical recovery of the *illud tempus* of the 'beginnings'."[7] For Eliade, "liturgical Time is a circular Time."[8]

It would take us too far afield to attempt here an adequate critique of Eliade's view. Suffice to say that though there are similarities between the liturgies of the Old Testament and of Christianity on the one hand, and the liturgies of mythical religions on the other, the similarities are superficial, especially insofar as Christian liturgy is concerned. We have seen that Israel, along with its linear view of time, did have its cycles of festivals, some of which, by an extrapolation of nature, were historicized seasonal feasts. But the celebration of these festivals not only united the participants with the past, it also projected them into the future. The Christian liturgy, however, recaptures the past, and at the same time anticipates and even summons the future in a way that goes infinitely beyond anything found in either the mythical and mystery religions or the liturgies of the Old Testament.

This point is of great importance for the question of Christian fulfillment. For the whole process of fulfillment calls for a linear, forward moving time. Fulfillment can never be achieved by simply moving in circles and always coming back to the same point of departure. Though liturgical cycles may seem to be circles, they are in fact spirals. For if, in and through the liturgy, Christians are really caught up in the saving and sanctifying acts of salvation history, going through a liturgical cycle inevitably means that they are lifted up to a higher spiritual plane, in such a way that the recurring cycles of time become a spiral which continually propels them upward and onward toward the God of the future, in whom alone they find fulfillment.

*   *   *

All I have said in this chapter about the relation of the biblical person with his environment makes it clear, I think, that he was indeed an existentialist. He was also a personalist. The first suggestion of personalism in the Bible is found at the very beginning when God created man in his image and likeness (Gn 1:26) and brought all the wild beasts and the birds of heaven to see if he could find a companion and helpmate among them (Gn 2: 18-24). When man failed to find a suitable companion, God fashioned another human person, saying: "it is not good that man should be alone." But the full meaning of personalism was not revealed until toward the end of the Bible when Jesus made the astounding and incomprehensible revelation that, not only is it not good for one human person to be alone, it is also not good, nor even metaphysically possible (though the human mind cannot understand why), for a divine person to be alone. Not only a human person, but also a divine person needs to be with other persons sharing the same nature. In the case of Adam, it was sufficient that his companion have human nature, a nature only similar to his own. In the case of the divine person, "to be means to be with" two other persons, two other "Thous," whose nature is not only similar to his own, but actually identical with it. Christian personalism gets its inspiration first and foremost from this amazing revelation that the "I" of each divine person has no meaning, and indeed no existence, apart from the community of divine persons, in which each one is a living relation of love to the other two. It is the almost incredible vocation of the Christian to be called to share in the "I-Thou" relationships of that divine community which we call the Blessed Trinity.

When their pilgrimage is over, Christians will finally realize fully why the Bible and their Christian vocation have called them to be personalists in a sense and to a degree that philosphers of personalism could never possibly grasp. Having been made one with the divine person of Christ in the intimacy of his ecclesial Body while on earth, they will be introduced, in and through Christ Jesus, into the depths of the triune life of God, in which the very personhood of each person consists in a total self-gift of love to the other two. They will then be sharing fully in that fullness of existence possessed by Existence himself, who revealed his name as "I am who I am." (Ex 3:14). Then at last the Christian person will be able to say: "I finally am who I am." This is Christian fulfillment.

Notes

1. See, for example, James Barr, *Biblical Words for Time* (London: SCM Press, 1962).

2. *Understanding the Old Testament* (Englewood Cliffs, N.J.: Prentice-Hall, 1966), p. 2.

3. (Greenwich, Conn.: Fawcett World Library, 1967), pp. 1051-1052.

4. Trans. Willard R. Trask (London: Routledge and Kegan Paul, 1955).

5. Trans. Willard R. Trask (New York: Harper Torchbooks, 1963). *Cf.* e.g., pp. 168-170.

6. Trans. Philip Mairet (New York: Harper Torchbooks, 1967). *Cf.* e.g., pp. 30-31.

7. *Myth and Reality*, pp. 168-169.

8. Ibid., p. 169.

Bibliography

Besides the works already mentioned which throw light upon the existentialism of the Bible, the following books deserve particular mention here: Jean de Fraine's *Adam and the Family of Man*, trans. Daniel Raible (New York: Alba House, 1965) is a detailed and very informative study of the concept of corporate personality in the Bible. Gerhard von Rad, in his *Old Testament Theology*, 2 vols. (New York: Harper and Row, 1962, 1965) gives an excellent presentation of "Israel's Ideas About Time and History, and the Prophetic Eschatology," II, 99-125. *The Fullness of Time* (New York: Harper and Bros., 1952) by John Marsh is a discussion of various questions pertaining to time encountered in reading Scripture.

Part III

PEOPLE

CHAPTER SEVEN

LOVE AND EXISTENCE

OF ALL THE BONDS which make Christians one with their environment, the most important by far is the bond which makes them
persons-with-others, persons-for-others, persons-in-community.
This bond is love.

The significance of this hyphenation for the existential Christian can be fully grasped only when it is seen in relation to the
statement of St. John: "God is love" (1 Jn 4:8). John does not say
that God is loving or that God has love; he simply identifies God
with love, and in so doing identifies the fullness of existence with
the fullness of love. Just as God, because he is the absolute fullness of existence, is the only being who cannot not be, so also, because he is the fullness of love, he is the only one in existence who
cannot not love. The pagan mind, unaided by revelation, proved
able to rise to great heights in trying to understand the nature of
God. Aristotle defined him as "a thinking Thought." But no one,
without revelation, ever dreamed of conceiving God as "a loving
Love." Yet that is what St. John tells us God is.

The fullness of being is found only in persons. If it had not been
for the revelation of the Trinity, we would have assumed that one
infinite person would be an adequate expression of infinite love.
Now we know that, though the absolute fullness of love can be
"contained" within one nature, it cannot be "contained" within
one person, but breaks through the "limitations" of a single unlimited personhood and flowers into a plurality of persons who
form a communion in love which we call the Blessed Trinity.
Without the revelation of the existence of this community we
would not have been able to grasp fully the meaning of the statement that God is love; we would not have been able to really
grasp the profound relation between love and existence.

The fullness of being which is the richness of personhood tends
to "overflow," to communicate itself to others, to give itself to

others. Persons who are not the absolute fullness of existence have to go outside themselves to find others with whom to communicate, others upon whom they can pour out the riches and fullness of their being, and to whom they can give themselves in love. As the absolute plenitude of being and therefore the unbounded richness of personhood, God is the only one who does not have to go outside himself to communicate with others, to give himself to others.[1] Because he is a community of persons, he can give himself to himself. His existence consists in being a community of persons, each of whom is a communication and a gift of self to the others. He is a communion of love. He not only has social life, he is social life.

Some Greek philosophers speculated that if there were only one God, he would be a lonely God, living in isolated splendor. Christian revelation has solved the problem of God's loneliness; it has revealed that God, while being only one, is nevertheless not just one person, but a community of three persons living in a communion of mutual love. Each divine person is a living relation of love to the other two, and the personhood of each person is constituted, so to speak, by the living relations of love that he has with the others. The three persons are not distinguished by anything absolute; if they were, they would not be perfectly equal. They are distinguished by something relative, by the interpersonal relationships of love they have with each other.

The biblical person's concept of the holiness of God was based on the fact that he was the "Wholly Other," the one who was infinitely other in relation to all created beings. But not until the Christian revelation did it become known that, not only is God by his nature wholly other, but sharing in this divine nature are three persons, each of whom is infinitely distinct, and therefore infinitely other in relation to the other two. The self of each person consists in a total self-giving to the others. The infinite otherness of each person "elicits" the totally altruistic love and the self-giving of the other persons. Here there can be no selfishness, no self-seeking, no return upon self, simply because if the love were to try to return to self it would return to a self that is self-gift, that is an absolute outpouring of love to the other persons. Because there is no "self-satisfaction," no "possession" in this love, Maurice Zundell can write: "The eternal purity of boundless love discloses in the treasure of its abysses a glimpse of Poverty's holiest and most sublime Countenance."[2]

Jesus became incarnate and died on the cross to communicate to us the total outpouring of the Father upon the Son in which, in a sense, the Father empties himself completely to give his all to the Son, but in so doing achieves the fullness of his own personhood, which is to be Father. "As the Father has loved me, so I have loved you . . . . I have made known to you everything I have learned from my Father" (Jn 15:9, 15; cf. 3:35; 5:19-26,36; 6:36,57; 10:15). Jesus, the image of the Father (Col 1:15; Heb 1:3), came to live a life and to die a death which would image in the world the absolute gift, the total outpouring of the Father in giving birth to the Son, and, at the same time, to draw us into the total surrender of the Son to the Father in love. The exterior poverty of Jesus was a sign of "Poverty's holiest and most sublime Countenance" found in the life of the Trinity. The profound *kenosis*, the radical emptying described in Paul's Christological hymn in his letter to the Philippians (2:6-8) was a reflection of the "emptying" of the Father in the generation of his only Son, and of the Son's total giving of himself to the Father in love.

Knowing the deepest meaning of the life of Christ, one could almost have predicted how it would end. There are many ways in which a human person can pour out his love for others. But the ultimate expression of a total gift of self is the shedding of every red drop that has ever visited one's heart—the outpouring of one's blood, which, for the biblical person, is synonymous with life itself. In this perspective we can accept the daring statement of Raimundo Panikkar when he speaks of "the Cross of the Trinity, i.e. the integral immolation of God, of which the Cross of Christ and his immolation are only the images and the revelations."[3]

One could almost have anticipated the institution of the eucharist as the sacrament of love. In the "Cross of the Trinity" the outpouring of self happens once and for all, and yet is eternally continuous, without any repetition. Would not Christ have wanted his once-and-for-all immolation of self to be prolonged across all time through a continuous reenactment, without any repetition? Moreover, one could almost have predicted that if the Son of God came to earth to communicate the love of the Trinity, in which the three persons, through their absolutely altruistic mutual gift of self, constitute a holy communion in love, this love would be imaged in a holy communion that would not only unite individual Christians with Christ, but also bind them all together in a community, the Church, a people made one with a oneness that shares in the unity of the persons of the Trinity (cf. C 4c).

*　　*　　*

Meditating on the triune life of God provides insight into the
meaning of human love and of Christian love especially. Back in
the twelfth century Richard of St. Victor, in his treatise on the
Trinity, followed an opposite course: by reflecting on human
love and interpersonal relations he discovered a number of insights regarding the inner life of the Trinity.[4] As Ewert Cousins
has pointed out,

> Richard's concern for interpersonal relations and his exploration of
> human love as self-transcendence link him with twentieth-century
> personalism, both philosophical and theological. His minute and
> penetrating analyses of affective states have much in common with
> contemporary phenomenology and psychology, especially existential
> psychiatry.[5]

Richard finds in self-transcending love for other persons the
fullest and most perfect expression of personhood and the only
means of achieving full human happiness. The only way to be
truly a self is by having the capacity to transcend self through
altruistic love. The only way to truly posses oneself is by giving
oneself away. The only way to achieve genuine autonomy and
freedom is by intimate union with other persons through self-
transcendent love. "In other words," writes Cousins, "Richard
is attempting to get beneath the surface of isolation and separation to the spiritual depth where persons are intimately united
at the core of their being."[6]

In the capacity of human love to transcend self, Richard sees a
reflection of the mutual transcendent love of the divine persons.
Because in self-transcendent love between human persons the
fullness of autonomy and freedom is achieved through the most
intimate kind of union and oneness, we have a reflection of both
the distinction and autonomy of persons, and the unity of nature
found in the Trinity.

To be a person-with-others and a person-for-others through
self-transcendent love means to be in the world a resplendent
reflection of the Trinity. No wonder the New Testament, in which
the mystery of the Trinity is revealed, insists so much on this
kind of love.

*   *   *

Two particular aspects of human love call for special attention in the present context. The first is that although persons have two distinctive qualities, intellectual knowledge and altruistic love, and therefore two distinctive ways of communicating to others the riches of their being, it is particularly through altruistic love that the richness of personhood is revealed to us. A person may be brilliant as an intellectual and as a teacher in communicating knowledge, but if her or his capacity for altruistic love is limited, we do not feel that we are in the presence of an especially rich and fully developed personality. On the other hand, a person may not be especially brilliant intellectually, but if he has an extraordinary capacity for selfless love, if he is open and generous to others, if he is expansive in friendship and capable of entering into warm, intimate interpersonal relationships, if he is a loving, giving, and forgiving person, we spontaneously exclaim: "There is a beautiful person." Openness in communicating knowledge seems of little importance for our appreciation of someone as a person in comparison to the openness that love gives. God did not explicitly reveal himself as "a thinking Thought," even though that is what he really is; he left that to Aristotle. He knew it would mean much more to us, and give us a deeper insight into the fullness of his existence and the infinite richness of his being to reveal himself as "a loving Love."

The second aspect of human love that calls for attention here is its poverty. We have seen that Zundell associates divine love with poverty. But in human love there are two kinds of poverty because there are two kinds of love.

There is a love which desires and reaches out to another person not for that person's sake but for what he or she can do to satisfy a selfish need, to fill an interior emptiness. The awareness of the inner poverty of one's *being* leads to compensation by *having*, by possessing, by grasping, sometimes frantically. Here a person is loved, not as a subject but as an object; the love is not an "I-Thou" but an "I-It" relationship. In an "I-Thou" relationship the love is altruistic. This kind of love is often spoken of as "benevolent love." It seeks and rejoices in the good of the persons loved, without any desire to use, exploit, or manipulate them. True love knows that freedom is an essential element of the uniqueness of the persons loved. It sets them free to grow ever more fully in their uniqueness, in their otherness. Precisely because the love is so intimate, it gives the persons loved all the distance they need to become ever more truly themselves, knowing that the more they become themselves, the more loving and lovable they become. Only in this love can there be true inter-subjective communion; only here does the lover experience what is most incommunicable and therefore most mysterious and precious in the beloved. Only those who are not poor in being can afford to be poor in possessing; only they enjoy fully the blessedness of the first beatitude; only they share in that spirit of poverty which Maurice Zundell attributes to the mututal love of the three divine persons.

In *Being and Having* Gabriel Marcel writes:

> Charity thought of as presence, as absolute disposability; I have never before seen its link with poverty so clearly. To possess is almost inevitably to be possessed. Things possessed get in the way . . . . At the heart of charity is presence in the sense of absolute gift of one's self, a gift which implies no impoverishment to the giver. . . . I wonder if we could not define the whole spiritual life as the sum of activities by which we try to reduce in ourselves the part played by non-disaposability.[7]

What Marcel says here finds a striking verification in the nascent Church described in Acts: "The whole group of believers was united, heart and soul; no one claimed for his own use anything that he had, as everything they owned was held in common" (Ac 4:32; cf. 2:44-45).

* 		* 		*

When the scribe asked Jesus: "Which is the first of all the commandments?" (Mk 12:28), he was asking for only one commandment. Jesus replied by giving him two. This was not an arbitrary decision on the part of Jesus to give the scribe twice as much as he asked for. Because of the profound and intimate unity between the two commandments, Jesus could not give the one without the other, especially since he had come, not simply to speak in the name of the monopersonal God of the Hebrews, but to reveal and to give us a participation in the love of the divine community in which he had shared for all eternity. If this Trinitarian love was to be reproduced on earth, it would have to be in a communion of human persons loving each other.

The profound unity between the first and the second commandments would later find expression in the common doctrine of theologians that love of God and love of neighbor are not two distinct virtues but one and the same, because they both have the same formal object. Supernatural love of neighbor means that we love others precisely in terms of their relationship with God himself.

This does not mean, however, that we can prescind from what is uniquely personal in our neighbors, for our supernatural love must be incarnational; it must be incarnated in all that is best in human love, insofar as this is possible. Our neighbors are unique human persons who are to be loved for themselves, but a part of their selves is that they are related to God. The virtues of faith, hope, and charity are called theological virtues because their direct object is God himself. If therefore love of neighbor belongs to the same infused theological virtue by which we love God, this must mean that in loving our neighbor we are loving God himself. Love of neighbor is not just a fruit, an effect or a condition of love of God: it is in itself an act of love of God. At the same time, it is erroneous to suggest, as some do, that God can be loved only in one's neighbor and never in and for himself.

Because the scribe's question referred to commandments already contained in the Law (cf. Mt 22:36), Jesus used the formulation of the second commandment found in Leviticus (19:18). His own formulation, however, was significantly different. On the night before he died out of love, Jesus said his disciples: "I give you a new commandment: love one another" (Jn 13:34). We may very well wonder in what sense this commandment was new. For apart from the fact that fraternal charity had already been commanded in Leviticus, people had been loving each other, sometimes with great altruistic love, since the beginning of time. Aristotle and Cicero had written inspiring treatises on friendship. In Genesis we read that Jacob loved Rachael with such a great love that the seven years he had to work to win her passed like a few days (Gn 29:20). We are told that the love between Jonathan and David was so great that the soul of Jonathan was knit with the soul of David, and Jonathan loved him as his own soul (1 S 18:1 R.S.V.). So what is new about the commandment of Jesus? What is new is found in the little phrase he tacked on at the end: "as I have loved you." Never before in history had anyone loved the way Jesus loved; no one ever could. For the love of Jesus was a human love totally impregnated with divine love. Yet it is with this new, this divine kind of love that all Christians are commanded to love others. And if we ask what this love means we have the beginning of an answer in Christ's own words: "As the Father has loved me, so I have loved you.

Remain in my love'" (Jn 15:9). In other words, Christians are hyphenated with others in somewhat the same way as the Father and the Son are "hyphenated" in love in the bosom of the Trinity. Obviously, the hyphenation cannot be exactly the same; but there must be some similitude, for Jesus never talked in meaningless hyperboles.

The altruism of divine love is so absolute that it does not call for, or depend upon, any lovableness in the person or thing loved. Divine love and human love work in opposite directions. Human love is an effect caused by lovable qualities seen or imagined in the person loved. Divine love, on the contrary, is not an effect but a cause. It does not presuppose lovable qualities in order to love. If any lovable qualities exist anywhere they do so because God first loved when there was nothing there to love, and his love called the lovable qualities into existence. Christian love must be projective and creative. It must find a way of calling into existence lovable qualities even when at first they do not seem to exist. Experience shows that this can and does work. It shows that Christians who try to make their love projective and creative gradually begin to discover lovable qualities that in the beginning did not seem to exist.

*   *   *

We usually refer to Jesus' answer to the scribe as the twin commandments of love. Actually, we are dealing not just with twins but with triplets: love of God, love of neighbor, and love of self. These three are intimately connected. Just as we cannot love God without loving others, so we cannot love either God or others without first loving ourselves. Usually it is simply taken for granted that everyone loves himself; but things are not quite that simple. For many, perhaps the greatest obstacle to loving others and being loved by them is that they have never learned to love themselves properly.

It has often been said that a friend is an _alter ego_, another self. But if we do not truly love ourselves, we cannot love another self. Only insofar as we cherish ourselves and can grasp in some way what it means for us to be able to say "I am," can we enter into a communion of love with another self. Then, by experiencing this communion, our own self is in turn confirmed as a unique and irreplaceable value.

The perception of one's own personal worth, the recognition of oneself as lovable cannot be taught in the ordinary sense of the term. Love cannot be demonstrated speculatively as truth is demonstrated; it can be demonstrated only by a demonstration of love on the part of others. It cannot be communicated by books or by ordinary classroom techniques. It must come from a living existential experience.

We have our first experience of intimacy when we are completely defenseless children, and what happens then strongly influences our experience with intimacy throughout life. Need for the warmth of constant love on the part of their parents and their siblings, acceptance and approval by them, being cherished by them as persons of unique worth, awareness of a respect for them as persons who have their own rights and their own dignity—all these things are as important to children psychologically as shelter and nourishment are physically. Through the love of others we as children learn that we are lovable and that we have a personal worth all our own. In this way we learn to accept ourselves and to feel secure about ourselves. Only then will we be able to love another self. If, on the contrary, we are rejected, if we experience severity where there should be love, if we are made to feel inferior, it will be difficult for us later in life to be convinced that we can be loved for our own sakes by others, including God.

If we have experienced affection, esteem, and respect, we will be prepared to have a wholesome self-love, which might be called a selfless self-love. This may seem a contradiction in terms. In reality it is not. Indeed, it is precisely the kind of love we find in God. Nor is it a contradiction in a human person. Self-love shows its selflessness in its delight in giving itself away; it shows its love in its confidence in having a self worth giving.

If, on the other hand, persons have not discovered that they are lovable by being loved early in life, the kind of love they will ordinarily have for themselves is a selfish self-love: their insecurity, their feeling of emptiness will drive them to grasp for what they do not believe they possess. To fill the vacuum they will try to possess and manipulate not only things but other people as well. They will not know how to open themselves to genuine friendship, because, having been deeply hurt when they were defenseless, they will instinctively fear exposing themselves to being hurt again. They will not know how to identify with others because they are not sure of their own idenity. In the measure in which persons are unloving they will be unlovable and if others show signs of loving them, it will be hard for them to be convinced that they are being loved for their own sakes. They will constantly feel the need of probing and testing, in all kinds of subtle ways, to keep seeking reassurance that they are loved and accepted by others.

There are many defense mechanisms by which people may seek to save themselves from the risk of entering into close, open friendships for fear that others will discover the secret of their own lack of personal acceptance and their desperate need of acceptance by others. Sometimes these mechanisms have such a variety of disguises and are so extremely subtle and refined that the self-seeking is often below the conscious level and can be recognized only with the shrewdest kind of discernment, and at times only with some kind of psychological analysis. Moreover, what sometimes passes as love for God can be the expression of subtle, hidden, and disguised neurotic and self-seeking motivations. The kind of spiritual life in which one is not only faithful but even a slave to one's duties, and in which life is so highly organized and meticulously budgeted that there is plenty of time for spiritual exercises but no time for friendships, is at least suspect.

One of the basic secrets, not only of personal equanimity and a happy life, but also of a successful spiritual life, is acceptance. It is often hard enough to accept the people and things that make up the context of our lives, but the hardest thing of all is the acceptance of ourselves; and that means our historical selves, just as we have actually lived and evolved to the present moment. This is our only existential self, no matter how much we might wish that it were different; it is therefore the only self we have to offer to God. It is the only self that God loves, and the fact that he does love this unique, historical, and existential self should be a sufficient reason for our loving this self also. Unfortunately, those who, during their most plastic years, have formed a poor image of themselves find it difficult to existentially "feel" this love of God. They have *experienced* a lack of love; God's love cannot be experienced in the ordinary sense of the word. It frequently happens that people with excellent qualities, which should be enough to demonstrate objectively that they are persons of worth, count them as nothing. This worth remains for them in the speculative order. Their qualities do not succeed in supplanting the feeling of lack of worth that was built into their very being during the most crucial time when they were growing existentially as human persons.

Though these persons are seriously handicapped in their efforts to grow in Christian love, their condition should never be considered hopeless. The gospels show us Jesus as a healer, and we should never underestimate the healing power of the Christian experience. Though spiritual direction, counseling, prayer, and the healing grace of Jesus, progress can be made in triumphing over this handicap.

Our reflections on the response of Jesus to the scribe's question concerning the greatest commandment in the law can be summed up by saying that there are three commands of love in the Christian life: to love God with all one's mind, heart, soul, and strength; to love others, including enemies and persecutors, not merely as we love ourselves, but as Christ has loved us; to love ourselves as Christ has loved us, that is to say, with a selfless self-love. It is through the mediation of human love and intimacy that one can begin to grasp and to enter into divine intimacy. But in order to have this experience of love of others, we must first love ourselves with a selfless love.[8] To love oneself selflessly is, therefore, a basic Christian imperative.[9]

*   *   *

Our understanding of human love can be clarified and deepened by reflecting on how it is related to knowledge. For existentialists only the human persons exist in the full sense of the word, because only they have a depth of existential interiority; only they are conscious of their existence; only they are present to themselves; only they belong to themselves in absolute immediacy; only they are subjects with a conscious, free relation to reality as a whole. Therefore, to really know persons it is not sufficient that we know them as we know things; it is not sufficient that we know them from the outside; we must know them from the inside. The knower must somehow penetrate into the other person's interiority and know him or her, not simply as an object, but precisely as a subject.

In discussing the difference between Greek and Hebrew knowledge, I said that the former tends to know others through abstraction, and that abstract knowledge can only know others as objects. Such knowledge may give the impresssion of penetrating into the inner depths of the human person by being able to define his or her very essence. But a general definition does not tell us who a particular human person is; it does not say anything about what is absolutely unique and most personal in the interiority of a self. The biblical person seeks to know the singular object in its singularity, and when it is a question of a human person he seeks to know him or her not just from without but from within. For this reason I said that the Hebrews spoke of marital intercourse in terms of knowledge. Nothing could emphasize more strikingly that for the biblical person there is a kind of knowledge which is an engagement of the whole person, which is a total commitment and involvement of one's whole being, and which is the most intense kind of intimacy. The person known somehow becomes a part of one's own inner experience of life and existence. Let us try to capture if we can the meaning of this unique existential kind of knowledge.

The experience of knowing produces an image or representation of the person or thing known in the mind of the knower. There it is conditioned and adapted to the mind's mode of being. In this sense, knowing, taken by itself, draws the object known away from its own concrete, existential reality. In the experience of love the direction is the opposite. Love is a movement of the lover toward the beloved, who draws to himself the lover as a subject living in his or her own unique concrete existentiality. Here again we see the relation between love and existence. If, for example, a man loves a consecrated virgin or a married woman, his love may be very authentic and legitimate, provided he loves her in her concrete, actual, existential state. He will love her not as he would love another man, but precisely as a woman, for existentially that is what she is. But existentially she is also a woman who is consecrated by a vow of virginity or by marriage vows, and he must love her precisely as such. If he begins to love her in a way that is not consonant with the way she actually exists, he is no longer related to her concrete existence; he is abstracting.

Because human knowledge adapts the objects known to the condition of the knower, whereas love goes directly to the persons loved as they are in their unique act of subsisting, in this life the experience of loving God is superior to the experience of knowing him. As the mystics have often told us, God is in this life surrounded by a "cloud of unknowing." There is relatively little we can get to know about him, and what we do know is by way of analogical images whose similarity with God is infinitely less than their dissimilarity. But our love for him can penetrate through the "cloud of unknowing" and reach him directly as he exists in himself.

Though knowing and loving are two distinct experiences, they both take place in the same concrete person. For this reason they are intimately related in a variety of ways. It is possible for knowing and loving to be so "fused" that we can have a loving knowledge and a knowing love. Love makes the beloved "another self," and thus makes it possible for the lover to know the "other self" as a subject. Knowledge is so "fused" with love that it can reach out and touch the beloved in his or her innermost being, in somewhat the same way as love can. Knowledge suffused with love becomes an experience of intersubjectivity. The beloved is present to the lover precisely as a self, from the depths of her or his unique interiority.

It is proverbial that love is blind; it can often be extremely clairvoyant. Love can give to knowledge a profoundly penetrating intuition that becomes almost an instinct. Two persons who have established a deep intersubjective communion get to know each other so well through their mutual love that each can "instinctively" tell what the other is thinking, feeling, enjoying, and suffering without any ordinary means of communication. They know, and they are sure that they know with great accuracy, without being able to explain just how they know. Between them a mysterious kind of nonverbal communication is constantly taking place. They have a loving knowledge and a knowing love.

This helps us to understand how the Holy Spirit, who is Love, works in us. In the Trinity the Word proceeds from the Father by way of intellectual light, while the Spirit proceeds from the Father and the Son by way of love. But frequently the Church invites us to pray to the Holy Spirit for light and truth. We find Jesus telling his apostles that the mission of the Spirit who was to come would be to lead them into all truth: "But when the Spirit of truth comes he will lead you to the complete truth" (Jn 16:13). Frequently in the liturgy the Church prays to the Holy Spirit for light. Why should this be so?

If we read the complete text of St. John just quoted we shall find Jesus telling the Apostles that the Spirit will lead them to the complete truth, "since he will not be speaking as from himself but will say only what he has learned. . . . All that he tells you will be taken from what is mine" (Jn 16:13-14). Truth is not complete unless somehow it issues into love. The Spirit takes the truth from the Word and completes it by suffusing it with love. In almost every instance in which the Church prays to the Spirit for light, it prays not for the light of the intellect but for the light of the heart. In the traditional sequence for the Mass of Pentecost it prays: "*Veni lumen cordium,* come light of *hearts.*" In the most common prayer offered to the Holy Spirit we say: "O God, who by the light of the Holy Spirit, has instructed the *hearts* of the faithful . . . ." When divine love is poured forth in our hearts by the Spirit (Rm 5:5), he gives us the grace to enter into an intersubjective communion with God and with others in such a way that we know

God and others with a loving knowledge and love them with a knowing love.

Not infrequently we find this kind of knowledge in persons who have had little or no schooling, but who, because they are holy and therefore Spirit-filled, have an unerring "instinct" for what is right and what is true in the Christian life, an uncanny ability to discern the will of God in the complexities of human life. They may know nothing of theory, speculation, or abstraction; they think existentially in things pertaining to God. They may not be able to define, explain, or demonstrate; yet they have a surety that goes beyond all logical demonstration. They may not possess the wisdom of philosophers or theologians; but they possess the most precious wisdom of all, the supernatural wisdom which is one of the gifts of the Spirit, and which does not grow by study and learning, but by an increase of charity and progress in prayer. Here we have the kind of loving knowledge and knowing love that is the essence of all advanced forms of prayer. This is the most existential kind of knowledge, and for this reason we can say that the Church is most existential in its mystics. Love confers upon this knowledge its own ability to contact and to enter profoundly into existence. It gives to knowledge the power not only to know something, but to "taste" and "relish" it. In the commonly used prayer to the Holy Spirit mentioned above, the Latin phrase *recta sapere* is often translated incorrectly as "to know what is right." Its real meaning is "to relish what is right." Of the five senses, touch and taste are the most existential because they come into immediate contact with their objects. This is why we have nothing corresponding to radio or television for these senses. So the psalmist is inviting us to enter into a close existential union with God when he invites us to taste and see the goodness of the Lord (Ps 34:8).

Even on the purely natural level, knowledge suffused with love gives the ability to know someone, not just from the outside but from the inside. St. Augustine tells us that no one is really known except through friendship. The more intense and profound love is, the greater is the acuity it gives to the insight and intuition of the one who loves; the greater also is his or her capacity to penetrate into the existence and the interiority of the person loved. When persons open themselves to the infinite love of the Spirit, there is no limit to the powers of intuition they may receive, no limit to the capacity they may be given for existential knowledge of God and of others. The knowing love and loving knowledge brings about in existential Christians who are filled with the

Spirit a profound and intimate hyphenation with others. At the same time, it prepares them for, and even anticipates the ecstatic experience of seeing God face to face, of penetrating into the existence of the one who is Existence, and of entering into the infinite interiority of the one whose knowledge is his love because he is all love.

Notes

1. For an excellent discussion of this point and of its implications for friendship, see Robert Johann, "A Meditation on Friendship," *The Modern Schoolman*, XXV (January 1948), 126-131.

2. *The Splendour of the Liturgy* (New York: Sheed and Ward, 1939), p. 21.

3. *The Trinity and the Religious Experience of Man* (New York: Orbis Books, 1973), p. 46.

4. These reflections are found in bk. 3 of his *De Trinitate*, which has recently been published in English in a collection of some of his writings: *Richard of St. Victor*, trans. Grover A. Zinn (New York: Paulist Press, 1979), pp. 373-397. This volume is one of a series entitled "The Classics of Western Spirituality."

5. "A Theology of Personal Relations," *Thought*, XLV (Spring 1970), 56.

6. Ibid., p. 69.

7. Trans. Katherine Farrer (Westminister: Dacre Press, 1949), p. 69.

8. We have already seen that Jean-Paul Sartre, in contrast to other existentialists like Marcel and Buber, takes an extremely negative view of the human person's relation with others. He holds that man is born and dies alone and that it is only by deluding himself, between these two events, that he can believe he is not alone. For Sartre, love and friendship are only illusions which come from an unconscious "bad faith"—from a cowardice which refuses to recognize and admit his own solitude. The "other" for Sartre is necessarily, though perhaps in hidden ways, the enemy. Love is only hatred in disguise, just as faith is necessarily bad faith. This means that those around us, instead of helping us to rise above our isolation, only make us feel more profoundly alone, and thus increase our sense of isolation. Sartre holds this opinion because he believes that all love is reducible to self-love. In a sense he is correct. All genuine, all altruistic love is reducible to what I have called selfless self-love. On the other hand, all self-seeking love is reducible to egocentric and selfish self-love. The great error of Sartre consists in trying to reduce even what is truly altruistic love to egocentric self-love.

9. Johannes Metz has an excellent treatment of this point in *Poverty of Spirit*, trans. John Drury (New York: Paulist Press, 1968); see especially pp. 7-8: "Understood correctly, man's love for himself, his 'yes' to his

self, may be regarded as the 'categorical imperative' of the Christian faith: You shall lovingly accept the humanity entrusted to you!... You shall embrace yourself!... Man's self-acceptance is the basis of the Christian creed. Assent to God starts in man's sincere assent to himself. ... Knowing how difficult it is for man not to hate himself (as Bernanos points out), we can then understand why God had to prescribe 'self-love' as a virtue and one of the great commandments.... We can then realize how much easier it is to say 'no' instead of 'yes' to oneself, and that all asceticism is first designed to serve this great 'yes'."

Bibliography

Among the spiritual classics dealing with love, perhaps the best known and most universally appreciated treatises are those of St. Bernard and St. Francis de Sales. The relatively short work of St. Bernard *On the Love of God* is published together with numerous selections from his Sermons on the Canticle of Canticles, whose basic theme is also that of love, in a volume entitled *Saint Bernard on the Love of God*, trans. Terence L. Connolly (New York: Spiritual Books Associates, 1937). The classical work of St. Francis de Sales is entitled *The Love of God* (Westminister, Md.: Newman Press, 1962). A brief but extremely clear presentation and correlation of all the texts in the New Testament pertaining to love is found in *Christianity: Mystery of Love* by Thomas Barrosse (Notre Dame, In.: Fides Publishers, 1964). Robert Johann's essay on the metaphysics of love, *The Meaning of Love* (Glen Rock, N.J.: Paulist Press, 1966) is an extraordinarily lucid and profound analysis of love in its deepest dimensions. Among the many other books on love published in modern times the following deserve mention: Martin C. D'Arcy's *The Mind and Heart of Love* (New York: Meridian Books, 1956); Maurice Nédoncell's *Love and the Person*, trans. Sr. Ruth Adelaide (New York: Sheed and Ward, 1966); Vander Kerken's *Loneliness and Love*, trans. J. Donceel (New York: Sheed and Ward, 1966); and John Cowburn's *The Person and Love* (New York: Alba House, 1967). This last book is extremely rich in bibliographical references.

CHAPTER EIGHT

FRIENDSHIP AND FELLOWSHIP

FRIENDSHIP HAS ALWAYS PLAYED an important role in the spiritual life. St. Jerome, St. Augustine, and St. Bernard are only a few examples among the many saints who had friendships of great depth and intimacy. The strong, close friendship between St. Gregory of Nazianzen and St. Basil the Great is especially well known. Of this friendship St. Gregory writes: "It seemed that in us there was but one soul dwelling in two bodies; and if those are not to be believed who say that all things are in all things, yet of us two you may believe that we were both in each other." There are notable examples of friendship between men and women saints, even (perhaps we should say especially) among those committed to consecrated celibacy, such as the friendships between St. Francis of Assisi and St. Clare, between St. John of the Cross and St. Teresa of Avila, between St. Francis de Sales and St. Jane Frances de Chantal. Some of the most beautiful and inspiring reflections on friendship were written by saints, such as St. Aelred of Rievaulx[1] and St. Francis de Sales,[2] and by theologians, like Thomas Aquinas, who taught that in order to be truly happy a person needs friends.[3] St. Augustine, in one of his sermons, summed up his view on friendship by saying: "Nothing is friendly to a man who is without friends."

It is to be expected that friendship in its finest and fullest dimensions should characterize the lives of the saints. For holiness is a participation in an eminent degree in the life of God, and the divine life is friendship. But to see why this is so let us first reflect on the nature of friendship in general and on human friendship in particular.

Friendship is benevolent love, but it has two distinctive qualities not found in all altruistic love. First, friendship is necessarily reciprocal; there must be between friends mutual knowledge and love. Benevolence may inspire a person to sacrifice some of his possessions for the benefit of needy people whom he does not know personally; the ones who receive the benefaction may not know who their benefactor is. There is no friendship here. The love of enemies and persecutors is one of the highest kinds of benevolence, but it is not friendship because the love is not reciprocal. Besides mutuality of knowledge and love, there must be in friendship another quality which is often called "community of life." This means a mutual sharing of life, not necessarily in the sense of living together, but in the sense of sharing with each other those aspects of life that can be shared and that the friends consider precious. Only when all these three qualities of friendship are present can we speak of a true "I-Thou" relationship.

All friendship consists in the self of the lover who is present to himself in his own interiority becoming present to another self in his interiority. And in this mutual indwelling friends not only retain the distinctness of their own personalities but actually enhance it. But in human friendship the personal communion cannot consist simply in two or more persons contemplating each other, enjoying each other, and remaining enclosed within each other. Paradoxically, true human intimacy must look beyond itself to some kind of transcendence; otherwise it breeds narcissism.

There are profound potentialities in every human person that only loving and being loved can awaken. Hence, human friendship means mutual enrichment and constant growth in existence and in personhood, for, as I have already suggested, to be a person does not mean to be enclosed within self but to have the capacity "to stand out," *ex-sistere*, and to go beyond oneself. Authentic mutual love engages persons in the existential reality of each other. It is both an open revelation of self and an acceptance of others, and this acceptance calls into fuller existence both one's own self and the self of others. Often the dawn of a new love gives the lovers the feeling of entering into a whole new level of being.

True human love always means enrichment of one's being, but one does not love for this reason. At times, this enrichment comes about, at least in part, by a complementarity in the persons who enter into a communion of love, but again it is not for this complementarity that one loves. In any case, in true love this complementarity will be a positive thing, something quite different from the negative complementarity of neurotic friendships and marriages in which the neurosis of one person is supported by a complementary neurosis in the other.

To be a friend is to live in a state of openness, of availability and disposability in relation to others. This means living in a state of "presence" to others, a state of readiness to give oneself to others in ways that are not limited or particularized in advance. Though mutual love is a kind of covenant, it is not a contract that spells out in advance what each person is willing to be called upon to do. The covenant of friendship is a commitment to a mutual acceptance of the actual, concrete, existential being of others, with whatever limitations and weaknesses might be there, in such a way that each person truly shares in the existential reality of the others. Like all things existential, love is holistic: it loves the person as a whole, and not just certain qualities in him. This calls for a constant act of faith and hope, a readiness to respect and respond to the wholeness and the uniqueness of others.

Friendship, then, means mutual openness, mutual escape from loneliness, mutual confirmation in being, mutual indwelling. The delight that comes from this kind of love comes basically because the loved person exists. The "We" that results from an "I-Thou" relationship is not a whole made up of parts, but a whole made up of wholes. Similarly, a true community, which is a communion in altruistic love, is also a whole made up of wholes.

Friendship is a unique kind of relation and commitment. Commitments to a marriage partner or to the priesthood are governed by public law. A commitment to the religious life is expressed by public vows that are seriously binding. Legally binding contracts sanction other serious commitments. But, though friendship can and should exist in every state of life, it does not depend upon any binding force extrinsic to itself. It stands on its own. The gift of self is utterly gratuitous; it has no strings attached.

A beautiful and splendid thing is this mutual love, freely given and freely received. Love alone is its binding force; there are no external sanctions. But it is also a great risk. The love freely given can be withdrawn; it can even turn into hostility. The psalmist had this experience: "Even my closest and more trusted friend, who shared my table, rebels against me" (41:9; cf. 55:13). And Jesus himself had occasion to quote this line when his heart was broken because of the risk he had taken with Judas (Jn 13:18). But this experience did not deter him from continuing to take the risk of friendship down through the centuries. Though we may withdraw our love, he never withdraws his. That is why he instituted a special sacrament of reconciliation whose purpose it is to restore the splendor of friendship once it has been lost.

*   *   *

The three elements which make up the essence of friendship are found in their fullest possible measure in the friendships between the persons of the Trinity. Between these three friends there is infinite altruism and mutuality, and such absolute community of life that they all share in one simple nature. God is friendship and fellowship. He is a communion of lovers in which each person, while being infinitely present to himself in his own interiority, is at the same time infinitely present to the other persons in their own unique interiority. Unlike human intimacy, this divine intimacy does not have to look beyond itself, because it is itself absolute transcendence. Yet, it is a part of that mystery of love which is God, that it freely chose to look beyond itself, to create other intelligent and loving beings, and to invite them to share in its intimacy.

Aristotle explicitly denied the possibility of God loving human beings or having a relation of friendship with them. They were so far below God that he and they had nothing in common. They had nothing to offer him that could arouse desire. On the other hand, the most important thing that revelation tells us is that God loves us with an infinite love, and that he made it possible for us to enter into a real communion of friendship with him.

Adam could not find a suitable companion among all the animals that God had created, and God had to create another human person who shared Adam's human nature (Gn 2:18-24). No matter how often people may say that their dog is their best friend, it remains impossible for friendship to exist between a human being and any creature which is by nature lower than himself. The astounding thing is that God made it possible for us to have a real communion in friendship with him by giving us a share in his own divine nature (2 P 1:4). Habitual grace infused into us at baptism is a real share in God's inner life. And besides this created gift of grace, God gives us the uncreated gift of himself. Christians in the state of grace have the Trinity really dwelling within them. "We shall come to him and make our home with him" (Jn 14:23; cf. 1 Co 6:19). In order to make this communion of friendship more intimate, he took to himself in the incarnation a share in our human nature. He thus established with us a profound community of life and made it possible for us to say that God is our best friend.

Richard of St. Victor, after discovering a "reason" for a plurality of persons in God in the fact that in human life mutual self-transcending love is the fullest expression of personhood and the richest source of happiness, discusses the question of the third person in God. He shows that for mutual human love to reach perfection it cannot consist in a closed "We." Not only must the "I" and the "Thou" be self-transcending, but the "We" must also. He writes: "Certainly in mutual and very fervent love nothing is rarer or more magnificent than to wish that another be loved equally by the one whom you love supremely and by whom you are supremely loved. And so the proof of perfected charity is a willing sharing of the love that has been shown to you."[4]

Perfect friendship is free of all possessiveness and jealousy. It is free of every desire to keep the beloved a captive. The very selflessness that makes it possible for persons to transcend themselves in loving another must move them to transcend the exclusivity and the limitations of an enclosed "We," and to share their love and the person loved with others. The transcendence of the "We" is often more difficult to achieve than the transcendence of the "I." Yet the same love which enables persons to break through their individual isolation by entering into an intimate interpersonal relationship should impel them to break through any tendency to isolate themselves and their love from others. Here again the Trinity is the perfect model of totally transcendent love. Not only is there infinitely altruistic love between two persons, but this love is shared with a third person in absolute altruism.

At the same time, it is a part of the mystery of the love which is God that it consists in a communion of friends who constitute a "closed We," in the sense that there is no fourth divine person to whom it can open itself. But because this communion of friends enjoys infinite blessedness, the enclosure does not in any way imply the limitations and the impoverishment which a closed human "We" would necessarily suffer. But it is also a part of the profound mystery of the love which is God that it should freely decide to open, in a certain sense, the enclosed "We" and invite us to enter into it and share in its infinite blessedness. Christ Jesus came to earth to extend this invitation to us.

He came to us after living from all eternity a life of the most intimate and ecstatic friendship with the Father and the Spirit, and he incarnated his friendship in human life. He brought to earth in human form the other-centerdness of his divine personality, and became "a man for others," as Bonhoeffer has called him. Christ loved everyone, of course, but he had his favorites. Out of the crowds that followed him he chose seventy-two to share his mission. He chose twelve to be close to him in a special way. When Mark recounts the choosing of the twelve he writes: "they

were to be his companions and to be sent out to preach" (Mk
3:14). They were his companions first and only second his missionaries. To these chosen twelve he said: "I shall not call you
servants any more . . . I call you friends" (Jn 15:14-15).

Out of the twelve Jesus chose three, Peter, James and John, to
be especially close to him in both the moments of his glory and
joy (Mt 17:1-8), and the moments of his deepest sadness and
humiliation (Mt 26:36-46). Out of these three he chose one, John,
to be his closest friend. On more than one occasion John refers to
himself, in utter simplicity, as "the disciple Jesus loved" (Jn
13:23; 21:20), as though he were the only one that Jesus really
loved. Some persons have such an extraordinary capacity for
love and friendship that, though they may have numerous friends,
they are able to love each one in such a unique way that it seems
that the totality of their love is concentrated on him or her alone.
This is the way God loves; it was undoubtedly the way Jesus
loved. When we develop our capacity for friendship we are imi-
tating Jesus himself. Self-enclosure is an obstacle not only to human happiness, but also to the following of Jesus.

Jesus had other close personal friends, like the three living in
Bethany: Mary, Martha and Lazarus. When Lazarus became ill,
the message Martha and Mary sent to him was simply: "Lord,
the man you love is ill" (Jn 11:4). At the graveside of Lazarus
"Jesus wept, and the Jews said, 'See how much he loved him' "
(Jn 11:36). It is always a dramatic experience to see a strong,
fully grown man crying in public, and perhaps in no other way
can we get a deeper insight into the meaning of Christian friendship than by stopping to realize that these tears were the tears of
God. Nor was this the only time Jesus wept in public. His love for
his own people was so deep, so strong, and so passionate that on
one occasion as he drew near the city of Jerusalem he shed tears
over it because he already saw what was in store for this city and
his people who were rejecting him (Lk 19:41). The tears of Christ
reveal that his love was truly incarnate.

*   *   *

The Christian vocation is a call to prolong the love and friendship of Jesus in the world by living an other-centered life as he
did. This can be done only by participating ever more fully in the
friendship that is God, who loves us with an infinitely altruistic
love and calls us to love him with all the selfless love of which our
self is capable. He shares his divine life with us in the sacra-

ments, especially the eucharist, and in all the aspects of our life in which we allow his life to penetrate ours. He is continually calling us to enter into ever more intense and intimate intersubjective communion with him, especially by advancing to higher forms of prayer, contemplation, and mystical union.

The closest approach to this fullness of friendship with the Lord is the spiritual friendship between two or more persons who love each other intensely with the love that the Holy Spirit has poured into their hearts, who share a common desire for sanctity, who reach out together toward that transcendent friendship which is God, who share with each other the superabundant graces of life, light, and love which come from him, and who minister to each other with the power of the charismatic gifts coming from the Spirit. From one point of view, loving one's enemies may seem to be the most divine kind of love. Jesus seems to suggest this when he tells us that this kind of love makes us sons of our Father in heaven, who "causes his sun to rise on bad men as well as good" (Mt 5: 43-45). Such a love is like God's love because it does not presuppose any lovable qualities in the person loved. But Christian friendship can be an even deeper share in God's love. For if both lover and beloved are made one with Christ in the intimacy of his Body, the mutual self-giving means that they are giving Christ to Christ, and therefore God to God. Here we have a reflection of the love of the Blessed Trinity which consists in God's giving himself to himself.

The authentic spiritual person is one in whose life fellowship has an important part. This fellowship is not a superficial gregariousness; it is not the fellowship of the "jolly good fellow." It is something far more profound, something that the Spirit himself creates to give us an anticipation of the joy of the intersubjective communion found in the Trinity. It takes delight in sharing, not only things, but oneself with others. It finds joy in being with others, who are loved, not in order to achieve some ulterior goal, but simply to rest in the delight of entering into communion with them. One of the things often overlooked in the spiritual life is the basic human need for experiencing delight. This experience may take various forms, but fellowship is one of the most basic. Truly spiritual persons will not allow themselves to develop an introverted spirituality, with a lonely and rigid piety of prayer and asceticism, but with little attention to the importance of friendship and fellowship. They will not allow things and duties to get in the way of spending time with friends, for no other purpose than to share themselves with them and be enriched by them.

They will not look on this as wasting time. Community and frater-
nity will be high on their scale of spiritual values. They know that
though community in its juridicial structure and legal procedures
may be a ready-made and given thing, in its deepest dimensions
as a communion in love it is not; it is something which must be
continually created and sustained by constant giving of self on
the part of all its members.

Two states of life in the Church have as their special purpose
to create a resplendent reflection of the self-transcending love of
the Trinity: marriage and the religious life.

In many ways marriage offers the most favorable conditions
for bringing Christian friendship to fulfillment. Not only does it
continually demand mutual self-transcending love, but it also
provides the most intimate community of life. The transcendence
of the "We" which is necessary for perfect friendship does not
necessarily mean that all the specific qualities of every interpersonal relation can be shared with others. This is particularly true
of marital love, which demands exclusivity in all the aspects of
love which make it specifically conjugal. But married love will be
all the richer and deeper if the spouses share their love with
others in the many ways in which it can be shared. The natural
third parties in married love are children. Here, in a very special
way, the "We" of the married couple opens to embrace those who
are the fruit of their love. The Christian family is a unique symbol
of the Trinity.

Until the recent past, it was common to find in religious communities a strong suspicion regarding friendship. One of the
sources of this suspicion was the fear that religious, after break-
ing through the barriers of their individual isolation through
friendship, would then build barriers between their "We" and the
rest of the community. In a life which is designed to be in the
Church an especially eloquent testimony to the social life of God,
an enclosed "We" is indeed an anomaly. But repeated warnings
against the dangers of "particular friendships" are not the best
way to avoid this anomaly. There should be a positive education
of religious in their formative period concerning the true meaning of Christian friendship. Young religious should be taught that
though friendship can be stronger than death, it is at the same
time an exquisitely fragile thing, like so many other precious
things, and that it has many counterfeits. They should be taught
how to distinguish between authentic Christian friendship and
these counterfeits. Some psychologists today believe that it is

impossible, or at least extremely difficult, to enter fully into community life without having experienced close interpersonal relations with at least one or a few friends. Persons who have never experienced the warmth and intimacy of personal friendships will not be community persons. They will be withdrawn and isolated. At best, their community life will be a superficial thing which leaves intact the walls around the self.

Not all love between Christians is Christian love. Friendship between Christians can be either a "flesh" friendship or a "spirit" friendship. The former is a friendship which, though not necessarily involving anything sensuous or dangerous, is, nevertheless, not permeated by the Spirit of agape. A pneumatic friendship, on the other hand, is one that is indeed based on all that is best in human nature, one that can even give mutual support for many of the basic weaknesses of human nature, but one that is completely dominated and directed by the love that has been poured into our hearts by the Spirit who inhabits them (Rm 5:5).

All Christian friendship and fellowship have their source in the Holy Spirit, and it is important to see why. Some terms used in reference to the Trinity can be applied with equal appropriateness to all three persons, while others are appropriate to one rather than to the others. The term "gift" applies in a very special way to the Holy Spirit, because every true gift comes from love, and the Holy Spirit is the love binding together the Father and the Son. The mutual, utterly altruistic love in which Christian friendship and fellowship essentially consist can have no other ultimate source than that infinitely gratuitous gift which is the Holy Spirit himself. Moreover, all spiritual communion is attributed to the Spirit because in the inner life of the Trinity he is the living flame who "hyphenates" the Father and the Son in an infinitely intimate union of love. It is he who binds together the members of that communion of love which is the Body of the Lord. He is the ultimate principle of community, of intersubjective union, of fellowship and friendship.

Fellowship has always been considered a distinctive and essential characteristic of Christian existence since the coming of the Spirit at Pentecost called into existence that first communion in his love which Luke describes in Acts (2:42-47; 4:32-35). St. Paul brings his second letter to the Corinthians to a close with the greeting: "The grace of the Lord Jesus Christ, the love of God and *the fellowship of the Holy Spirit* be with you all." It is believed that this Trinitarian formula was probably taken by Paul from liturgical usage. It has now been restored to this usage as a greeting of the celebrant to the liturgical assembly at the beginning of Mass.

The indwelling of the Spirit in the Christian is a mutual thing, a mutual compenetration, an interindwelling (cf. 1 Jn 4:13; 3:24; Jn 15:10-15). There is a mutuality of interpersonal intimacy which consists in knowing, loving, and enjoying. The Spirit knows, loves, and enjoys us, and we in turn know, love, and enjoy him. This joy we share with Jesus, who, St. Luke tells us, was filled with joy by the Holy Spirit (10:21). When a truly pneumatic friendship exists between Christians, their intersubjective communion is bound up with the interindwelling of the Spirit. In the Spirit, they know, love and enjoy each other.

*　　*　　*

The more profound and the more intense the existential communion we call friendship is, the more is there a reaching out for supreme transcendence and absolute communion. In heaven this supreme transcendence and absolute communion will finally be attained. In this personal, existential communion we shall achieve the deepest possible penetration into reality. Having become one with Christ through love, we shall be introduced by him into the friendships which bind together the persons of the Trinity. We shall be united and made one with the total otherness of each of the divine persons in an intimate bond of friendship. Love of God will bring about in us the fullest possible love of self, which is beatitude.

Not only will our friendship with God reach consummation, but our friendships with others will also. No matter how profound, how intense and how all-consuming a love for another person may seem in this life, it will seem as nothing when we are finally united with him in heaven in a communion which is one with our communion with God. Not only will the intimacy and the intensity of our love of friendship go immeasurably beyond anything we can now imagine, but our capacity for love and friendship will know no limitations. In this life, although our Christian love is universal, it is necessarily only a kind of generalized love, except for the relatively few persons whom we know. And of these it is only with a very few that we can actually have that intersubjective communion in love which we call friendship. But God's love is not only a generalized thing; he loves every person as though that person were the only one in existence. In heaven we shall share in God's capacity for love and friendship. We shall have an intimate friendship with all the members of the society of the blessed, which includes not only all the human persons in heaven but also all the angels. I have said that it is impossible to have true friendship with anyone who does not have the same nature as our own. However, the angels have also been given a share in the nature of God as we have. This makes them connatural not only with God but also with ourselves.

If even one great friendship with a finite friend here on earth can so enrich our existence and give us such a greater appreciation of the meaning of life that it seems to draw us into a whole new level of being, what shall we say about the ecstatic friendship in heaven with the one who is Existence! What shall we say about sharing profoundly in the infinitely intimate and intense friendships of the three persons who make up the very life of Existence! If the relatively few intimate friendships we are able to have in this life can bring us an ever richer and fuller existence, what shall we say about the intimate friendship in heaven with each of the innumerable human persons in the society of the blessed, and with each of the myriads of angelic persons (cf. Dn 7:10; Rv 5:11), every one of whom is a kind of luminous universe by himself! And we shall have the capacity to love every person in the society of the blessed as though he were the only person in existence.

"Hell is other people," writes Sartre in *No Exit*. For a Christian heaven is other persons. Personalism could ask for nothing more.

In heaven, all the sacraments, having fulfilled their purpose, will have passed away. They are given to the *homo viator*, the pilgrim person, to help him along the way of his pilgrimage to reach his homeland. Once the homeland is reached they no longer have any meaning. All the charismatic gifts of the Spirit will have passed away, for they were given to serve others, and others are no longer in need. Faith and hope will have attained supreme truth and goodness. Only love remains. Friendship is forever.

The society of the blessed, which is a participation in the communal life of the Trinity, is in some measure prepared for, and already anticipated by a society here on earth, a communion in love, which we call the Church. Heaven invites us to reflect upon the mystery of God's pilgrim people.

Notes

1. *Spiritual Friendship*, trans. Mary Eugenia Laker (Washington: Cistertian Publications, Consortium Press, 1974).

2. *Introduction to the Devout Life*, trans. and ed. John K. Ryan (New York: Harper and Row, 1966), pt. 3, chs. 17-22.

3. *Summa Theologiae*, first pt. of the second pt., q. 4, art. 8. Aquinas treats of friendship not only in this *Summa* (cf. e.g., first pt. of the second pt., q. 4, art. 8; q. 27, art. 3; q. 65, art. 5), but also in his commentary on Aristotle's treatise on friendship in the Nichomachean Ethics, bks. 8 and 9. See *St. Thomas Aquinas on Aristotle's Love and Friendship*, trans. and ed. Pierre Conway (Providence: The Providence College Press, 1951).

4. *De Trinitate*, ch. 11. See *Richard of St. Victor*, trans. Grover A. Zinn (New York: Paulist Press, 1979), p. 384.

Bibliography

The works mentioned in the bibliography of the last chapter will, in many ways, serve this chapter also. Aelred of Rievaulx, one of the most outstanding spiritual writers of the early middle ages, has given us a treatise on friendship which is charming in its simplicity: *Spiritual Friendship*, trans. Mary Eugenia Laker (Washington: Cistertian Publications, Consortium Press, 1974). Perhaps the most profound analysis of the part played by friendship in the Christian life is Paul Philippe's *Le rôle de l'amitié dans la vie chrétienne* (Rome: Angelicum, 1938). Three other contemporary works deserve mention: Ignace Lepp, *The Ways of Friendship*, trans. Bernard Murchland (New York: Macmillan, 1966); Christopher Kiesling, *Celibacy, Prayer and Friendship* (New York: Alba House, 1978); and Paul Hinnebusch, *Friendship in the Lord* (Notre Dame, In.: Ave Maria Press, 1974).

CHAPTER NINE

A PILGRIM PEOPLE

THE EXISTENTIAL CHRISTIAN is called to be a person-with-others-in-community. The basic Christian community is the Body of the Lord.

In an existential approach to the spiritual life, the Church plays a central role. The life of the Spirit of the risen Jesus is communicated first and foremost to that communion in love which we call the Church. By participating in this communion individual persons share in the life of the Spirit. My intention here is not to deny the possibility of the Spirit's working in the hearts of persons outside the limits of the official Church: the Spirit breathes wherever he wills (cf. Jn 3:8). But normally it is by sharing in the communion of love which the Spirit has formed to be the Body of Christ that the Christian lives and grows in the Spirit.

In and through the Church a person achieves wholeness as a Christian—and in many respects as a human person. We have seen that in its sacramental life the Church does not think of its members as souls but as whole human persons. We have noted the extraordinary attention that this sacramental life gives to the human body; indeed the sacramental life of the Church is simply inconceivable except in the perspective of the human person as a kind of "sacrament" in which the body is the outward visible sign in and through which the soul lives and manifests itself.

The Christian also achieves extrinsic wholeness through the Church. The *Constitution on the Church* treats of the Church in terms of a communion in which the oneness is so great and so intimate that it can be defined in the words of St. Cyprian as "a people made one with the unity of the Father, the Son, and the Holy Spirit" (C 4c). We enter into this communion through baptism; we are actually baptized not only into Christ but also into one another. No purely natural love, friendship, fellowship, or community can give a person a wholeness that is in any way, even remotely, comparable to this communion. Through the Church the Christian is in some way made whole with the whole-ness of the Blessed Trinity.

Through the Church the Christian also achieves an extraordi-nary wholeness with respect to the world, so much so that it might be said that no one can be considered to be more "worldly" than the person who is living the Christian ecclesial life in its fullness. When Christ became incarnate in the material flesh of Mary, he actually drew the whole world to himself in a warm and loving embrace, and, in spite of all its sinning, the world will never be able to extricate itself from that embrace. In analogical terms, we may speak of three "incarnations" of the Word. The first is the incarnation in the full and theologically proper sense of the term: the incarnation in the flesh of Mary. But this incarnation necessarily called for two further "incarnations." There is first of all the "incarnation" in the Body which is the Church, and which in a sense extends and prolongs the first incarnation across space and time. Having drawn a body to himself from the flesh of Mary, the Word drew to himself the members of this ecclesial Body. The incarnate Word is the head of this Body, and he continues to live, work, and manifest himself in and through it. In fact, the Word has identified with himself the members of this Body, as Paul found out on the road to Damascus (Ac 9:1-9).

But this Body does not live in a vacuum. It lives and moves and has its being in a material universe, whose nature, historical movement, and destinies it shares. In this sense we can speak of the world as being the "body" of the Body of Christ, and of Christ as being "incarnated" in it. In the hymn, *Pange Lingua,* the Church sings of the rivers of Christ's blood bathing, not only the human person, but earth, sea, stars, and universe. St. Ambrose tells us that when Christ rose from the dead the whole world rose with him.

It is likewise in and through the Church that Christians can achieve wholeness with regard to time and history. There is such a thing as Church-time, which coincides with Spirit-time. It is the "time-in-between," the time which extends from Pentecost to the second coming of the Lord. Before Pentecost the Church did not exist, except in the prefigurement of the Hebrew Qahal; after the Parousia it will continue to exist, but no longer in time. In the time-in-between the Church carries forward salvation history, working on and with human history to make it salvation history, making secular time something sacred for its members, with-out, however, losing sight of the important values inherent in secular time and history. As we have already noted, the Greeks had two words for time: *chronos*, which is the homogeneous flow of duration measured by clocks and calendars, and *kairos*, which is a time of special significance. During the time-in-between, it is principally through the Church, though not exclusively, that the Spirit carries on his transformation of *chronos* into *kairos*, making it a time of decision, a time of vast opportunity, a time of great eventfulness, a time pregnant with eternity.

Anyone who examines the life of the Church as lived in its liturgy cannot fail to see how deeply its existence is time-conditioned. Church-time is made up of periods and cycles, which, as I pointed out earlier, are not just cycles continually repeating themselves, but onward and upward going spirals. Of the Church one cannot say what has been said of some of its saints, that it is so engrossed in its concern for eternity that it has no concern for time. Thus, in all the ways in which a Christian is made existentially whole, the Church plays a principal role. For the Church, holiness is always wholeness.

*　　*　　*

The existential character of the *Church Constitution* becomes immediately apparent when it is viewed in comparison with, or more exactly, in contrast to the preparatory document on the Church. Instead of seeing the Church in canonical terms as a perfect society, the Council presented it in concrete, existential, and biblical terms, as a pilgrim people constantly in a state of promise, constantly moving through time and history towards its eschatological fulfillment in the second coming of Jesus as Lord of the universe and of all history. The former preference for scholastic categories and subtleties gave way to a preference for biblical notions, images, and language. Instead of beginning with the hierarchial structure of the Church as the preparatory document had done, the *Constitution* begins with the Church as a mystery. Because it is a mystery it cannot be strictly defined; rather it can best be presented in the concrete images of the Bible (6). It is a little flock, a sheepfold, a kingdom, a tract of land to be cultivated, a spouse of the Lamb, a mother, a vineyard. Gone is the triumphalism that so often characterized treatises on the Church in the past (cf. e.g., 8c-e; 9g; 15b; 40b).

Of all the biblical notions which the Church makes its own, the most important and central is that of a pilgrim people, a notion which the liturgy had never lost sight of. Whereas the notion of "institution" usually dominated documents on the Church in the past, the notion of "people" dominates this document. No notion could be more existential than "people." The term immediately suggests history. A people is a group of real persons who over a period of time have had common historical experiences. As Yves Congar has pointed out, we tend to associate this term with the people of "my village, my city, my property,...of the train on which I travel, the hospital in which I am recuperating."[1]

The *Church Constitution* presents the Church as a historical phenomenon that reaches back in time to the first people of God and indeed to Abraham, our father in faith, and also forward in time to its final fulfillment in the society of the blessed. The document invites us to see the Church as caught up in history dominated by God's master plan for salvation. The notion of the people of God immediately brings out the continuity of the Church with Israel, and this continuity is strongly emphasized by the *Constitution* (cf. e.g., 2b; 9). As St. Augustine points out, the New Testament lies hidden in the Old, and the Old is manifest in the New. The Church was already present in the people of Israel, for the history of Israel was already the Christ-Event in the process of coming to be. At the same time, the society of the blessed is already present in a fuller sense in the pilgrim Church, since the Church, though still a pilgrim, already shares in the communion of love which is God.

There is both continuity and discontinuity between the old and the new people of God. We have seen that Israel began as a "flesh" community. The new people did not, except perhaps in the sense in which the Word became flesh, which means that he came to share in the same concrete human condition which we all share with one another. The new people are essentially a "spirit" community. Pentecost was the day on which the Hebrews celebrated their Sinai experience which made one people out of the heterogeneous crowd that fled together from Egypt. On this feast the Spirit of the risen Jesus fused into an unspeakably intimate communion the vastly heterogeneous peoples of the world. Here there was no question of an extension of "flesh" either horizontally or vertically. All were made one in the living flame of the one Spirit. It was on this day that mankind discovered fire for the second time, to use a phrase of Teilhard de Chardin.

We have seen that a certain "consanguinity" was established among the members of the old people of God when Moses sprinkled them with the blood of the victim of the sacrifice offered up to seal the old covenant. If this blood could bring about a unity and oneness among them, what shall be said of the unifying power of the blood of the Lamb by which the new covenant was sealed? This blood made of the peoples of the most diverse ethnic origins "blood relations" (cf. C 9e).

The old people of God were made one by believing in and remaining faithful to a unique transcendent God. The new people are made one by an immanent God, by the indwelling of the same Spirit who is the "principle" of unity and communion in the Trinity. The Spirit brings about the fulfillment of the prayer of Christ offered on the same occasion when he promised the coming of the Spirit: "May they all be one. Father, may they be one in us, as you are in me and I am in you, so that the world may believe it was you who sent me. I have given them the glory you gave me, that they may be one as we are one. With me in them and you in me, may they be completely one" (Jn 17:21-22).

For Paul, Christ and his people were identified in a real, onto-logical sense. In his Body Christ exercises a causality of grace in relation to his members, so that, in a sense, Christ dynamically is all Christians. Here the influence exercised personally by Christ on his members is something of an entirely different order from the relation of ancestors or leaders in the Old Testament. While it would be a theological error to extend the hypostatic union to the Christ's Body, we can say that this Body is continually receiving the first fruits of this union. The body of the risen Jesus, filled to overflowing with his divinity, is continually carrying on a sanctifying influence on the members of his Body. "In his body lives the fulness of divinity, and in him too you find your own fulfillment" (Col 2:9).

The unity of the Body of the Lord which is his Church is something that goes far beyond, indeed infinitely beyond, the extraordinary corporate personality of Israel. Here we have something of an entirely different order from a moral unity based on love, friendship, blood relationship, or a common cause. The members of the Church are bound together by the ontological reality which is the grace of Christ and which is a real participation in the absolute unity of God's own inner life.[2]

The new Israel differs from the old not only by its oneness but also by its universality. It is not a small group closed in upon itself, but a communion open to the limits of the world—and beyond. "While she transcends all limits of time and of race, the Church is destined to extend to all regions of the earth and so to enter into the history of mankind" (C 9g). "This characteristic of universality which adorns the People of God is a gift from the

Lord Himself. By reason of it, the Catholic Church strives energetically and constantly to bring all humanity with all its riches
back to Christ, its Head in the unity of His Spirit" (C 13b). The
Body of Christ extends beyond all the limits of the universe and
of time, for the Church lives in heaven and in purgatory as well as
on earth. This is why Chesterton could say that the Church is far
too universal to be called international. Incalculable are the possibilities of wholeness given to those who share in the life of the
Church, whose vastness transcends all the limits of space and
time, and whose oneness is a share in the unity of the Holy
Trinity.

It is in this perspective that we must view the search for self-
realization and self-fulfillment which has been so strongly emphasized in our times. For many this search seems very egocentric. Everything depends, however, upon what one considers the
self to be. Several process theologians, like Bernard Loomer
(who first gave the title "process thought" to the school of philosophy and theology which now bears that name) and Bernard
Lee, make much of a principle known as "Size" in questions such
as this. If the notion of self is limited to what is contained within
one's own skin, then seeking for self-fulfillment is indeed a very
egocentric enterprise. If, however, one expands the notion of self
to reach any place where a person is having influence or being
influenced, to reach anyone or anything that can make him or her
cry, that can make him or her happy or sad, then self-fulfillment
takes on a whole new meaning, and indeed a formidable one.
Size means stature; it means a huge range of relationships to persons one can respond to in pain and in joy. Ghandi's self had this
size, for on one occasion he remarked that when any person in
the world lacked bread he lacked bread. The self of Martin Luther
King, Jr. also had great size, for he once said: "Whenever anyone
in the world is not free, I am not free." But throughout history,
the self with the greatest size is that of Christ, who once said:
"Insofar as you did this to one of the least of these brothers of
mine, you did it to me" (Mt 25:40). In a sense, the self of the individual Christian becomes identified with this self of Christ
through an all-embracing love in the intimacy of his Body. In this
perspective, the question of self-fulfillment takes on dimensions
that stagger the imagination. The true self of the Christian extends
not only to every corner of the earth, but beyond the whole cosmos to heaven and purgatory. And the self of the Christian becomes coextensive with the self of Christ not only horizontally in
space, but also vertically in time.

There are two pivotal doctrines which members of the Church must keep in mind if they are to understand and appreciate the way in which the communal life of the Trinity is expressed and realized in the Christian life: the Mystical Body and the indwelling of the Blessed Trinity. The whole of the Christian life is caught up into the social life of the Body of the Lord. We share the Christ-life with all the other members of this Body, and from this communion we can never withdraw into the isolation of our own individualism. At the same time, we are temples of the Blessed Trinity; at every moment of our life, which coincides with the unique, unchanging moment of God's eternal "now," the Father is giving birth to the Son within us, and they are expressing their mutual love in the flame of the Spirit. If we turn within ourselves we find community—the communal life of the Holy Trinity; if we turn outside ourselves we find community—the community of the Mystical Body. No matter which way we turn we cannot escape community. Our vocation as Christians is to be transparent: we must allow the intimate and intense communal life of the Trinity dwelling within us to radiate through us to all the social relationships which constitute life in the Body of the Lord. St. Augustine, dreaming of the consummation of the union of this Body in which all its members will achieve the fullest love of Christ by loving one another in him, says: "There will be just one Christ loving himself."

What better preparation could there be for the final and total immersion of triumphant Christians in the life of the Trinity for all eternity than their immersion, both inside and out, so to speak, in the triune life all during their earthly pilgrimage? Because of the community within, we can be interior without being introverted; because of the community without, we can be exterior without becoming dissipated either psychologically or spiritually.

*   *   *

Although the notion of the Church as the people of God is central and dominant in the *Constitution on the Church*, the Council also presents it under other closely related aspects. At the beginning of the document it is viewed as a sacrament, a notion to which the Council returns later. It is called a sacrament "of intimate union with God, and of the unity of all mankind" (1b), and later a sacrament of saving unity (9f). In adopting this view, the Council returned to the patristic use of the term "sacrament,"

which modern ecclesiology had already begun to bring back into
focus. In its original and broader meaning, it was used as synonymous with "mystery," a term which became the title of the first
chapter of the *Constitution*. Like each of the seven sacraments,
the Church has both an external and an inner meaning, for it is
an outward, visible, and social sign of an inner communion in
love and grace. Just as the visible, tangible humanity of Christ
was the outward sign of the presence and activity of the Word
(8a), so the visible institutional community of the Church is an
outward sign of Christ's redemption, his grace, his love, and the
communion in love which the Spirit brought into existence. It is
also an efficacious sign: it makes the kingdom of God already
present, though not yet in its fullness.

Thus the Church is at one and the same time a visible society
which is hierarchically structured and juridically organized, and
a communion of faith, hope, and love, which is both a participation in, and a manifestation of that communion in love which is
the Blessed Trinity. As in his parables Jesus chose very ordinary,
and sometimes insignificant metaphors to be signs of his sublime
spiritual message, like the lost groat and the grass of the fields
that is here today but thrown into the oven tomorrow, so he also
chose as signs for his sacraments, not magnificent and stupendous things, but very commonplace, insignificant and often very
imperfect things: bread (which may or may not be pleasing to
the taste), wine (whose occasional bitterness does not make it
any less a sign of the true presence of Christ than sweet and
pleasant wine), water, oil, and so forth. Similarly, in the hier-
archical structure of his Church, Christ does not always choose
geniuses and saints; he more often chooses very limited, very
imperfect people, and even sinners. As the risen and glorified
Christ who is present and operative in all the seven sacraments
does not do away with the limitations of the signs, so the same
risen and glorified Christ does not do away with the limitations of
the sign of him which is the Church. The sign, which is human, is
vulnerable to all the influences of the human condition; the
Church bears the marks and even the scars of human history. It
is, and will always remain, a mystery of faith, just as the eucharist and all the other sacraments are mysteries of faith. It is not
the Church's fidelity to Christ which makes it a living sacrament,
but rather Christ's fidelity to the Church.

It is ironical and even a tragic anachronism to find, in this age
of existentialism, so many afflicted with what one can only call a

Platonic ecclesiology. It seems to have become fashionable in our times, not only to criticize, but to castigate mercilessly what is called "the institutional Church," as though it were a body completely exterior to the true spiritual Church of Christ. The impression is given that this "institutional Church" is not the Church of Christ, that the true Church is some kind of disincarnate, pneumatic, or charismatic Church, some kind of spiritual communion which exists somewhere apart from the "institutional Church." The term "institution" no doubt seems a cold and forbidding word, and the overemphasis on certain institutional aspects of the Church in the past is largely responsible for the anti-institutional and anti-juridical bias which is so strong in our times.[3]

Nonetheless, as the *Church Constitution* points out (8a), the communal structure of the Church can no more be separated from the spiritual aspect of the Church than the humanity of Christ can be separated from his divinity. Schillebeeckx is quite right in saying that "any attempt to introduce a dualism here is the work of evil—as if one could play off the inward communion in grace with Christ against the juridical society of the Church, or vice versa."[4] Ecclesiological Platonism utterly destroys the sacramental character of the Church; it is a kind of ecclesiological Nestorianism, a heresy which divided the two natures in Christ and denied that they were united in one person. A genuine incarnational spirituality is not reconcilable with a disincarnate vision of the Church; it calls for an ecclesial existentialism and personalism, and therefore an ecclesial wholeness; it calls for an acceptance and allowance for the bodily limitations of the human condition. Anyone who really understands the sacramentality of the Church will never belittle or disparage the external, visible, structural, and sociological aspects of the Church of Christ.

The Council had made it clear that, because of the weakness and the limitations of the human condition, the external aspects of the Church must always be going through some kind of renewal—*ecclesia semper reformanda* (cf. C 8d; 15b; E 6). There are many times when dissent and criticism are legitimate. But they must always be respectful and constructive. One does not disparage someone he loves with venom, ridicule, sarcasm, and caricature. He criticizes as little as possible and always in a loving way. A sincere and devoted love for the concrete, historical Church (the only one that has ever existed) is a primary and essential requisite for authentic Christian spirituality. "Christ loved the Church and sacrificed himself for her .... A man never hates his own body, but he feeds it and looks after it; and that is the way Christ treats the Church, because it is his own body—and we are its living parts" (Ep 5:25, 29-30). St. Paul's ecclesiology was always existential.

*   *   *

Once the Council Fathers began to take a more existential approach to the Church, once they began to view its life in a dynamic rather than a static way and to recognize the fact that it is always existing in history, in a condition of process, it was inevitable that they should emphasize strongly its eschatological nature, and its condition as a pilgrim, a wayfarer in a state of exile. We find evidences of this in a number of the Council documents: the *Constitution on the Liturgy* (8), the *Pastoral Constitution on the Church in the Modern World* (1, 57a), and the *Decree on the Church's Missionary Activity* (2a).

But it is especially in the *Church Constitution* that the Council focuses on the pilgrim character of the Church. After discussing this character in a number of texts in the first two chapters (cf. 7f; 8e; 9f,g; 14a), this document devotes the whole of chapter 7 to the question of the Church's eschatological nature, and in doing so goes back to the concept of eschatology found in Scripture and the early Church. The preconciliar document had presented the Church as a perfect city which is the kingdom of God. The Council document prefers to see the Church, not as a perfect city, but as a nomad, a pilgrim hastening on its way, manifesting the mystery of Christ in shadow until at the end it will be disclosed in full light (8e). In this document we find a profound change from a static, individualistic, and marginal theology of eschatology, which had developed after the sixteenth century, to a dynamic, social, and central notion, which theologians had begun to rediscover during the years prior to the Council. For centuries there had always been in theology a discussion of the *eschata*, "the last things," usually in a tract entitled *De Novissimis*, "On the Last Things." But this was a static consideration of the death of the individual Christian and what comes after. The dynamic concept sees the *eschaton*, the end-time, as having already invaded history in the incarnation, and thus the Church is essentially an eschatological people in the last times of salvation history, moving like a pilgrim, making its way over the roads of the world and continually straining toward its final fulfillment in the Parousia.[5] Eschatology is no longer a minor, isolated tract; it pervades the whole of theology. This contemporary view stems from two main sources: a rediscovery of the major role which eschatology plays in the Bible, and an awareness of the evolutionary character and the strong future thrust of our present culture (cf. CW 5). Because eschatology is one of the most characteristic aspects of contemporary theology, it should also be a distinctive characteristic of contemporary spirituality in general, and of contemporary prayer in particular.

One of the most interesting and significant aspects of the Council's vision of the Church is found at the beginning of chapter 7 (48d), and it calls for some reflection.

> The final age of the world has already come upon us (cf. 1 Cor. 10: 11). The renovation of the world has been irrevocably decreed and in this age is already anticipated in some real way. For even now on this earth the Church is marked with a genuine though imperfect holiness. However, until there is a new earth where justice dwells (cf. 2 Pet. 3:13), the pilgrim Church in her sacraments and institutions, which pertain to this present time, takes on the appearance of this passing world. She herself dwells among creatures who groan and travail in pain until now and await the revelation of the sons of God (cf. Rom. 8:19-22).

This text seems to say that the destiny of the Church is bound up with the destiny of the world, that the world and all creation have an eschatology which is intimately related to the eschatological nature of the Church. A somewhat similar idea had already been expressed earlier in connection with the statement that "the Church is destined to extend to all regions of the earth, and so to enter into the history of mankind" (9g). It is clear that the Council viewed the Church in the perspective of human history. The text quoted above (48) seems to suggest that, just as St. Paul can say that "the world as we know it is passing away" (1 Co 7:31), so it can be said that the Church as we know it, in its earthly sacramental and institutional forms, is also passing away. The present Church, like the world, has a provisional character, not in the sense that it is destined to go out of existence, but, on the contrary, in the sense that it is destined to enter into the fullness of existence, a transfigured existence, in which present sacramental and institutional forms will no longer be relevant.

An important conclusion might be drawn from this: not only are the Church and the individual Christian in a state of exile as long as they remain in this world, but the world itself is also in a kind of exile from the definitive transfigured state for which it is destined. The redemption of Christ has invaded, and is in the process of transforming, every dimension of human existence, the world, and the entire creation. The world, the Christian, and the Church share a common eschatological destiny which is in the process of becoming (cf. Rm 8:23). Perhaps we have here an insight which might help in understanding, and, to some extent in solving, the antinomy between the strong emphasis on the exile character of the Christian's existence in this world, which was often characteristic of spirituality in the past, and the contemporary emphasis on the fact that the world is the natural habitat of human persons and becoming increasingly more so as they, through the powers of science and technology, make the world more and more their own abode. The traditional flight *from* the world must be conditioned and have its meaning clarified by a flight *with* the world toward the future.[6] In other words, there are two aspects to the future of Christians: they have a historical future which calls them to collaborate with the building of a better world, as the *Pastoral Constitution* has insisted so strongly; they also have a transcendental, metahistorical future, towards which they must always keep straining as pilgrims in exile. What the *Church Constitution* says about the eschatology of the Church makes it clear that the environment of Christians is not static but extremely dynamic. We are members of a community which is in constant flight, in company with the world, through the rapid flow of time and history, toward a final point of absolute rest, which itself will not be static but intensely dynamic.

Sacraments by their very nature hide at the same time as they reveal what they signify. They are destined to pass away once the goal of the pilgrim way has been reached. The earthly sacramental character of the pilgrim Church will also pass away. Then there will be no hiddenness; there will only be pure revelation. The Church will be a pure communion of love in which all the members of Christ's Body love him and one another with a total love. Then indeed will Augustine's dream be finally and fully realized: there will be just one Christ loving himself for all eternity.

Notes

1. *This Church That I Love*, trans. Lucien Delafuente (Denville, N.J.: Dimension Books, 1969), pp. 26-27.

2. Jacques Maritain holds that the Church is a person in the strict, formal, metaphysical sense of the term. See *On The Church of Christ*, trans. Joseph Evans (Notre Dame, In.: University of Notre Dame Press, 1973), ch. 3, "The Personality of the Church." *Cf.* also *The Peasant of the Garonne*, trans. Michael Cuddihy and Elizabeth Hughes (New York: Holt, Rinehart and Winston, 1968), pp. 175-176. This question is too complex and too technical for us to consider it here.

3. In the past the institutional aspect of the Church was often given primacy over its other aspects. This is what Avery Dulles calls "institutionalism." But, as he rightly points out, "a Christian believer may energetically oppose institutionalism and still be very much committed to the Church as institution." *Models of the Church* (Garden City, N.Y.: Doubleday, 1974), p. 32. Not giving primacy to the institutional aspect of the Church is something quite different from sweeping denunciations of the "institutional Church."

4. *Christ, the Sacrament of Encounter with God*, trans. Paul Barrett (New York: Sheed and Ward, 1963), p. 48.

5. See the excellent article on the pilgrim and eschatological character of the Church and of the Christian by Paolo Molinari, "Charactère Eschatologique de L'Église Pérégrinante et ses Rapports avec L'Église Céleste," *Unam Sanctam* theological studies (Paris: Les Éditions du Cerf, 1967), LI, tome 3, 1193-1216.

6. *Cf.* Johannes Metz, *Theology of the World*, trans. William Glen-Doepel (New York: Herder and Herder, 1969), p. 92.

Bibliography

It goes without saying that the primary source for this chapter is the *Dogmatic Constitution on the Church*, considered by many to be the most important document of the Council. I recommend again the two scholarly commentaries mentioned in the bibliography of chapter 2. The first volume of the *Commentary on the Documents of Vatican II*, ed. Herbert Vorgrimler (New York: Herder and Herder, 1969), and volume 51 of the *Unam Sanctam* series, ed. G. Baraúna (Paris: Les Éditions du Cerf, 1966) contain articles by highly competent theologians. A much briefer, less scholarly, but still helpful commentary is found in *Vatican II: The Church Constitution*, ed. Austin Flannery (Chicago: The Priory Press, 1966). The first volume of *Concilium*, entitled *The Church and Mankind*, ed. Edward Schillebeeckx (Glen Rock, N.Y.: Paulist Press, 1965) contains several worthwhile articles. Among the many books inspired by the Church Constitution, I recommend the following: Karl Rahner, *The*

Church After the Council, trans. D. C. Herron and R. Albrecht (New York: Herder and Herder, 1966); Yves Congar, *This Church that I Love*, trans. Lucien Delafuente (Denville, N.J.: Dimension Books, 1969); Henri de Lubac, *The Church: Paradox and Mystery*, trans. James R. Dunne (New York: Alba House, 1969); and Georges Tavard, *The Pilgrim Church* (New York: Herder and Herder, 1967). The work of Avery Dulles, *Models of the Church* (Garden City, N.Y.: Doubleday, 1974), has made an especially significant contribution to contemporary ecclesiology.

Part IV

THE WORLD

CHAPTER TEN

WORLDLY HOLINESS

AN EXISTENTIAL VIEW of human persons sees them as profoundly hyphenated with the world. We are not, as Plato thought, heterogeneous beings introduced into the world from the outside. We have our origin and our continued existence from the world; cosmic stuff enters into our very essence. Julian Huxley called man "the flower on the stem of the world"—a concept reminiscent of the biblical image of the human person. The world is our natural habitat, but it much more than that. The science of ecology has demonstrated how much human life is dependent on environment, how much environment actually enters into and becomes a part of human life. External things are not just external.

We are a part of the world, as the world is a part of us. So true is this that Alexis Carrel could write some years ago in *Man The Unknown*: "Personality is rightly believed to extend outside the physical continuum. Its limits seem to be situated beyond the surface of the skin. The definiteness of the anatomical contours is partly an illusion. Each one of us is certainly far larger and more diffuse than his body."[1] Karl Rahner has expressed a similar view in his work, *On the Theology of Death*:

> It should . . . be borne in mind that, even in her lifetime, as informing the body, the spiritual soul is an open system towards the world. It might also be remembered with profit that natural philosophy finds it almost impossible to restrict the idea of the human "body" to what is covered by the skin. The spiritual soul, moreover, through her essential relationship to the body, is basically open to the world in such a manner that she is never a monad without windows, but always in communication with the whole of the world.[2]

We are a part of the world, not just in a static but in a very dynamic sense. We are caught up in the evolution of the universe.

We are the goal, even though not the ultimate end, of its upward thrust and of all its strivings. We and the world are continually interacting in manifold ways, continually conditioning and shaping each other. The world is not just a kind of stage on which the drama of human life, including the drama of the spiritual life, is played out. It is a protangonist in this drama. Because of this, the spiritual life must be worldly. Prior to our own times this statement would have sounded like a contradiction in terms. Yet expressions like "worldly holiness" and "worldly prayer" have now become current. Contemporary spiritual persons prefer to see the world as a mediation of God to them rather than as a separation.

Spiritual ecology must assume as one of its primary tasks the dissipation of the many ambiguities in the term "world" which have bedevilled the whole history of Christian spirituality. The Council was quite conscious of these ambiguities, as is evident in a number of passages in its documents (cf. e.g., CW 2b; 37).

Many seek a solution of this problem in a simple distinction between the positive and the negative meanings of the term. In its positive meaning, it signifies the world as created by God's love and repeatedly pronounced by him to be good, and even very good (cf. Gn 1:10, 12, 18, 21, 25, 31), the world as the locus of God's self-communication, especially in the incarnation, the world as redeemed along with the human person and given a Christian destiny, the world as the habitat and environment of the human person which is constantly enriching human life in countless ways. In its perjorative meaning, it signifies the world as alienated from God by sin, and therefore hostile to God and in constant conflict with the saving action of Christ, the world as ruled by evil principalities and powers. In this view, Christians are in the world in both senses (Jn 17:14-15), but they must not be "of the world" in its pejorative sense (Jn 18:36). With regard to the world in its positive meaning, the Christian stance is one of affirmation; with regard to the world in its negative meaning, the Christian attitude is one of withdrawal, according to the Christian tradition of "flight from the world," *fuga mundi*.

This solution of the question of the ambiguity of the term "world" is far too simplistic. The problem is much more complex than this solution suggests. And I know of no way of laying definitively to rest this ghost which has haunted the spiritual life over the centuries except by inviting the reader to accompany me through what might at first seem like a thicket of distinctions and definitions.

In the New Testament it is possible to distinguish five basic meanings of the term "world."[3] The first meaning signifies the totality of reality brought into existence and maintained in existence by God. This may be taken either in a purely cosmological sense to indicate the cosmos as it exists by itself, or in a more theological and spiritual sense, to refer to the world as a revelation in the purely natural order of God's loving kindness, his wisdom, and his power.[4]

The second meaning signifies the environment in which human beings live. Here the world may be taken in at least three different senses: It may simply signify the physical environment of the human person and of human society. It can also mean the earthly city, which the Christian has the responsibility to develop, to change, to improve, to build up—in a word, to hominize. It might also be considered from a more supernatural point of view as the world in which God's self-communication in Christ Jesus took place, the world to which Christ, the Apostles, and indeed all Christians have been sent to sanctify and to imbue with the spirit of Christ.[5]

The third basic meaning of the term is the pejorative sense mentioned above. It signifies the world as sinful, the world which is under the dominion of hostile powers that are constantly in conflict with all things pertaining to God, the world that incites to sin, along with the flesh and the devil. The world in this meaning is found very frequently in the New Testament, almost exclusively in John and Paul.[6]

The fourth meaning signifies the world considered as the object of salvation. This is the same world as the world of sin; however, it is seen as not being irremediably evil and definitively lost, but rather as still open to salvation and to the fullness of liberation from sin. Here it is important to note that the text of John (3:16), which is most frequently quoted to demonstrate the goodness of the world, is not necessarily restricted to the world in the positive sense: "God loved the world so much that he gave his only Son." For the love that the Father had in sending his Son was a redeeming and saving love; it was a love of compassion for a weak and sinful world; it was mercy responding to misery. We can, of course, also see in this text the positive love of gratuitous predilection by which God loved the world even before its foundation. In other words, in this text we can see the term "world" referring to both the second and the fourth meanings.[7]

A fifth meaning, found especially in St. Paul, refers to the world as redeemed and tending towards its eschatological fulfillment. Usually when Paul is speaking of the world in this sense, he does not use the ordinary Greek word *kosmos* but rather *ta panta*, which literally means all things or the whole of creation. Here the implications of the term "universe" include, but go far beyond, what is found in the first meaning. Here the universe is seen as embracing all things and all humanity in relation to the saving act of Christ which, having already taken place and continuing in an ongoing action, is tending towards its echatological fulfillment. Here *ta panta*, all things, are ordained towards Christ and depend on him for their fulfillment. The universe is viewed in relation to its Christian destiny. Here we see the cosmic dimensions of the Pauline Mystery of Christ and find a kind of meeting point of Christology, cosmology, and eschatology in one and the same vision. The future aeon of the world is seen as already at the heart of the present aeon.[8]

*   *   *

These distinctions help us to understand the meaning of expressions like "worldly spirituality," "worldly holiness," and "worldly prayer," which refer especially to the second, fourth, and fifth meanings given above. They also help us to interpret correctly the Council documents and other documents of the Church. With these distinctions in mind we can appreciate the inadequacies of the simplistic division between the positive and negative meanings of the world, with the corresponding duties of affirmation of the first and flight from the second. Actually, this explanation of the traditional flight from the world is erroneous on several accounts. It ignores the difference between the third and fourth meanings—the world as sinful and the world as the object of salvation—and it thus fails to emphasize that Christians are called not only to withdraw from the sins of the world but also to reach out, as Christ did, in mercy, compassion, and apostolic zeal, to the sinful world, and to carry out the ongoing redemption of this world by ministering to it and bringing to it the redeeming love of Jesus. Many of the saints who were most ruthlessly severe in renouncing the world in the third meaning were most zealous in bringing to the sinful world the compassionate and redeeming love of the Lord, and they were able to do so precisely because of their total detachment from the sinful world.

The simplistic explanation also fails to take into account the important fact that Christian withdrawal from the world is not by any means limited to the evil in the world. All Christians, each according to his or her state in life, particular ministries, and charismata, are called to withdraw from many of the good things offered by the world. It is important to see just why this is so.

Israel, conscious of having been chosen and set apart by Yahweh as a people peculiarly his own (cf. Ex 19:5-6), felt called to separate itself from the peoples living around it in order to preserve its identity and its mission in their purity and integrity. With the coming of Christ, the walls of separation were torn down, and the new people of God were chosen to be open to the world of God. Yet they were also called to accept a certain rupture with the world, and in a sense it is true to say that no one has ever insisted more emphatically on this rupture than Christ himself. "If any man comes to me without hating his father, mother, wife, children, brothers and sisters, yes and his own life too, he cannot be my disciple" (Lk 14:26). Here, of course, the word "hate" is not to be taken literally; yet it is a Hebraism which means *total* detachment.

In baptism and confirmation Christians are consecrated, and, like all consecrated persons and things, are set aside in a very special manner for Christ and for God. This consecration involves a certain otherness that distinguishes them from non-baptized persons. Even apart from this special otherness, all life is a continual series of options which, if they are to be consistent, must be coherent with one's fundamental option. Every option is a choice of one thing, and so a flight from other things not chosen. It does not mean that these other things are not good; indeed, they may be recognized as having great intrinsic value. But they are not coherent with the option made.

The option made in baptism is radical; it is the option of a life totally consecrated to God in Christ Jesus. It is an option for a participation in God's own inner life, and for a life totally dominated by the paschal mystery. From this fundamental option there continues to flow an unending series of options throughout life which must be consistent with the basic option. Always the choice of one thing necessarily involves a turning aside from many other potentially good things. If the paschal event, the radically transforming event of baptism, does not produce a profound otherness in one's life, if participation in God's inner life does not initiate a series of options different in many ways from the options of those not sharing in the divine life, of those not called to prolong Christ's passion and death in the world, it cannot be much of an event. "Do not harness yourselves in an uneven team with unbelievers (2 Co 6:13).

Here, as everywhere, the model of the Christian life is the life of Christ himself, who, while always showing a great love for the world, and while never manifesting even the slightest trace of Manicheism or Jansenism, deliberately made options which resulted in a life of great detachment from many of the good things of life. Detachment derives from the fact that the Christian life is a pilgrimage and not a sedentary existence. A pilgrim is one who must constantly be in a state of withdrawal, who must constantly be letting things go, not necessarily because they are evil or inducive to sin, but because they will make his or her life sedentary. Christians can never hope to have their pilgrimage lead to the fullness of charity, which is the goal and ultimately the whole meaning of the Christian life, without distancing themselves, not only from evil things, but also from many things good in themselves and having great intrinsic secular value. Indeed, the highest forms of beauty and goodness, as well as of culture and civilization, can at times be more seductive than evil things: an inordinate pursuit of beauty in the human arts, of scholarship, and even of apostolic action can paralyze the spiritual life in much more insidious ways than can evil things.

Since the Christian life finds its fulfillment in the fullness of love of God and neighbor, it calls for a life of intense concentration of one's whole being on this love. This concentration requires a distinctive and specific lifestyle which involves a certain existential discontinuity and rupture with many of the positive values of the world. Just as in all highly intense concentrations, such as that of the artist, the scholar, the musician, the explorer, and even the athlete, the specific focusing and concentration of the Christian life, calls for the sacrifice of many things which, though perfectly good and legitimate in themselves, do not fall within the focus. Every act of concentration means distancing oneself from all those things that do not fall within the chosen zone of concentration. Every free option for a particular lifestyle means distancing oneself from all those things which do not fit into the chosen pattern.

Christians are called to be continually making options consistent with the Christian lifestyle that flows from the basic option of baptism, and coherent with the essence and goal of the Christian life—the fullness of love of God and neighbor. Through these free options they deliberately limit quantitatively their experience with the world in an effort to improve the quality demanded by the exigencies of the otherness brought about by the radical consecration of baptism. It is only in terms of this otherness, this distancing from many of the positive values of the world, that Christians can be witnesses to the world of the presence of an "other-than-the-world," signs pointing to the new aeon, to the existence of the future in the present, heralds proclaiming that the world needs to be drawn beyond itself into the mystery realized in Christ Jesus.

When Christians are told that they must not conform their lives to the present world (cf. e.g., Rm 12:2), this does not mean simply a withdrawal which abandons the world to its own present conditions. The *fuga mundi* must also mean transforming the present world into a better world, working to actualize its almost unlimited potentialities, to hominize and humanize it, indeed, even to Christify it. Christians must feel a responsibility for their world, understood in its second meaning as the environment of humanity. They must contribute their efforts in helping it achieve both its secular and its Christian destinies.

Not all Christians are called to have the same relation to the world, taken in all of its five meanings, for in the Church a great variety of ministries and states of life determine each one's relation with the world. Lay people in the Church have a special relationship that differs from that of the members of secular institutes, as theirs differs from that of the apostolic religious, who in turn have a different relationship from that of contemplative religious. The *Church Constitution* states: "A secular quality is proper and special to laymen" (31b), and in a number of other texts the Council makes it clear that lay people, as distinct especially from religious, have a unique role to play in relation to the world and the temporal order (cf. e.g., C 36d).

The "flight from the world," though in a sense applicable to all Christians, has over the centuries been applied especially to religious. It does have a special and distinctive meaning for them, since along with their baptismal consecration, they have also been consecrated (see p. 158 below), and therefore given a special otherness by their profession. This religious consecration is a peculiarly intense concentration of one's whole being on the task of actualizing in the most direct and fruitful way all the potentialities of the paschal event that took place in baptism. It is a special free option made under the inspiration of the Spirit that brings about a distinctive lifestyle involving a more decisive existential discontinuity and rupture with the ordinary structures and many of the human values of the world. Religious can never forget this nor fail to realize that their role in relation to secular realities and the temporal order is meant to be something different from that of laymen. Only in this way can they fulfill their vocation to be in the Church and the world especially eloquent signs and heralds of the new aeon.

Despite their various lifestyles, the life of all Christians is a combination of both engagement and disengagement in relation to the world. In the concrete, actual circumstances of human life, where the elements entering into an existential situation are multiple and variable, one has to depend upon a supernaturally enlightened prudential judgment and a discernment of spirits coming from the Holy Spirit to know just exactly where to draw the line between involvement in the world and flight from it, and how to establish a balance between engagement and disengagement. Only the Spirit can teach us how we can best go to God and grow in his love through affirmation or through negation of earthly values.

*   *   *

Just as there can be in the Christian life both a "flesh" friendship and a "spirit" friendship, so also the Christian's relationship to the world can be either a "flesh" or a "spirit" relationship. In a "flesh" relationship, we approach the world and secular values on a purely natural plane. In a "spirit" relationship, we approach terrestrial realities under the guidance and inspiration of the Holy Spirit. Such a relationship is based on the belief that the Spirit is carrying on his mission in the world in this time-in-between, that he is constantly working to "renew the face of the earth," that he is present as the divine depth-dimension of the world. But while the Holy Spirit is present, making already present in the world the new aeon and preparing the world for its ultimate fulfillment in "the new creation," there are also present in the world other spirits that are not holy. The powers of evil, the demonic forces of the old aeon are also working in the world, in conflict with the work of the Spirit of Jesus. Christians can never forget that, whether they like it or not, they are caught up in that conflict (cf. CW 37b-c). If they do not approach the world as *pneumatikoi*, as spiritual persons, if they approach it "in the flesh," in their weak human condition, they can easily be naive, and their naiveté can lead them to become victims to the demonic forces working in the world, in its institutions, in human society, and most of all, in their own hearts.

At the heart of the Gospel message is the paradox that one

gets by giving away (cf. Mk 10:28-31). This paradox was the fundamental principle in the life of Francis of Assisi. From the time he stripped himself naked in the presence of the bishop no one ever renounced the things of the world more truly than he; no one was ever more detached or lived in a greater spirit of poverty. Yet no one ever loved the good and beautiful things of the world more than he. He sang an ecstatic canticle of praise to God for all his earthly creatures, for "our dear Brother Sun .... fair is he, in spendor radiant, bearing your very likeness, O Lord; for our Sister Moon, and for the bright, shining stars .... for our Brother Wind .... for our Sister Water, so useful, lowly, precious and pure .... for our Brother Fire .... beauful is he and eager .... for our Mother Earth .... producing fair fruits, many-colored flowers and herbs ...." St. Francis looked upon the things of the earth around him as his brothers and sisters: the birds, the animals, and even the Umbrian dust. He gave up the world "in the flesh" and received it back "in the spirit."

There are always two phases in the paradox of the Christian life: death leading to a new life in which what we lost in death is returned to us with new and radiant dimensions. Only the cross of Jesus can bring about these luminous new dimensions. Christians will be able to love and possess in the fullest measure only if they are willing to go through the death and rebirth which the first birth of baptism calls for. Only by dispossession can they achieve possession "in the spirit." As Teilhard de Chardin has remarked, "The Christian .... is at once the most attached and the most detached of men"[9] (cf. CW 37d-e).

In trying to judge the nature of the Christian relationship to the world, it is also important to distinguish between the speculative and the practical orders. The speculative order is abstract, and it strives to determine with absolute objectivity the nature and value of things. In the speculative order, theologians affirm the goodness of the things created by God and redeemed by Christ; they hold that grace does not destroy nature but presupposes and builds on it; they declare that nature was not totally vitiated by original sin. In the practical order, however, a value judgment is relative; it expresses, not the value things may have in themselves, but the value they have for a particular person. Things of great value in themselves may seem to be of little value in comparison with something of surpassing value.

St. Paul wrote to the Philippians: "I look on everything

as so much rubbish if only I can have Christ" (3:8). The Greek word translated here as rubbish also means excrement, and other versions use the words "dung" or "dungheap." It is not necessary for us to seek some kind of Platonic influence behind this statement. Paul is not speaking here as a theologian but as a person in love. He is saying that in comparison with the Christ he knew and loved, everything else seemed like so much rubbish. Throughout history there have been lovers who have been willing to give up everything, even kingdoms, for the sake of a human love. In comparison with the person they loved, even kingdoms seemed like dross. Should we be surprised or scandalized to find those great lovers, the saints, expressing contempt for the world and for all that it has to offer in comparison with Christ Jesus? Though the influence of Platonic philosophy undoubtedly made a contribution to the negative attitudes toward things of the world often found in the spirituality of the past, it would be a mistake not to recognize that much in these attitudes also came from this other source.

The ideal Christian attitude toward the world consists in having in the practical order such an all-consuming love for Christ Jesus that all the world has to offer will, as for Paul, seem like rubbish by comparison, while at the same time having in the speculative order a share in Paul's vision of the universe as profoundly Christic.

Notes

1. (New York: Harper and Brothers, 1935), p. 258.

2. Trans. Charles H. Henky (New York: Herder and Herder, 1961), p. 30.

3. See Yves Congar, "Église et Monde dans la perspective de Vatican II," *L'Église dans le monde de ce temps, Unam Sanctam* theological studies (Paris: Les Éditions du Cerf, 1967), LXV, tome 3, 38-41. See also Rudolf Schnackenburg, *The Church in the New Testament*, trans. W. J. O'Hara (New York: Herder and Herder, 1965), pp. 176-187.

4. Along with a great many texts in the Old Testament, a number of texts in the New Testament refer to the world in this first basic meaning. *Cf.* e.g., Mt 25:34; Mk 13:19; Lk 11:50; Jn 1:3,4; 17:5,24; Rm 1:20; Ep 1:4.

5. There are many texts, especially in St. John, in which the term "world" has this meaning. *Cf.* e.g., Jn 8:26; 9:39; 10:36; 11:27; 12:46-47; 1 Co 5:10.

6. There are almost as many texts with this meaning as with the

other four meanings put together; more than enough, surely, to convince the spiritual person to beware of any naive and excessive optimism with regard to the world. *Cf.* e.g., Jn 8:23; 12:25-31; 14:30; 15:18-19; Rm 12:2; 1 Co 2:6; 15:24-25; 2 Co 4:4; Ga 1:4; 4:3; 6:14; Col 2:8,20; Ep 1:21; 3:10; 6:12; Lk 4:5-6; Ja 1:27; 4:4; 1 Jn 2:15-17; 5:19.

7. It is highly significant that St. John, who speaks so frequently of the world in its third meaning, is also the one who speaks most frequently of it in this meaning. *Cf.* e.g., Jn 3:16-17; 4:42; 6:33,51; 8:12; 9:5; 12:46-47; 1 Jn 4:14.

8. *Cf.* e.g., Rm 8:18-25; 11:36; 1 Co 8:6; 15:24-28; 2 Co 5:17-18; Ep 1:10-12,23; 3:9; 4:10; Col 1:20.

9. *The Divine Milieu*, trans. Bernard Wall (New York: Harper and Brothers, 1960), p. 42.

Bibliography

Because the world plays such an important role in contemporary spirituality a vast literature on the relation between the Christian life and the world has appeared in recent years. Only a few typical works can be mentioned here. Edward Schillebeeckx discusses with depth and clarity many aspects of the question in *World and Church*, trans. N. D. Smith (New York: Sheed and Ward, 1971). Karl Truhlar faces squarely the relation between the positive and the negative aspects of the Christian's relation to the world in an article entitled "Transformation of the World: Flight from the World," which is found in an excellent anthology edited by Robert Gleason under the title *Contemporary Spirituality* (New York: Macmillan, 1967), pp. 212-246. Joannes Metz in *Theology of the World*, trans. William Glen-Doepel (New York: Herder and Herder, 1969) relates the theology of the world with the theology of history and also with political theology. In a small book, *Théologie de la matière*, M. D. Chenu discusses the relation between our technological civilization and Christian spirituality (Paris: Les Éditions du Cerf, 1968). Alfons Auer's *Open to the World*, trans. Dennis Doherty and Carmel Callaghan (Baltimore: Helicon Press, 1966) provides an enlightening analysis of lay spirituality in the world. Finally, the Canisianum at Innsbruck has put together an excellent collection of articles in an anthology entitled *The Christian and the World* (New York: Kenedy, 1965).

CHAPTER ELEVEN

THE CHRISTIAN UNIVERSE

FOR ST. PAUL, Christ constitutes the first principle, the foundation, and the deepest inner meaning of the whole cosmos—and all this in virtue of several titles. The first title of Christ's headship of the universe is found in the act of creation. "All things were created through him and for him. Before anything was created, he existed and he holds all things in unity" (Col 1:16-17). As the image of the Father, pre-existing with him from all eternity, he is both the source and the end of all creation. "I am the Alpha and the Omega, the Beginning and the End" (Rv 21:6; cf. 22:13). All cosmic realities find in him their image, the source of their intelligibility, as well as of their existence and their activity (I Co 8:6; Col 1:15-17; Heb 1:3). The whole cosmos is a kind of reflection of the unique Word uttered by the Father from all eternity in the bosom of the Trinity. This is what St. John had in mind when he wrote: "Through him all things came to be, not one thing had its being but through him" (Jn 1:3). To approach the world "in the spirit" and not "in the flesh" means to approach it conscious that the world was created in, through, and for the Word, that in a sense the whole universe is a spoken word of God. "By the word of Yahweh the heavens were made, their whole array by the breath of his mouth" (Ps 33:6). It means the ability to read the word of God in the world.

When the Word became flesh Christ became Lord of the universe by a new title. Through the incarnation all reality became Christologically oriented. Thereafter no cosmic reality could ever be unaffected by, or unrelated to, that central event of all history. By entering into the heart of his created universe Christ became its redeeming Lord.

In the first creation our planet is far from being the center of the cosmos. It is only a minor planet of the sun, which is one of the vast number of stars that make up only one of the innumerable galaxies in the universe. But in the "new creation" our planet is the center of the cosmos. For it was on this planet earth that the Word of God became incarnate. By reason of what happened on our planet, Christ is the Lord of the whole universe.

By assuming a perfect human nature, Christ assumed to himself all temporal realities, in such a way that temporal values acquired a new dimension and a new worth. The lordship of Christ not only includes the persons who are members of the Church, but extends to all peoples, as well as to their arts and sciences, to their social institutions, and to all their relations with the natural and the hominized universe.

But Christ, according to the eternal plan of God, did not become fully the *Kyrios*, the Lord of the universe, until his resurrection, and this final title of his lordship will have fulfillment when not only human persons but the whole physical universe have finally participated in the glorification of the risen Christ (cf. Ep 1:20-23; Ph 2:9-11). Just as the fall of the human race had cosmic repercussions, so too the redeeming resurrection of Jesus necessarily involves the whole cosmos (cf. Rm 8:19-22; I Co 15:20-28; Ep 1:10; 4:10; Heb 2:5-9). Having been created in and through Christ, all things have also been re-created in and through him (cf. 2 Co 5:17; Col 1:18-20).

In the thought of St. Paul, the redemption and sanctification of the individual person is realized only in the measure in which this person is inserted into the total social context of his or her supernatural life which is the Mystical Body. But just as the individual Christian does not live independently of this Body, so in turn this Body is inserted into the larger context of the whole universe, which forms the environment of its very life and activity. For this reason I said earlier that the world may in a certain sense be called the body of the Body of the Lord. For St. Paul, Christ's headship of the Mystical Body and his headship of the universe are very intimately united: "He has put all things under his feet, and made him, as the ruler of everything, the head of the Church, which is his body, the fullness of him who fills the whole creation" (Ep 1:23).

This holistic view of the Christian life makes it clear that the effort to build up Christ's Body cannot be separated from the effort to build a better world. Salvation history is not a history of the salvation of human persons apart from the world. Much less is it a history of their salvation from a world that is hostile to them. It is a history of the salvation and glorification of the whole of creation.

What we are moving toward is not just the survival of the immortal soul, but a complete eternal life with all its human dimensions, corporeal, social, and cosmic. Hence the universe is not just a temporary companion of our brief stay on earth; it is something that will accompany us forever in the world to come. We must respect it and love it as our companion for time and eternity—but always "in the spirit," always in the Lord.

Although theologians agree that there will be a new glorified universe born from the present one, a universe which will have some connection with the present universe, they are unable to specify just how this will take place or to provide any kind of cosmological concept of it. The same is true of the glorification of the human body. It is certain that it will take place and that the glorified body will have some kind of continuity with our present body, but no one can specify in biological terms just how this will take place.

The spiritual life, therefore, consists in preparing for the total cosmic glorification. This point, though always recognized in theology, has recently become one of the most fruitful areas of theological development, and it implies a whole new outlook on the world and on the spiritual life. Our concept of salvation and sanctification is now universal and holistic; it is not just the saving and sanctifying of "my soul."

*   *   *

Among many aspects of the relationship between the spiritual life and the spiritualization and eventual glorification of the cosmos, two things in particular deserve mention: liturgy and Christian poverty. Both deal essentially with material things, but they might easily seem to be at odds in the way they go about it.[1] Poverty seems to consist essentially in a withdrawal; liturgy, on the contrary, seems intent on drawing cosmic matter into its worship. Actually, the two have exactly the same aim: the restoration of God's original plan for the universe and the gradual spiritualization of cosmic realities in preparation for their ultimate glorification.

God's original plan was for the whole of creation to constitute an harmonious act of praise to his glory. This plan was destroyed by sin; material things began to be turned aside from their original destiny and made to serve human selfish and sinful purposes, and our consumer society is ever intent on aiding and abetting this frustration of God's original plan (cf. Rm 8:19-22). Both liturgy and poverty, each in its own way, aim at freeing creation from the bonds of selfishness and restoring God's original plan.

To understand how the liturgy does this, we must begin by recognizing that prior to the liturgy and apart from it there is a natural sacramentality in cosmic matter, the sacramentality Gerard Manley Hopkins had in mind when he wrote: "The world is charged with the grandeur of God. It will flame out, like shining from shook foil."[2] For an authentic contemporary spirituality, secularity is not sufficient; it must be combined with sacramentality. But it is important to distinguish between a sacral world and a sacramental world, as we shall see in the next chapter. The sacramentality we are talking about here is not something overlayed on secularity; on the contrary, it shines forth from the inmost depths of secularity itself. No one has ever had a clearer vision of this luminous sacramentality radiating from the very heart of secularity than Teilhard de Chardin:

> Throughout my life, through my life, the world has little by little caught fire in my sight until, aflame all around me, it has become almost completely luminous from within. . . . Such has been my experience in contact with the earth—the diaphany of the divine at the heart of the universe on fire.[3]

Art and technology can give cosmic realities a higher kind of sacramentality by imparting to them something of the luminous intelligibility of the human mind. The liturgy takes to itself the natural sacramentality of secular reality, and often the sacramentality of sacred art, and elevates them to the supernatural order, where we find the sacramentals and the sacraments, in which God's goodness is not only reflected but made efficacious. The sacraments are already a preparation for, and in a sense an anticipation of, the final transfiguration of the world. In none of the sacraments is this so true as in the eucharist, in which the cosmic materials of bread and wine make the humanity and the divinity of Christ present physically and substantially, and in which all human work represented in the making of bread and wine from cultivated wheat and grapes is taken up into glory.

This role of the eucharist in preparing for and already anticipating the transfiguration of the universe is one of the central
themes in the thought of Teilhard de Chardin:

> As our humanity assimilates the material world, and as the Host
> assimilates our humanity, the eucharistic transformation goes beyond
> and completes the transubstantiation of the bread on the altar. Step
> by step it irresistibly invades the universe. It is a fire that sweeps
> over the heath; the stroke that vibrates through the bronze. In a
> secondary and generalized sense, but in a true sense, the sacramental
> Species are formed by the totality of the world, and the duration of
> the creation is the time needed for its consecration.[4]

In God's plan for the whole of creation to be a canticle
of love and of praise, he destined the human person to be
the "high priest in the lofty temple of nature."[5] For the human
person alone can give articulate and intelligent voice to creation. He ministers in this priestly function particularly in
the liturgy, and above all in the celebration of the eucharist.
Before the reform of the liturgy, the celebrant of Mass was
instructed to begin his thanksgiving on his way back to the
sacristy by reciting the Canticle of Daniel (3:57-87) in which
all creatures are called upon to praise the Lord: the sun,
moon, and stars, the mountains and hills, everything growing
from the earth, all beasts wild and tame, all water creatures
and birds, the springs, the rivers, and the seas. The appropriateness of this canticle as the beginning of thanksgiving after
Mass was not always apparent to everyone. Yet it was most
fitting that the priest, standing at the pinnacle of the whole
of creation and having just offered on the earth by means of
the cosmic materials of bread and wine the most sublime act of
worship and praise, should call out to all creatures to join him in
his canticle of love. Once again, no one, to my knowledge, has
expressed so profoundly and so lyrically the meaning of all this as
Teilhard de Chardin in his *Hymn of the Universe.*
   Only one whose mind and heart have been caught up in the
spirit of evangelical poverty can fully appreciate this meaning. For the essential aim of Christian poverty is to liberate
material things from human selfishness and sinfulness and
to dedicate them to God's glory. It is not just a negative
ascetical practice. As consecrated virginity is not just a denial,
but a positive consecration of the sacramentalized Christian
body to God's glory, so, in somewhat the same way, evangelical
poverty is not just a rejection of material things, but a positive

dedication of them to the glory of God. Evangelical poverty is a "chaste" way of using the things of the world. Its purpose is to help Christians achieve more fully the ultimate aim of the Christian life, which is to share as fully as possible in the life of God. In a sense, God is the poorest being in existence. He does not have anything; whatever we say he has, he is. He is infinitely poor in having because he is infinitely rich in being, in existence. Evangelical poverty aims at making us poor in having so that we can become rich in being to an ever fuller degree.

Christian poverty, then, does not stand back from material things because it hates them as something evil, but on the contrary because it loves them so intensely that it does not want to allow selfishness, avarice, pride, or sensuality on our part to mar in any way the reflection in them of God's beauty and goodness. St. Ambrose tells us that the poor are given a participation in the sovereignty of God over the whole world. Christ manifested his absolute lordship and mastery over all created things by living a life of stark poverty. No material thing, nor all material things together, were able to master him. Christian poverty gives a share in Christ's mastery of the entire cosmos. John of the Cross, after achieving a total detachment from material things, could sing: "Mine are the heavens and mine is the earth." This is the Christian paradox I spoke of earlier: we get by giving away.

Closely allied to both evangelical poverty and liturgy in relation to cosmic realities is the virtue of magnificence, about which we hear very little these days. This virtue directs the way in which Christians make things; it inclines them to make them with beauty, nobility, and even at times with a certain grandeur, according to what the situation calls for and the means allow. There must be nothing "cheap" or ersatz about Christians, even in their poverty. In building and making things they must lift up cosmic realities to share in some way in the beauty and nobility of the Christian life. Aristotle taught that the virtue of magnificence, though operative in many aspects of human life, is called for especially in whatever pertains to divine worship.

The destiny of the whole cosmos for redemption, resurrection, and glorification gives a special significance to human labor. The works of art, industry, and technology, the practice of the various professions, the efforts to master the universe (cf. Gn 1:28) and to bring to light its secrets can begin to take on a spiritual meaning, a redemptive value, an eternal significance. God has placed into our hands an unfinished universe, giving us the glorious mission of perfecting his work, of bringing it to fulfillment, of preparing it for its glorification, of continuing the work of creation, and of guiding the universe in the direction for which it was created. Thus it is possible for Christians to put the universe more and more at the service of human and divine love and to make it ready to be spiritualized with the love of the Holy Spirit: "Send forth thy Spirit and all shall be created, and thou shalt renew the face of the earth." In this way we are, as the *Pastoral Constitution* has suggested, aiding the body of the new human family to grow, and this is already a kind of beginning of the world to come (39c).[6]

Seeing the Christian life in this perspective makes it possible to discover many implications in the statement at the end of Mark's gospel that the Good News must be proclaimed to the *whole of creation* (16:16). The Good News must be brought not only to human persons in isolation but to their whole environment. It must be expressed in a great variety of magnificent ways in all the arts. It must be built into the structure of human society. It must provide a pattern for the efforts of Christians to refashion the universe. Cultural, scientific, and technological progress is not, of course, the measure of the coming of the kingdom. There is an otherness of the kingdom which purely secular progress can never be identified with or compensate for. But we shall find all the fruits of our nature and of our industry purified, illuminated, and transfigured when the Lord Jesus will finally present the kingdom to his Father (cf. CW 39). In this sense, progress in the world has an intrinsic relationship with the kingdom of God. Hence the concern of contemporary spirituality to participate in the growth, development, and fulfillment of the world. Hence the broad horizons and extensive dimensions of this spirituality, which sees as its task, not just to spiritualize our spirit with the life of the Holy Spirit, but also to spiritualize our body and indeed the whole universe.

It would be difficult to find a more fitting conclusion of this chapter than the following quotation from Karl Rahner:

> But he himself has come to us. And he has transformed what we are and what we still want to consider as the gloomy, earthly dwelling place of our "spiritual nature": he has transformed *the flesh*. Ever since that event, mother earth bears nothing but transformed children. For his resurrection is the beginning of the resurrection of all flesh.
> One thing, of course, is necessary, for his event—which we can never undo—to become the blessedness of our existence: he must burst forth

from the grave of our hearts. He must rise from the core of our being, where he is a power and a promise. He is there, and yet something remains to be done. He is there, yet it is still Holy Saturday until the last day, until that day that will be a cosmic Easter. And this rising takes place beneath the freedom of our faith. It is taking place as an event of living faith that draws us into the colossal eruption of all earthly reality into its glorification, the splendid transfiguration that has already begun with the resurrection of Christ.[7]

Notes

1. See my article on this question, "The Spirit of Poverty," *Worship*, XXVIII (April 1954), 224-232. See also my discussion of a doctrinal-sacramental approach to poverty in "Sanctification Through the Vows," *Proceedings of the 1955 Sisters' Institute of Spirituality* (Notre Dame, In.: Notre Dame University Press, 1955), pp. 105-120.

2. "The Grandeur of God," *Poems of Gerard Manley Hopkins*, ed. Robert Bridges and W. H. Gardner (London: Oxford University Press), p. 70.

3. *The Divine Milieu*, trans. Bernard Wall (New York: Harper and Brothers, 1960) p. 14 (note). See also pp. 110, 127, etc.

4. Ibid., p. 104. *Cf.* also pp. 102-105. For a fuller appreciation of Teilhard's poetical and even mystical fascination with the relation between the eucharist and the universe, see *Hymn of the Universe*, trans. Simon Bartholomew (New York: Harper and Row, 1965), especially "The Mass on the World," pp. 19-37; "The Monstrance," pp. 46-49; and "The Pyx," pp. 50-55.

5. Etienne Gilson, *The Unity of Philosophical Experience* (New York: Charles Scribner's Sons, 1954), p. 50.

6. This is something of the vision of Teilhard de Chardin regarding the human person's activities in the world. *Cf.* e.g., *The Divine Milieu*, pt. 1, "The Divinization of Our Activites," pp. 17-43.

7. *The Eternal Year*, trans. John Shea (Baltimore: Helicon Press, 1964), pp. 94-95.

Bibliography

George Maloney's *The Cosmic Christ* (New York: Sheed and Ward, 1968) gives an excellent historical survey of theological reflections on the role the cosmos has played in Christology from St. Paul to Teilhard de Chardin. I shall have more to say about Teilhard's teachings in the last chapter. For the present let it suffice to recommend two of his books which are the most popular among his many writings, and also the most spiritual and the easiest to read: *The Divine Milieu*, trans. Bernard Wall (New York: Harper and Brothers, 1960) and *Hymn of the Universe*, trans.

Simon Bartholomew (New York: Harper and Row, 1965). Sister Maria
Gratis Martin gives a brief, compact overview of Teilhard's teaching in
the perspective of his spirituality in *The Spirituality of Teilhard de Chardin* (Westminister, Md.: Newman Press, 1968). I also recommend Robert
Faricy's *Building God's World* (Denville, N.J.: Dimension Books, 1976),
which is a readable small volume on the theology of Christian involvement in the world.

CHAPTER TWELVE

THE SACRED AND THE SECULAR

IT MIGHT BE ARGUED, indeed it seems beyond dispute, that among all the signs of the times which spiritual ecology must study and evaluate, the most obvious and the most significant is the process of secularization, a process which began with the dissolution of the Holy Roman Empire and what came to be known as Christendom, which has gathered momentum ever since, and which has reached its peak in our generation. Nothing has had a more profound and pervasive influence on the evolution of our present culture, including our spiritual culture and hence the distinctive style characteristic of contemporary spirituality, than this process. Expressions such as "secular spirituality," "secular holiness," and "secular worship," which would in former times have seemed contradictions in terms, have now become common. Not long ago any identification of the holy with the profane would have seemed heresy, if not blasphemy; yet we now hear Malcolm Boyd, speaking in the introduction to his book of prayers, *Are You Running With Me, Jesus?*, about the "heretical gulf" between the holy and the profane.[1] Even more: what has always been considered the most sacred act that could ever have taken place, the sacrifice of Christ on Calvary, is now being called a secular event.[2]

We are faced here with one of the most acute problems relating to the spiritual life in our times. The context and environment of the spiritual life today is thoroughly secularized; and it is only in learning how to come to terms with a secularized culture that a valid spirituality for our times can develop.

In attempting to assess the impact of our secularized culture upon the spiritual life, spiritual ecology inevitably gets involved in semantics. Whereas in the last chapter the semantic problem involved only the one word "world," here we are confronted with a whole vocabulary: secular, profane, sacred, holy, secularization, secularism, consecration, sacralization. Not only is each of these terms surrounded with ambiguities, but the ambiguities are compounded when these words are seen in relation to each other.

Secularization has been defined as "the massive assertion of the autonomy of the secular,"[3] or as "the phenomenon whereby, in relation to any sacred, religious and ecclesial order, the realities of the world and of human life tend to be grounded in an every growing autonomy."[4] These working definitions can provide a starting point for our reflections. But it is important at the outset to make a clear distinction between secularization and secularism. The former is the assertion of the place, the value, and the intrinsic and legitimate autonomy of the secular; it does not deny the sacred and the transcendent but simply prescinds from them. The latter, on the contrary, is the denial and the positive exclusion of the sacred or transcendent. As Harvey Cox has pointed out, it is "the name for an ideology, a new closed worldview, which functions very much like a new religion."[5]

The problem we are faced with here is that of the true meaning of the cosmic dimensions of the Mystery of Christ which will be discussed in the last chapters of this book. The central question is whether for Christ to recapitulate all things and draw them to himself in a transfigured and glorified universe, whether in order to speak of a cosmic Christ and Christification of the universe, it is necessary that all that is secular be made sacred, that the realm of the temporal and profane surrender its autonomy.

Although the term "sacred" is often used in a great variety of meanings, in its most proper sense it signifies something consecrated and hence set apart and given a special "otherness" by being drawn into the realm proper to God alone, even though not necessarily removed totally and exclusively from ordinary relationships to the natural order. Persons consecrated by baptism and confirmation, and perhaps further consecrated by holy orders or religious profession, receive a special sacral quality, which does not, however, exclude participation in things pertaining to the secular order. The sacred in this sense is exemplified by Christian lay persons, who, as the Council tells us, have a special secular quality (C 31b), by diocesan priests, who for centuries have been called "secular," and finally by religious, who may have many secular tasks to perform. Some things, however, are so consecrated as to become totally other, completely lifted out of the order of the secular, such as the eucharist and the whole sacramental order in general.

The realm of the secular embraces everything that has not been sacralized by being consecrated. But though contradistinguished from the sacred, the secular is not contradistinguished from the holy, for the holy has a much broader meaning than the sacred. The term "holy" includes everything explicitly pertaining or related to the supernatural order. For example, the Christian meal, blessed and offered to God, carried out in a spirit of mutual charity, and reflecting the fellowship of the eucharist, is holy, but still secular, since it has not, like the eucharistic meal itself, been consecrated and set aside from the secular order. Sacred secularity is a contradiction in terms; secular holiness is not.

Even when the secular is not made holy by being explicitly related to the supernatural order, it does not mean, as many either consciously or unconsciously assume, a godless section of life, but precisely God's world. Indeed, even when secular realities have not been made explicitly holy or actually transformed into the sacred, a foundation for the sacred is already present. For the world of the secular has been created by God, and is thus a sacrament of his goodness, power, and beauty. Having been created in, through, and for the Word (Col. 1:16), it is open to, and oriented toward, the order of grace. Though the purely secular has its own finalities within certain spheres, it has no ultimate end of its own. Its ultimate end is supernatural; it has been given a Christian destiny. In this sense Teilhard de Chardin can say that everything is sacred, nothing is profane.[6]

Since the sacred properly so called comes into existence through an act of consecration, to understand the sacred we must try to analyze the meaning of consecration. We are involved here with consecration in its strict and proper sense as an act which sacralizes persons or things, which removes them either totally or partially from the realm of the secular, and which gives a special share in the otherness of the Wholly Other, who is God. It is important to distinguish this proper sense of the term "consecration" from several loose and improper senses in which it is commonly used.

In the French school of spirituality, for example, Cardinal Bérulle, St. John Eudes, St. Grignon de Montfort and others made much of the "consecration" of oneself, one's home, and even the entire human race to the Sacred Hearts of Jesus and Mary. Taken in this sense, "consecration" merely means a devotional dedication of oneself in love to Christ or his mother. In the heyday of Catholic Action there was much talk about "consecrating" one's work, one's milieu, indeed all aspects of human life and society.[7] This is also an improper use of the word which confuses consecration with sanctification. It is true that the Martyrology of Christmas night does speak of Christ coming into the world because he wishes to consecrate it. But here again the more proper word would be "sanctify." The Council used the phrase "consecration of the world" just once (C 34b), and after that sedulously avoided it. The mission of the Church is not to sacralize secular realities but to sanctify them. This distinction is of great importance, for sacralization takes away either totally or partially the secularity proper to persons and things of the world; sanctification does not. To sanctify simply means to make holy.

The mission of the Church is to strive to make the secular order holy by communicating to it the redeeming love of Jesus, thus bringing it under the higher order of grace. But this higher order of grace is not to be identified with the ecclesiastical order of the institutional Church. As an institution, the Church has no jurisdiction over secular realities. Moreover, the outpouring of the grace and redeeming love of Jesus, as well as the operation of his Spirit of holiness, are not by any means restricted to the ecclesiastical order. Christianity and the Christian life are not coterminous with the life of the Church.

The Church's blessings fall into two categories: invocative and constitutive. Invocative blessings given to persons and things do not bring about any fundamental change in their secular status. The persons and things are not set apart for special religious and cultic purposes. These blessings aim simply at helping Christians sanctify themselves, especially through the things that enter into their lives. They do not aim in any way at sacralizing persons or cosmic realities. Rather, they seek to impart to experience with secular realities a special association with the ongoing redemptive process by which Christians, and through them their entire world, are being gradually spiritualized and drawn towards their ultimate glorification. If at times these blessings seem to be excessively multiplied, the purpose is to show that nothing in the universe is unrelated to this ongoing process. Constitutive blessings, on the other hand, when understood in their most proper sense, bring about a consecration, a sacralization of the persons or the things blessed, which are thereby set apart and given a special "otherness" for religious and cultic purposes.

Consecration in the strict sense is an act by which persons or things are rendered sacred by being drawn into the order of the divine. This implies a certain withdrawal from ordinary circumstances in order to be wholly at the disposal of God. The persons or things acquire a new character which distinguishes them from the ordinary. They become the special possession of God and are set apart for his service and glory.

The fundamental notion of God and of his holiness among the Hebrews was that of the "Wholly Other." When persons or things, through consecration, entered into the sphere of the divine, there was a communication of this "otherness" which set them apart. For the biblical person not only were individual persons and things consecrated to God, but the whole nation was a consecrated people, a sacred people, a people set apart from all others (cf. e.g. Ex 19:5-6; Lv 20:26; Dt 7:6; 26:18-19).

The incarnation was the fulfillment of this consecration of the Old Testament, at the same time giving it an entirely new perspective. The man Jesus was the Holy One of God par excellence (cf. Ac 4:27-30). His very title, "Christ," means "the anointed one" and hence "the consecrated one." He called himself the one whom "the Father consecrated and sent into the world" (Jn 10:36). And in his great sacerdotal prayer, speaking to the Father of his apostles, he said: "For their sake I consecrate myself so that they too may be consecrated in truth." (Jn 17:19). Jesus was consecrated not by ordinary oil but by the unction of the Holy Spirit (cf. Ac 10:38; Is 61:1; Ac 4:26-27).

Jesus was consecrated by the hypostatic union with the "Wholly Other," and yet, while remaining "Wholly Other," he became a brother to all mankind, and entered intimately into every aspect of human life. From then on the sharing of the Christian in the consecration of the Lord would have to find a way of combining these two paradoxical aspects.

The new covenant of baptism and confirmation is a profound consecration of our whole being which gives a participation in the consecration of Jesus himself (cf. 1 Co 6:11; Ep 1:3-5; 5:25-27). It makes us a special possession of the Father by giving us a share in the filiation of his Son. This consecration is a deep, intrinsic reality which sets us apart from ordinary profane existence and introduces us into the most sacred of all situations, the inner, personal life of the Trinity. We are drawn into the very "otherness" of God himself. Our consecration does not simply associate us or relate us to God; it actually makes us live with his inner life.

Baptismal consecration is profound and all-pervasive. Yet other consecrations are possible in the Christian life. Holy Orders is a consecration which sets the priest apart in a special way. Religious profession has for many centuries been referred to as a consecration, particularly in relation to the liturgical consecration of virgins, but also by extension to religious profession in general. The term has been used extensively in relation to the religious life since Pius XII, and it occurs frequently in the Council documents (cf. e.g., C 44b; 45d; 46c). Some theologians question the propriety of speaking of religious profession as a true consecration. The principal reason is that God alone can consecrate a person; no one, simply of his own initiative, can make himself sacred, introduce himself into God's own sphere of life, and make himself the unique, total, and exclusive possession of God. Yet the assumption that in religious profession the initiative is taken solely by the person professed seems to me unacceptable. For, apart from the initiative taken by God in calling a person to the religious life, there is the fact that the public vows taken in the Church involve a public and official action on the part of the Church of God, and therefore on the part of God himself working through his Church. Precisely because profession truly consecrates and sacralizes the religious, a dispensation from religious vows has traditionally been called an "indult of secularization." But while holding that religious profession is a true consecration, I think it a mistake to refer to the religious life as "the consecrated life," for this implies that the life of the baptized, confirmed, and perhaps ordained Christian is not consecrated.

Consecrated persons have been sacralized, and therefore made sacred and holy by being drawn into the sphere of the all holy God. This may be called ontological holiness because it is associated with the very being of persons who have been set apart for religious purposes. But besides this there is personal Christian sanctity which consists in a practice of the virtues to an eminent degree, and especially the virtue of charity, which informs and motivates all the others. The ontological holiness of persons who have been sacralized calls for a high degree of personal sanctity. Unfortunately the two do not always go together. It has been traditional in the Church to accord special reverence to persons who have been consecrated and sacralized in a special way, even though they may be lacking in personal sanctity. Indeed, Canon law has punished with *ipso facto* excommunication anyone who "lays violent hands" on persons in sacred orders or on religious.[8] It may be that in the past some bishops, priests and religious have presumed too much on their ontological holiness in expecting special reverence and respect. In any case, the temper of our times is not inclined to honor those who have not merited reverence and respect by their own efforts.

Was the man Jesus sacred or secular? He was both. Because of the unique kind of consecration that was his, he was the most sacred person who ever lived. But he was at the same time secular, since he entered fully into every aspect of human life except sin. He could apply to himself the words of Terence: "I am a man and I consider nothing human alien to me." Like Jesus, the Christian must be both secular and sacred. Not even the hermit or the strictly cloistered religious can every fully rupture the bond which links him to the secular world. But he must also, like Jesus, have that distinctive otherness which identifies him as a consecrated person. Otherness and presence to the world are not mutually exclusive; indeed, they are correlatives. Otherness does not in any way mean irrelevance; and it is only by realizing this that we can hope to keep the profane and the sacred both distinct and united—a task that is not easy but necessary for an authentic contemporary spiritual life.

Is it legitimate to speak of the sacrifice of Christ on Calvary as secular worship? It is, if by this we mean that it was not a sacred ritual, carried out through sacralized signs. It was not something that was performed apart from the secular order. It was an historical act that took place in the world as a result of what Schillebeeckx has called "a secular combination of circumstances."[9] The vocation of the Christian is to live a life of secular as well as of sacred worship. St. Paul tells us as much when he exhorts the Romans to offer their living bodies as a holy sacrifice, truly pleasing to God, and then immediately tells them not to model themselves on the behaviour of the world around them (Rm 12:1-2). It is clear that for Paul one kind of behaviour in the world was a worship of God and another was not. In other words, there were two kinds of secularity, the one Christian and the other non-Christian.

When Paul exhorts the Romans to offer their living bodies, he is writing as a Hebrew and therefore means their whole lives. This is clear from the first letter to the Corinthians: "Whatever you eat, whatever you drink, whatever you do at all, do it for the glory of God" (1 Co 10:31). Peter tells the early Christians that they are "the holy priesthood that offers the spiritual sacrifices which Jesus Christ has made acceptable to God" (1 P 2:5). Through the common priesthood of baptism and confirmation, the whole secular life of the Christian can and should become a constant worship of God. The *Church Constitution*, speaking of the laity, expresses this beautifully:

> For all their works, prayers, and apostolic endeavors, their ordinary married and family life, their daily labor, their mental and physical relaxation, if carried out in the Spirit, and even the hardship of life, if patiently borne—all these become spiritual sacrifices acceptable to God through Jesus Christ (cf. 1 Pet. 2:5). During the celebration of the Eucharist, these sacrifices are most lovingly offered to the Father along with the Lord's body. Thus, as worshippers whose every deed is holy, the laity consecrate the world itself to God (34b).

The early Christians were very conscious that in their lives there was to be both secular worship and sacred worship, that the two were intimately united in such a way that the first flowed from the second and led back to it again, and that the second would lose its full meaning without the first. Sometimes they united the two very intimately, as in their love feasts, when a Christian secular meal, in which they ate and drank for the glory of God, was closely associated with the celebration of the eucharist. Christian secular worship and Christian sacred worship should go together to form the total expression of the one Christian sacrifice of love. At the same time they must be kept clearly distinct. The celebration of the eucharist, for example, should never be "secularized" (as it has often been, especially since Vatican II) by disregard for the directives of the Church by which it has labored over the centuries and continues to labor to preserve and enhance the sacred character of its most sacred act of worship.

In speaking of the consecration of Jesus, I said that in his own person he brought to fulfillment the sacralization begun in the Old Testament. At the same time, he did try to eliminate all excessive and false instances of sacralization. He tore down the wall that had separated the sacred Hebrews from the profane Gentiles (cf. Ep 2:14; Ac 10:28). Time and time again his voice echoed the voices of the prophets who had castigated their people for the excessive externalism, legalism, and ritualism to which their concept of the sacred had degenerated. On the other hand, he was ever faithful to all the legitimate demands of the religion of his people (cf. e.g., Lk 2:22ff.; 4:16). Moreover, he founded a religion in which the sacral would play an essential part, as is evidenced by his institution of the sacraments. Paradoxically, it was the sacral element at the heart of Christianity that made it possible historically for the secular to achieve its proper autonomy.

*   *   *

In antiquity, and in pagan religions in general, nature possessed a numinous and sacral quality. It was inhabited by a variety of deities, and natural forces and processes were identified with their operations and influences. There was a constant appeal to the sacred and the religious for the understanding and use of nature. The order of the divine or the numinous was not clearly distinguished from the cosmic order and its laws. Something hieratic was constantly being associated with even the most ordinary processes of nature. A similar tendency was carried over to human society in the sense that the gods were, in one way or another, a part of the civic polity. Even the advanced civilization of the Roman Empire was no exception.

To all this the Hebrews were a striking exception. The creation story in Genesis, even though it borrowed some elements from other peoples, was unique in making Yahweh a sole and totally transcendent God to whom alone divinity could be attributed. At one stroke it cast out all deities from nature; it brought about what Max Weber has called the "disenchantment of nature." It was the beginning of a long process of secularization. But because of the apartness of the Hebrews, this disenchantment stayed within their own small enclave; secularization did not extend to the world at large.

Christianity, as it spread across the world, appeared as a challenge to the whole concept of nature and society that had been an essential part of ancient cultures. Rightly understood, the Mystery of Christ calls for the world to be itself, that is to say, non-divine. Moreover, it is the great paradox of Christianity that in the incarnation God, by drawing the whole universe to himself in the close embrace of the hypostatic union, by entering into the world and nature, and by becoming a part of human society, liberated the world and human society from the numinous and hieratic, and left them free to be themselves.

The political state too was freed of all divinities and acknowledged to be what it is supposed to be, simply a political state: "Give back to Caesar what belongs to Caesar—and to God what belongs to God" (Mt 22:21). It was precisely because the early Christians rejected the various divinities thought to inhabit nature, because they refused to accept the official gods of the state, that they were accused of being "atheists" and persecuted as such. In other words, Christianity desacralized the universe and the state by casting out their deities. It brought about a process of desacralization and therefore of secularization in the world; it distinguished the sacred from the secular and restored the realm of the temporal and the profane. In this sense we can agree with Johannes Metz that it is of the very nature of the incarnation to secularize the world.[10]

Unfortunately, the Church throughout history did not always understand with sufficient clarity the relationship of the incarnation to the secular order. In a sense, although Christianity had desacralized the political order of the Roman world, it nonetheless modelled itself on that order and at the same time claimed for itself something like the Roman state's prerogatives. Thus in the Middle Ages there developed what came to be known as Christendom, when the Church became wedded to the political, social, and economic order. A theandric state and a sacred culture developed which tended to absorb the temporal and to subjugate it to its own purposes. The sanctifying of the temporal order was seen mainly in terms of clericalism and ecclesiasticism which did not sufficiently respect the intrinsic autonomy of the secular order. The Church established a kind of monopoly over many activities and institutions which the secular order could very well have taken care of by itself. It did indeed teach a doctrine of the "two swords," but the secular sword was viewed as something granted by the Church and destined to be used primarily in the interests of the Church. Temporal, profane, and terrestrial realities tended to be looked upon as constituting only a temporary situation in which the Christian had to work out his own salvation. At best they were indifferent in themselves, without any intrinsic relation with the Kingdom of God, whose earthly presence was thought to be coterminous with the Church.

Through a series of political revolutions and evolutions, through the development of empirical science, technology and industrialization, through the laicization of human society, there gradually evolved in the West a secular culture which was often judged to be hostile to the Church, or which at best seemed to leave the Church on the margin of things as something largely irrelevant. Empirical science and technology opened up the mysteries of the universe, brought about a disenchantment of nature and dissipated all sense of the numinous or the sacral in relation to it. People became increasingly conscious of their power over nature and of their ability to dominate its forces. The development of the secular state and the evolution of the social sciences gave them a sense of the autonomy of human society, of its rightful aspirations, and of their power to engineer its development towards an ever greater realization of these aspirations. And the end product of all these developments is known as the secular city, a pluralistic society committed to no particular faith or supernatural ideology, the human city conscious of its own rightful autonomy, of its intrinsic destiny, and of the power it possesses to evolve towards the fulfillment of that destiny.

Secularization in its development has not infrequently been associated with secularism, and has been historically accompanied by a process of de-Christianization. As a result, many tend to take a negative view of the secular city, to look upon it as something intrinsically anti-Christian. Others, on the contrary, distinguishing between the process of secularization and the process of de-Christianization, see in it not only a purification of false elements in the Christianity of the past, but actually a product, at least in part, of the most authentic tradition in Christianity. Bonhoeffer has hailed the development of secularization as "clearing the decks for the God of the Bible." For him secularization has resulted in "man come of age."

*   *   *

At the time of Vatican II, this problem of the relationship between the Christian life and the world presented itself as one of the most acute questions which the Council felt obliged to face. This it did principally in the *Pastoral Constitution of the Church in the Modern World*, (cf. e.g., 26, 36, 38, 42, 43, 57, 58, 76, 93), but also in other documents, notably the *Constitution on the Church* (cf. e.g., 31, 34) and the *Decree on the Apostolate of the Laity* (cf. e.g., 5, 7, 31). It would prolong unduly our discussion of secularity to attempt to summarize and evaluate all the statements of the Council which relate to this subject either directly or indirectly. Nor is it necessary, for these statements are sufficiently clear in themselves. Let it suffice to say that, after reflecting on all the relevant teachings of the Council, it is difficult not to agree with Thomas Clarke when he says: "I would venture to guess that ... Vatican II may well live in history as the council in which the Church inaugurated the age of Christian secularity."[11]

The growing autonomy of the secular in general has been accompanied by a growing realization of the autonomy of the spirituality of the lay person. The spirituality of the medieval sacral culture tended to take monastic spirituality as its model. Although the Church has always held that the call to holiness is universal, although theologians have taught that perfection consists in love and not necessarily in the profession of the evangelical counsels, "striving for perfection" was all too often identified with "leaving the world" and entering a monastery. When secular realities were not recognized for their true worth, lay people, whose lives were most closely associated with these realities, were often not considered to have a spirituality of their own. Indeed, it sometimes seemed that they were looked upon as "second class citizens" as far as the spiritual life and holiness were concerned. And it was only after the true meaning of secular realities was restored through the process of secularization that the spirituality of lay people began to claim attention once again. All this explains why the Council felt it necessary to devote the whole of chapter 5 in the *Constitution on the Church* to the universal call of all to genuine holiness. In restating this traditional doctrine, and, in particular, in emphasizing that lay persons with their special secular quality are called to the same holiness as members of the hierarchy and religious, the Council was saying implicitly that there is such a thing as secular holiness.

But while insisting that all Christians are called to the same holiness, the Council makes it clear that there is a diversity of ways in which Christians attain this holiness (39b, 41), since there is a diversity of sacral vocations in the Church. The laity have been consecrated and made sacred by baptism and confirmation (41g-h); others have been further consecrated by holy orders (41b-f); still others have received the special consecration of religious profession (39b; 42e-g). Since each of the various Christian states of life has its own special kind of sacrality, each will have its own special kind of secularity. Each will become holy by bringing its own special sacrality to bear upon its own special kind of secularity.

The Council recognized that the temporal order does not mean merely a temporary order, in the sense that the world and the cosmos are here only for a fleeting moment. It recognized the everlasting character of the temporal world, and the fact that it too is destined to be drawn into the glorification of humanity (cf. CW 39). At the same time, the Church clarified its true nature as Christ intended it to be, that of a servant Church. It realized that if the risen Christ is to draw the whole universe to himself, and if his magnetism is to be exercized upon the world principally through the Church, it must fulfill this role, not through power, domination, political activity, jurisdiction, clerical and ecclesiastical monopoly, not by attempting to absorb the world and contain it within a sacral order, but through the humble and vivifying role of serving the world's needs and thus suffusing into it the agape of Christ (cf. CW 42).

The loving and humble service of the Church is the leaven of the "new creation" working in the dough of the first creation. The supernatural action of Jesus through the Church must not only respect the intrinsic values and aspirations of the world, but incorporate all of them that are valid into his saving action and thus help to bring them to fulfillment. For, since we are already living in the last times, the human city has become intimately bound up with the coming of the kingdom, already here in mystery (cf. CW 40d). Thus the Christian experience consists simply in participating in the Mystery of Christ, in the plan of God which embraces all reality, both secular and sacred, both divine and human work. The spiritual life cannot be too "churchy." It must enter into the world in and with Christ, must see his cosmic and historical lordship everywhere and at all times, and work to bring the newness of life, which is the fruit of the resurrection, to all creatures, while leaving them free, as the incarnation did, to be themselves, to retain their secular identity (cf. CW 36).

But to achieve this end, the identity of the sacred must also be preserved. Even though the Mystery of Christ is not limited to the sacral realm of the Church, even though the spirit and the ferment of the gospel are at work beyond the limits of the Church, and even though the lordship of Jesus is not restricted to the Church and its activities, the Church is the privileged medium through which the glorified Christ extends his newness of life to the world. But the Church can function in this capacity, it can carry on its servant role of sanctifying and Christifying the world, only in the measure in which it retains its own sacred identity. There is indeed such a thing as Christian secularity, but this cannot mean that the Church itself becomes secular. The

Church cannot fulfill its role of bringing holiness to the world except by retaining all that is truly sacred. Similarly, the specific mission of Christians in the midst of secular civilization is to be witnesses to the reality of the sacred. We are not called to sacralize the secular, but to sanctify it, which, however, cannot be done unless we retain and develop within ourselves those special sacral qualities with which we were endowed by the consecration of baptism and confirmation (and possibly by the consecrations of holy orders and of religious profession). The slogan today is holy worldliness, or secular holiness, but the holy will soon evaporate if the sacred in us does not retain its identity, for without this identity our role in the world, however altruistic and self-sacrificing, will be nothing more than secular humanism. We shall be unable to find Christ in the secular if we do not find him in the sacred. To be *in* the world and *with* the world cannot mean to be *like* the world in all things. To be a sign or witness necessarily means being other. To be *with* and to be *other*— this is our role as Christians in the world.

*   *   *

More than any other single factor, the process of secularization is responsible for the vast difference between the spiritual climate of our times and the spiritual climate of Christendom. It is the task of spiritual ecology to evaluate this profound difference. A culture completely dominated by Christianity provided a climate which was in many ways favorable to the spiritual life; and this culture did indeed produce many great saints. Yet, however paradoxical it may seem, by the very fact that the culture of Christendom considered itself to be the culture of Christianity, it was not a Christian culture. For Christianity can never be identified with any one particular culture, nor is any culture authentically Christian which fails to recognize the proper autonomy and intrinsic worth of the secular order. The secular and the sacred do indeed have to be united, and often in intimate ways, but this union can be truly Christian only if the proper autonomy of each is clearly recognized and respected.

On the other hand, even when secularization does not degenerate into any form of secularism, it does not necessarily produce a climate unequivocally favorable to the development of the spiritual life. As Karl Rahner has pointed out, Christians today are living in a state of diaspora and will continue in this state for the forseeable future. The Christian today is surrounded on all sides by the purely secular, which has a constant and massive impact upon him in a great variety of ways, especially through the various highly developed forms of the communications media. In a climate of this kind it is all too easy to develop a "secularized" mind to which the voice of the sacred may seem extremely weak, and perhaps at times even alien. In many ways this kind of climate is not particularly favorable for the development of faith. On the other hand, faith which develops in a Christian culture may easily be a cultural faith, that is to say a faith which is simply accepted as a part of one's social heritage and environment. The secular city can serve to purify faith by strengthening its transcendent quality. Authentic faith cannot be reduced to element of culture; it must, independently of all culture, be a free and personal response and commitment to God.

A secular environment is a challenge to every Christian to strive to make Christian faith and Christian values penetrate society and thus promote the cosmic and social lordship of Jesus. The Christian may, and indeed must, aspire to the creation of a Christian society, even though this may be an ideal which will never be reached. A Christian society is something quite different from a Christian state, or from a single culture which becomes identified with Christianity.

George Bernanos is often quoted as having written: "When I am dead tell the kingdom of earth that I have loved it much more than I ever dared to say." We Christians of today need not hesitate to express our love for the world. For it is only in and through the world that we can achieve both our personal and our Christian fulfillment.

Notes

1. (New York: Holt, Reinhart and Winston, 1965), p. 5.

2. See Edward Schillebeeckx, *God the Future of Man*, trans. N. D. Smith (New York: Sheed and Ward, 1968), p. 99.

3. Charles Davis, *God's Grace in History* (London: Collins Fontana Books, 1966), p. 11.

4. René Marlé, *Lumen Vitae*, English ed., XXIII (December 1968), 583.

5. *The Secular City*, 2nd ed. (New York: Macmillan, 1966), p. 18.

6. *The Divine Milieu*, trans. Bernard Wall (New York: Harper and Brothers, 1960), p. 35.

7. At the Second World Congress of the Apostolate of the Laity, held in Rome, October 1957, Pius XII stated that the "consecration of the world" is the work of the laity. Cf. *Acta Apostolicae Sedis* (Vatican: Polyglot Press, 1957), XLIX, 927.

8. Canon 2343.

9. *God the Future of Man*, p. 99.

10. See his *Theology of the World*, trans. William Glen-Doepel (New York: Herder and Herder, 1969), especially chap. 1, "How Faith Sees the World. The Christian Orientation in the Secularity of the Contemporary World," pp. 13-55.

11. "Christian Secularity," *The Sacred and the Secular*, ed. Michael Taylor (Englewood Cliffs, N.J.: Prentice-Hall, 1968), p. 6.

Bibliography

For a number of years, two books in particular have been highly respected in this field. One is Rudolf Otto's *The Idea of the Holy*, trans. John W. Harvey (London: Oxford University Press, 1958). Another work, in some ways similar to it, is Mircea Eliade's *The Sacred and the Profane*, trans. Willard R. Trask (New York: Harcourt, Brace, 1959). Probably the most widely read and the most controversial book on this subject, at least in this country, is *The Secular City* (New York: Macmillan, 1966) by Harvey Cox. It is recommended that this book be read in the revised edition, for it contains a number of corrections and improvements which resulted from "the *Secular City* debate" that occurred after the publication of the first edition (cf. p. xii). *Secular Holiness, Spirituality for Modern Man* (Denville, N.J.: Dimension Books, 1971) by Paul Hinnebusch develops several points briefly touched upon in our discussion. Three lectures of Charles Davis published in a slim volume entitled *God's Grace in History* (London: Collins Fontana Books, 1966) are remarkable for their clarity and conciseness. Johannes Metz has made especially significant contributions to this question, particularly in the first chapter of his *Theology of the World*, trans. William Glen-Doepel (New York: Herder and Herder, 1969). Edward Schillebeeckx has a number of penetrating insights on this question in *God the Future of Man* (New York: Sheed and Ward, 1968) especially in chapter 3, "Secular Worship and Church Liturgy."

Several worthwhile articles are to be found in three volumes of the *Concilium* series: XIX, *Spirituality in the Secular City*, ed. Christian Duquoc (New York: Paulist Press, 1966); XLVII, *Sacralization and Secularization*, ed. Roger Aubert (New York: Paulist Press, 1969) and XLIX, *Secularization and Spirituality* ed. Christian Duquoc (New York: Paulist Press, 1969). Michael Taylor has collected an anthology of articles which provides an excellent sampling of the many discussions on this subject: *The Sacred and the Secular* (Englewood Cliffs, N.J.: Prentice-Hall, 1968). Another worthwhile collection of articles is found in *The Spirit and Power of Christian Secularity*, ed. Albert Schlitzer (Notre Dame, In.: Notre Dame University Press, 1969). Two other books deserve mention here: *God and Secularity* (Philadelphia: The Westminster Press, 1967) by John Macquarrie, and *Worship and Secular Man* (New York: Orbis Books, 1973) by Raimondo Panikkar.

Part V

TIME

CHAPTER THIRTEEN

THE FULLNESS OF TIME

NOTHING IS MORE FAMILIAR to us than time; our whole life is conditioned by it. Yet few things are so difficult to define or explain. The statement of St. Augustine is well known: "What . . . is time? If no one asks me, I know; if I want to explain it to someone who does ask me, I do not know."[1] But time also has spiritual and supernatural dimensions; it is a Christian mystery from which the spiritual life and spiritual theology cannot prescind without losing their proper orientation.

Time is not simply a condition of our universe; it belongs to its essence. The universe is not just a framework within which the process of time takes place; in a sense it is that process. The Latin word *saeculum* means both the world and a period of time, an age. Something similar is found in other languages. In English we often refer to the world by speaking of "temporal realities," a phrase which comes from the Latin word *tempus* meaning time. And when the term "spiritual" is contradistinguished from the term "temporal" it is considered to be antithetical not only to matter but also to time. The present chapter is concerned with this antithesis.

Time is the duration characteristic of all things terrestrial. It is a flowing and successive duration; the very existence and life of worldly realities are essentially fluid. The meaning of this fluid duration can best be seen by contrasting it to the duration of eternity, which is characteristic of the life of God. Eternity is not a continually flowing duration which never had a beginning and will never have an end; it is not simply a succession of instants which will never terminate. God possesses the whole fullness of his existence and his life in one instantaneous and simultaneous "now," called by scholastic philosophers the *nunc stans*, the "stationary now," as opposed to the "now" of all earthly beings, which is a *nunc fluens*, a "flowing now." In the constant flow of

earthly duration the very coming into existence of each successive "now" is simultaneously its going out of existence. It is as if
earthly realities were on a rapidly moving surface, such as a
moving belt, so that in order to remain in the same place they
must keep running rapidly.

Human existence is extended and dispersed in the rapidly flowing stream of time. We are never wholly present to ourselves; we
are never "all there"; our "now" is constantly eluding our grasp
and flowing down stream. Our life is continually in a state of dissipation; it is in a sense continually being drained into nothingness. Our existence is fragmented, and we possess it only through
the infinitesimal fragment of each passing instant. We are never
fully in a state of being, but always in a state of becoming. Since
we never fully possess ourselves, we are always, in a sense, be-
side ourselves.

Yet, as human persons we are not in time in the same way other
earthly realities are. We alone, through the self-awarensss proper to us, can truly experience what time is. Paradoxically, it is
precisely because we transcend time while existing in it that we
can grasp and appreciate the temporal character of our life. The
very fact that we are, through our spiritual powers, present to
ourselves makes it possible for us to realize that we are never
fully present to ourselves. Only a psyche can measure time and
bind it together in a unity of past, present, and future. We consciously convert the future into the past through the present instant in which we posses self-awareness. We alone can see time
as a process in which we are able to actualize ourselves and freely bring about our own fulfillment. Thus personal time is in many
ways similar to biblical time: it is qualitative; it has content and
is specified by the events which take place in it.

Throughout history time has been a mystery about which there
has been a great deal of speculation. But never before has this
mystery received so much attention as it does today. This wide-
spread interest makes it clear that we are faced here with an
especially important sign of our times. Indeed, it seems necessary to agree with Robert Johann when he writes: "Perhaps the
most characteristic aspect of modern thinking about man is its
emphasis on temporality."[2]

Since time is a measure of human existence, it is not surprising
to find that existentialists, from Kierkegaard to Heidegger and
Sartre, have been concerned with it. A holistic view of human
persons inevitably sees them as a beings-in-time. But their very

being in time is a sign of their limited wholeness, for their existence is spread out and fleeting. Moreover, any attempt to reflect upon the problem of how to achieve a fully authentic human existence must necessarily come to grips with the meaning of human history. For most existentialists, time is not simply an empty homogeneous duration, not simply a fourth dimension of the person. For it is in time that the human person must be in a constant state of bringing about accomplishments which enable him to really exist.

Not only existentialism but other schools of thought as well have been especially preoccupied with the problems of time and history. One of the strong attractions which Marxism offers is a pattern for the evolution of human history. But the developments that are particularly relevant for our purposes are the Scriptural and theological studies which have emphasized the great importance of time and history for an understanding of the Bible and of the Christian life.

The early Christians were conscious of the important role that time and history played in their lives. Some of the early Fathers of the Church, such as Irenaeus and particularly Augustine, reflected upon this role.[3] But throughout subsequent centuries the centrality of this role was to a large extent lost sight of, principally because of the influence of Greek thought in the development of Christian theology and philosophy. Because of its tendency to withdraw from the concrete existential order, Greek thought is not a particularly apt instrument with which to explore those dimensions of the mystery of time that go beyond Aristotle's notion of it as the measure of motion.

Not for centuries has there been as much stress as in recent times on the notion of salvation history, and on the importance of viewing it in its very historicity and not as a kind of framework within which the timeless truths of faith are to be contemplated. In the foreword of his book, *Salvation in History*, which is dedicated "to the Secretariat for Christian Unity as a token of thanks for the invitation to take part in the Second Vatican Council as a guest and observer," Oscar Cullmann writes:

This re-awakened interest in the salvation history of the Bible found expression in an address by Pope Paul VI before the non-Catholic observers at the Second Vatican Council when he said that 'a concrete, historical theology concentrated on salvation history' is the common basis of ecumenical dialogue. As a matter of fact, in the discussion of the Council's schemata between Roman and non-Roman theologians, mutual understanding was continually furthered when both sides spoke the language of salvation history and thought in its categories.[4]

Contemporary spiritual persons vigorously reject any opposition between the temporal and the spiritual. And the Second Vatican Council agrees with them wholeheartedly (cf. e.g., C 48; CW 36; 39; 76; L 5; 6). They refuse to conceive the spiritual life in terms of a static timelessness that abstracts from the existential order of time and history. They reject out of hand any form of "angelism," any kind of disincarnate spirituality which sees the spiritual life in isolation from the fourth dimension of time as well as the three dimensions of the body and of the world. Nor are they satisfied with attempting to sanctify time from the outside, so to speak, by purity of intention and the use of ejaculations. However important these practices may be, contemporary spiritual persons want to try to discover something within time which in some way reveals and communicates the spiritual and the divine.

*   *   *

In the incarnation the Lord Jesus entered into the depths of time, and in a certain sense sanctified it from within. Centuries before, Plato had defined time as "a moving image of eternity."[5] Christ transformed time into a moving image of eternity in a sense which Plato could never have imagined. And we can learn to sanctify the duration proper to us as human persons only by seeing the relation between Christ and time.

In "the fullness of time" Christ was born (cf. Ga. 4:4). During the long centuries before his arrival biblical time had been specified by its content. It now had a Content that should, it seems, burst all the limitations of time. The incarnation was indeed a breakthrough in time to something that infinitely transcends it. Transcendence became a historical event. The eternal began to be measured by time. This was an event that was not simply an action of God in history such as had often occurred before, but that actually contained God himself within time. His entrance into time became the point from which all future time would be computed forward and all past time backward.

But all time is related to the Christ-event not only because both past and future are computed from the midpoint of history which is the incarnation, but because the whole of cosmic time from beginning to its end is, in a very profound sense, Christ-time. Christ's possession of time goes all the way back to creation, and beyond. From all eternity the divine plan which is the Pauline Mystery of Christ was always present in the mind of the Father (Jn 17:24; Ep 1:4). Already present in that plan was the Easter Vigil proclamation: "Christ, yesterday and today, the Beginning and the End, the Alpha and the Omega. His are the centuries and the ages. To him be glory and sovereignty forever and ever!"

This plan began to unfold at the first moment of time at the beginning of creation. "In him were created all things in heaven and on earth . . . all things were created through him and for him" (Col 1:15-16; cf. Jn 1:3-4; 1 Co 8:6). Since time is a constitutive element of the universe, God, in creating the world in and through his Word, created time in and through him and gave it to the world. For the Christian, creation and redemption must be seen as a coherent process. One of the traditional hymns for paschaltime sings: "Eternal King of the elect, Creator of all things, workman since the foundation of the world, you imprinted the trace of your visage on Adam." All time, from the first moment of creation and especially from the election of Israel, is the Christ-event in the process of becoming. In this perspective, Matthew starts his gospel with a genealogy which goes all the way back to Abraham, thus bringing out the fact that Jesus is the fulfillment of the whole history of the chosen people of God (1:1-17). Luke goes a further step back with a genealogy which traces the origin of Christ all the way to Adam, and hence to the beginning of creation (3:23-38). John goes still further back to before the beginning of creation when the Word was in the bosom of the Father (1:1). Thus from the very foundations of the cosmos all cosmic time was in some sense Christ-time. But it did not become fully Christ-time until the incarnation. It was then that Christ drew time intimately to himself, and made its extended and successive flow the very duration of his own life and existence. Jesus has accurately been defined as God-in-time.

With the incarnation "the first days" of cosmic history were finished and "the last days" had begun (cf. C 48d). And all these "last days," which extend to the final moment in the history of the cosmos, are Christ-time in an even fuller sense than "the first days." Paul tells us that all things were created not only through, but also for the Word of God, who is Christ. Time is the process by which the universe moves towards its final fulfillment. It will find that fulfillment in Christ who is not only the Alpha but also the Omega.

Old Testament eschatology was pure expectancy for the end which was far off; in Christian eschatology the end has already come—but not fully. There is expectancy but it is based on the already present reality of what is expected. The present reality does not lessen the expectancy; it intensifies it immeasurably. In *Christ and Time,* Oscar Cullman repeatedly explains this paradox with the illustration of a war in which the decisive victory has already been won, even though battles may continue before the day when all hostitities will finally cease.[6] Redemption has already been decisively won by Christ, but battles (whose victories are also victories of Christ) will continue in the Church and in the lives of individual Christians until the Parousia. Matthew, who begins his gospel with a genealogy that goes back through the centuries, finishes it with a look into the future that extends to the end of time: "And know that I am with you always; yes, to the end of time" (Mt 28:20). John, who begins his gospel by looking back across the centuries to the "time" when there was no time, brings it to a close with Jesus alluding to the Parousia (Jn 21:22-23).

Thus, Christ-time spans the whole extent of cosmic time, of which the Lord of history is the source, the center, and the final end. It extends from creation to consummation. Through Christ all cosmic time is inserted into the eternal plan of the Father. Only in relation to him can history find its deepest meaning. Thus, the supreme norm by which all history is to be judged is not an abstract, transcendental principle but the Christ-event, which is in itself an historical event. Christ's lordship of history does not merely mean that he reigns over history and directs its on-going process; rather he reigns within history. His kingdom, in its present stage, is at the heart of history.

At the midpoint of history, the Word drew time intimately to himself, allowed himself to become immersed in it, and submitted himself to its laws and its limitations. Indeed, he seemed to have a special love for time. He immersed himself in it much more than would have been necessary. He could have assumed human nature in its fully developed state as a grown man, and he could have acquitted his task of redeeming the world with efficient dispatch by accomplishing it in a fleeting moment. Actually, he did neither. He deliberately chose to go through every successive stage of development that human life normally goes through, and to stretch out his work of redemption over days and months and years.

Coming from the perfectly simultaneous duration of eternity, the Word of God was introduced to our successive duration by the nine months period of embryonic development in the womb of Mary. Nothing could have been a more apt introduction to the meaning of time, to its laws and its limitation, than this. He for whom a thousand years had been like a day (Ps 90:4; 2 P 3:8), now began to experience the dragging succession of every moment of time. After birth came that long, slow process of development by which he grew into the maturity of manhood (cf. Lk 2:40, 52). The years at Nazareth gave him a feeling for the passage of time, for the variety of its seasons and its cycles, which only those who have lived the simple, slow-moving, uneventful life of a village like Nazareth, can understand. And the uneventfulness of the life at Nazareth was in itself a significant event in the history of salvation. Then came the three years of active, fleeting hours during the day, and of rapt, absorbed hours of prayer at night. Finally, there came the long agonizing hours of the Passion, and especially the last three hours on the Cross. Only those who have experienced intense pain over a long period can understand the relationship between suffering and time.

Perhaps the most striking thing about the existence of the eternal Word in time is that he was always at home in it. The impression is sometimes given that the Christian life consists in a flight from the body in order to attain the spiritual, and a flight from time in order to attain the eternal. Actually, there is no suggestion of anything like this in the life of Christ himself. Just as he never gives the impression of a spirit unnaturally and uneasily inhabiting a body that is alien to him, so there is never any suggestion of impatience with the limitations of time, with it slowness or its rapidity. If there is one thing Christ learned during his life on earth it was that time is not a homogeneous thing stretching out indefinitely, but rather a rhythmic thing with a variety of seasons and a succession of different stages. He learned that every period of human life has its own problems and needs, that every day and and every hour have their own sufferings and joys.

As Christ was caught up and carried along by the rhythmic flow of time, as he passed through the seasons and the stages of human life, as he took up the work and the problems of each hour and each day, he was "a moving image of eternity." He lifted up each moment of time as it came along and gave it a share in the eternal. He who had for all eternity been like a canticle of love in the bosom of the Father had come to earth to make it possible for time to share in that eternal canticle. At every moment of his existence there was going on in the heart and soul of that perfect mediator between God and man a constant exchange of love and life. At every moment human life, with its love, its work, its sorrows, its anguish, was being lifted up and consecrated to God in a never-ending hymn of praise and adoration. At every moment God was pouring out the riches of his divine life and love upon us through Christ. As the Christmas liturgy sings: "O wonderful exchange!"

But Christ sanctified time, and made it possible for us to sanctify it in our own lives, not only by descending into it and making himself subject to all its limitations, but also by rising above it and lifting it up to share, in some sense, in a new kind of duration. This he did by his resurrection and glorification. Through the resurrection, the man Jesus entered into the life and glory proper to him as the Son of God in the bosom of the Trinity. No longer is he subject to the limitations of being a son "according to the flesh." Christ as man has now entered into the kind of duration that is proper to him as the Son of God in the bosom of the Father. He is now the glorified man drawn into the eternity of God. He is now in the perfect unity of eternity (cf. Heb 9:24-26).

Christ has entered into the eternal "now" where there cannot be any repetition. His transcendent, glorified body is now detached from time, though it still remains united with our earthly bodies immersed in time. His "time" is now the Father's "time." Through his incarnation Christ was inserted into cosmic time; through the resurrection he has re-inserted cosmic time into God's eternal plan and into eternity. Insofar as the members of his Body are one with him, they too, in a certain sense, are inserted into his eternal present, even though they continue to struggle in the long duration proper to them.

Time is now rooted in eternity in a way that was not true before the incarnation. For it has now been assumed by the risen Jesus into the eternal "now" that is proper to him as Son of God. Christ's act of redemption is fixed in this eternal "now," while its effects continue throughout the flow of time. Because all the successive "nows" of time are centered in his eternal "now," he is personally present to them all.

The assumption of time into eternity by the risen Christ should help us to understand the unique and at the same time paradoxical situation of the Christian in the last times of salvation history. Because we are not yet finally risen and glorified, we are still subject to the limitations of time, to its continual succession and its rhythm. But because we are truly "in Christ," as St. Paul keeps telling us, because we are truly incorporated into the glorified Jesus, we already have the beginning of that triumph over the limitations of time brought about by Christ's resurrection and glorification. Precisely because we are baptized into the risen and glorified Christ, we are baptized into his death (Rm 6:3), an event which took place in the past. We can participate in acts accomplished in the past only because we are one with the Christ of the present, whose present moment includes both past and future. Hence, as Durrwell has pointed out, our participation in the saving acts of the past, particularly through the liturgy, does not mean that these acts are lifted out of the past and transplanted into our present, just as it does not mean that we somehow leave the present in order to be carried back to the past. "This action, performed once in the past, remains fixed in an everlasting actuality in the Christ of glory, where all the ages with which he coexists flow together, accessible to all who seek redemption."[7] The saving events of the past continue to take place in the Church only because we are intimately incorporated into Christ, "who is forever fixed in the act of redeeming us."[8]

The same must be said of the future (cf. C 48d). Because we are one with the risen and glorified Christ, the future does not mean only a promise, only a decision taken by God which is going to be put into effect sometime later. This future already exists in the Lord Jesus, with whom we have been made one, and consequently the future is already present for us, just as the past is.

A vast difference exists, therefore, between Christian time and Old Testament time. In an earlier chapter I said that in the celebration of the Jewish festivals, the Hebrews of every age, because of their intense feeling with regard to vertical corporate personality, had the conviction that through the rite and proclamation of the celebrations they were made contemporaneous with their ancestors and participants with them in the historical events of the past. But because their time had not yet been assumed into the eternal "now" as Christian time has, and because the "oneness" of their corporate personality did not have the reality of the "oneness" of Christ's Body, the saving actions of the past were not made present in the same way as the saving actions of Christ are made present to Christians of every age. This also holds true for the future.

* * *

Having once ascended beyond the heavens from the flow of time to the stationary "now" of eternity, Christ never descends into time again. But his Body, the Church, continues to live in the flow of time, where it will remain until the Parousia as the unglorified Body of a glorified head. Through the Church the Lord of time and history continues to make his influence felt in the flow of time. Throughout time, the Church continually summons the Christian to encounter this action of her Lord.

Church-time is "the last days" (I Jn 2:18), "the end of the ages" (1 P 1:5, 20; 1 Tm 4:1; cf. 1 Co. 10:11; Jude 18; Heb 1:2). The Church is the messianic community of the end-time. This does not mean anything apocalyptic; it does not suggest that the end of the world is imminent. It simply means that he who was to come has already come, even though he is to come again. It means that the *eschaton* is already present, while still remaining in the future, that the second aeon has already arrived in Christ Jesus, who, in a sense, makes the future simultaneous with the present. The first and the second coming of the Lord are basically one act of God, but separated by the time-in-between, the "little while" (Jn 16:16-19) that we call A.D., the time of the Church.

Church-time is the time-in-between Pentecost and the second coming of Jesus. Hence, the Church is always living an "in-between" existence. "My dear people, we are already the children of God but what we are to be in the future has not yet been revealed" (1 Jn 3:2). The Church is simultaneously a citizen of the earthly city and of the heavenly city (cf. CW 40d). It lives its earthly existence in history; but it also lives beyond history. Its heavenly existence is lived in mystery. In Church-time, the mysteries which transcend time are already present and active. The Christian, who lives in Church-time, can see the present only by constantly looking to both the past and the future. As Durrwell has put it: "Since Easter, human time has been advancing towards an event of the past, the resurrection of Christ, and it will only reach it at the end of history."[9] In one sense, the Church is being constantly drawn at one and the same time toward the past and the future; in another sense it is constantly drawing both the past and the future into the living present. It lives in constant tension between the "already" and the "not yet." The kingdom is already in its midst (cf. Lk 11:20; 17:21; Mt 13:17); but it is not yet present fully (cf. Mt 8:11-12; 25:13; Mk 8:38). The decisive battle has already been won and victory is now assured. Yet many fierce battles still remain to be fought, and the Church will remain militant until the end of time. Death and sin have already been definitively conquered; yet the Church must continue to struggle with them until the Parousia.

True Christian spirituality must be stamped with the "in-between" character of the Church. As Christians we must be "prepared for honour or disgrace, for blame or praise; taken for imposters while we are genuine; obscure yet famous; said to be dying and here we are alive; rumored to be executed before we are sentenced; thought most miserable and yet we are always rejoicing; taken for paupers though we make others rich, for people having nothing though we have everything" (2 Co 6:8-10).

Because the Church lives an "in-between" existence, its time will always have a certain paradoxical character. On the one hand, it lives a truly human kind of time, a time that moves forward and unfolds in the history of the universe. But this time remains profoundly rooted in the eternal redemptive act of its Lord and his eternal "now." The risen Jesus is ever present in his Body and this abiding presence makes both the past and the future somehow present at every moment of the life of the Church. Jesus did not simply tell his followers that he would be with them in the future; he said: "Know that I *am* with you always; yes, until the end of time" (Mt 28:20). Christ is contemporaneous with every Christian throughout history until at last the ultimate in contemporaneity is reached in ecstatic union. Every day of Church-time is a day of grace in which time and eternity meet and somehow become one. The "today," pronounced so frequently in the Old Testament, takes on a whole new meaning in Church-time. As Raymond Nogar has pointed out, in the Christian notion of time "both the excesses of the 'myth of the eternal return' in which time means nothing and the excesses of the 'myth of evolutionism' in which time means everything are avoided. Through salvation history, time and the timeless are harmonized in the divine."[10]

Just as Christ-time is essentially related to cosmic time, so also is Church-time. Christ, the Lord of history, has put all cosmic time at the service of his Body, which draws its rhythms into its own inner life in such a way that the various aspects of the total mystery of Christ are associated in the Church with these rhythms, especially through the liturgy. In its sacramental life, the Church is continually reliving the historical events of the mystery of redemption in a rhythmical way. It continues to dwell in cosmic time while continually giving it entirely new dimensions.

Christ, through his life on earth, linked the Christian with cos-

mic time by inserting it into salvation-time. The Church continues this mission, since in the Church Jesus is always present,
and through him time and eternity are continually united in an
intimate embrace. Though Church-time is distinct from cosmic
time, it continually draws the events of profane history into its
own saving purposes. The constant renewal of the paschal mystery in time draws into this mystery all the sufferings, the anguish, the needs, and the hopes of the world. The sufferings of
humanity are caught up into the redemptive act of Christ which
the Church is continually making present and thus become the
ongoing redemption of Christ in the members of his Body.

Having once been redeemed by Christ, time can never lose
that redemption again. And as Christ continues to live on earth
in the Church, so time continues to be redeemed, made holy,
made pregnant with eternity in and through the Church. Just as
the Church teaches its members not to despise their three dimensional extension of the body, but rather to sanctify it, sacra-
mentalize it, make it an object of reverence, and lift it up to a
share in divine worship, so it teaches them not to treat lightly
their fourth dimensional extension, but rather to look upon every
moment of it as something holy, something that constantly
touches eternity. It teaches them to sanctify the ebb and flow of
time, to be caught up in its rhythmic movement and to be borne
upward in its cyclic spirals closer and closer to eternity. All this
it does especially in its liturgy. It is particularly through the
liturgy that time becomes for the Christian a "moving image of
eternity." That is why the worship of the Church is always in
movement, why nothing is more characteristic of it than its temporal character, why it is so intimately related to the cycles and
seasons of time, and why practically all of its feasts are celebrations, not of abstract ideas or doctrines, but of historical events.

Church-time is Spirit-time (cf. Ac 2:16-21). The Spirit came
into our world on Pentecost, when the Church was born, and he
remains on mission in the world and in the hearts of people everywhere until the Parousia. The mission of the Word had a beginning and an end in time. We have feasts to celebrate the beginning and the end, Christmas and Ascension. We have Pentecost
to celebrate the beginning of the mission of the Spirit, but no feast
to celebrate its end; that celebration will be the Parousia. In the
time-in-between, the Spirit is the vital principle of the Church.
He is the earnest and the first fruits of the final fullness of redemption. In and through him the paschal power of the risen
Jesus is present to the Church.

Because Church-time coincides with the time of the mission of the Spirit, it is essentially mission time, the time during which the Good News must be preached to the whole of creation (cf. Mk 16:16; Ac 1:8). "The mission," says Jean Mouroux, "is the vital force that hurtles the Church through space and time from Pentecost to the Parousia."[11] One of the great merits of the *Constitution on the Church* is that it placed the mission at the very heart of the Church and not at the periphery (cf. e.g., 5a, d). *The Decree on the Missionary Activity of the Church* developed this point more fully: "The pilgrim Church," it states, "is missionary by her very nature" (2a). Later it relates mission time to the Parousia (9d).

Throughout the whole course of salvation history the Christ-event continues in the process of becoming. In the last times, it is the total Christ that is going through this process. The incarnation is being prolonged through space and time. And it is only in and through each Christian that Christ can become continually incarnate in every culture and be fully present to the world at every moment of time. As the Body of Christ grows, it must continually strive to bring about a transformation of all human history; it must strive to make this world in some sense an anticipation of the world to come. Church-time should be the time of a progressive union between the order of nature and the order of grace.

*   *   *

The Christian future is not simply something which comes inexorably into our lives with the measurable passing of moment after moment. Rather, it is an advent; it is something that God has planned for us before all time; it is something to which we can aspire and freely move through the exercise of our human liberty. As Christians we are not doomed to a future which is nothing more than a void. Rather, we are constantly being beckoned by God toward a future that can for us be the fullness of time in the sense of a fulfillment which comes into being by a free gift of God with the collaboration of human freedom. "We are fellow workers with God" (1 Co 3:9) as we move into the future. No one should value time more highly than we Christians, for it is through time that we can achieve Christian fulfillment. Time makes it possible for us to make ourselves what we choose to be through free acts inspired by grace. What is more important, it provides the duration for God to remake us according to the image of his only Son.

For existentialists, who distinguish between being and existence, human existence does not mean simply to be; it does not have its unique value from what is permanent and immutable but rather from the intensity of its becoming. A constant becoming, a constant state of evolving through the process of time is essential to the existence of the human person. As Kierkegaard has said, existence is not a thing but a task. In the perpetual becoming which constitutes the very existence of the human person there never comes before death a present moment when the process stops. Hence, there is never a past which consists in a finalized accomplishment. Each present moment is a continual projection toward the future and at the same time a continual transformation of the past. The person's awareness that he is an existent calls him to project himself into the future, and he begins by determining what the existentialists call his fundamental project, in relation to which he creates his aspirations and projects himself toward their future accomplishment.

The fundamental existential project of every Christian is, or should be, to become a saint. All Christians are called, according to their various states in life, to relate their most fundamental aspirations toward this project and to move resolutely in time toward their future accomplishment. For Sartre, the fundamental project of the human person, if one delves down deeply enough, is to aspire to become what men call God, and since this project cannot be realized, his total existence is bound to result in failure.[12] In baptism we Christians are given a real share in the divine life, and from then on our existential project is to strive to bring about, in the measure of time given us, the total transformation of our being into the life of God. This fundamental project is not only possible but mandatory. And if for Sartre the existential project ends in total disillusionment and desolation, the Christian project, when achieved, brings total happiness. But if it is not achieved, it does indeed bring desolation. "There is only one misery," writes Leon Bloy, "and that is not to be saints."[13]

To achieve this, we must be constantly redeeming time (Ep 5:16), constantly transforming *chronos*, cosmic time into *kairos*, a time filled with God's presence, a saving and sanctifying time, a time rich with possibilities. In Christian time, what is taken from the future is transformed in the present and therefore is never exactly the same when it is surrendered to the past. In a sense, nothing slips completely into the past forever; there is a continual gathering, a continual growth, a continual fulfillment. Suffering passes away; but having suffered in love with Christ will never pass away. Whatever has been done in love in the past enriches the present moment and is the source of a fuller future. Christian time is always a becoming, in the sense of coming to be ever more fully. Eternal life is not simply something that comes after time; it is rather something that comes as the fulfillment of time. The content of saving time will endure forever. We await not only a resurrection of our bodies and of the cosmos, but also the resurrection of content-time into eternity.

Because our being is extended in time we can give ourselves to God and sanctify ourselves only by doing so historically. For us Christians, to have time must mean to have time for God. We must sanctify time first of all by entering into it as Jesus did and making it a "moving image of eternity." We must be patient with both its slowness and its rapidity. We must be patient above all with God's process of sanctifying us in time. We must keep in mind the line of T. S. Eliot: "Only through time time is conquered."[14]

We must also sanctify ourselves by rising above time, as Christ did. We must be continually aware that every one of our fleeting present moments is rooted in, and centered on, the eternal "now" of the risen Jesus. Because we are members of the Body of which Christ is the glorified head, we share in some way in the infinite density of the "now" of Jesus. Every Christian moment is dense and pregnant with the past and the future, and is thus an anticipation of eternity. Hence the profound depth of the interiority of every Christian moment. Time should mean much more for us Christians than for those whose lives are completely immersed in the temporal order. For Christians time is one aspect of the paradox which runs throughout the whole Christian life. As many of the prayers of the liturgy suggest, we must learn to rise above the things of time in order to attain the things of eternity, just as we must learn to detach ourselves from material things in order to attain the things of the spirit. But this very detachment involves a love for time and matter which comes directly from the heart of Christ, who became incarnate in our duration as well as in our flesh.

A few examples will illustrate the practical implications of these considerations. As Christians we should take delight in meditating on the various mysteries of the life of Christ, from the mystery of his birth to the mystery of his resurrection and ascension. These meditations are not just the fruit of memory and imagination. The man Jesus is presently existing, and the events of his infancy, his childhood, his adolescence, and his young manhood are present to him, and through him to us, not only in the sense that childhood, youth and later age are present in some way in every existing person, but in an extraordinary and unique way. Because of the density of his eternal "now," which makes the past present to him, they are in a sense contemporaneous with him at the present moment, in which all our present moments are rooted. Because he is now his own history, all his earthly mysteries have, through his resurrection, attained a new existence and a contemporaneity. Thus we are able at any time to enter into the various mysteries of his life with an extraordinary realism.

Prayer makes it possible for the Christian to get a sense of what it means to rise above time with Christ and already to anticipate eternity. The pilgrimage of Christian prayer normally leads little by little from the first stages of discursive prayer, which, like time, are diffused, to an experience of contemplation that makes prayer converge ever more fully toward a point at which it becomes a simple resting in the presence of God through a knowing love and a loving knowledge. As the pilgrimage progresses, the Christian will begin to have experiences, at least at times, which make it seem that an hour of prayer has passed in a few moments. At first this experience may happen only occasionally and often give way to periods of prayer in which time seems to drag on. But as the progress continues, this experience normally becomes more frequent and more prolonged, as the Christian transcends time in an ever fuller measure by experiencing in ever greater depth the richness and the density of the "now" of the risen Jesus.[15]

The theological virtues of faith, hope, and charity make it posposible for us to rise above the limitations of time. By faith and hope we already know, and in some sense already experience the future. By hope we can lay hold of *now* what faith tells us future history will be, and this faith enables us to respond *now* to what will be. For example, we are able to love our brothers and sisters *now*, in spite of their present lack of lovable qualities, because we know *now* through faith what they will some day be when they share fully in the risen Christ.

But it is preeminently through the theological virtue of love that we are able to rise above the fleeting moments of time and above the transitoriness of human life in general.[16] Faith, hope, and love are all theological virtues because they all have God himself as their object. But love differs from faith and hope in two important ways. First, it alone will last forever. When heaven has been attained, faith will vanish in the presence of vision, and hope will come to an end in the actual possession of the Supreme Good. Only love will never pass away (cf. 1 Co 13:8). Already in this life supernatural love experienced at any moment is something eternal, transcending all process and becoming. The second important difference between love on the one hand and faith and hope on the other is that, even though all three have God as their object, faith and hope never succeed in actually possessing him. Faith is concerned with what is still unseen, and hope with what is not yet possessed. Hence faith and hope always remain at a distance from God. But the person who loves already in this life possesses the God whom he or she will possess in heaven when all time will have passed away, since love means an intersubjective communion by which the lover and the beloved abide in each other. "God is love, and anyone who lives in love lives in God, and God lives in him" (1 Jn 4:16).

Hence, the Christian who truly loves God in this life is already in communion with him, and this communion is in direct continuity with the communion that exists in eternity. The presence of God through this comunion is not a finite presence, even in this life. It does not come and go like the presence of finite persons. Hence, this presence is already a sharing in God's eternal presence to himself. The love of God lifts the Christian above the stream of process and becoming, above all the changes and vicissitudes of time. Only a sharing in the one "now" of God through an intimate communion of love can rescue us from the dispersal of the infinity of "nows" which constitute our natural duration. Insofar as the love of God fills our earthly existence, all the dispersed and dissipated moments of our lives are caught up in his wholeness, and we are thus given a sense of fulfillment. Only the love of God can gather up the fragments of time and make them whole. The degree to which it can do this depends upon the intensity of our love and the extent to which we allow it to fill all aspects of our life. The saints experienced this wholeness to an extraordinary degree because of the great intensity of their love for God, which dominated their whole lives. And if at times they seemed to look down on temporalities, it was because they could indeed look "down," since, while still existing in time, they were lifted "above" it by the love of God, which had already given them an anticipation of eternity.

In the last analysis, true fulfillment can be achieved only through an intense love for God, and it will attain its fullest measure only in heaven. In this life our existence is spread out very thinly in the fourth dimension of our duration. We may try to "taste fully each passing moment," to use a phrase of Camus, but each moment is actually going out of existence even before we begin to taste it. What, then, will it mean to have in heaven the totality of our existence gathered together and brought to a point of intense, profound, all-embracing concentration in a "now" that is not fleeting! The time of the Christian is a constant "moving image of eternity" until at last the image gives way to the reality.

Notes

1. *The Confessions of St. Augustine*, ed. and trans. John K. Ryan (Garden City, N.Y.: Doubleday Image Books, 1960), p. 287.

2. "Charity and Time," *Cross Currents*, IX (Spring 1959), 140.

3. *Cf. Confessions*, bk.11: "Time and Eternity."

4. Trans. Sidney G. Sowers (New York: Harper and Row, 1967), p. 11.

5. *Timaeus* 37d.

6. Trans. Floyd V. Filson (Philadelphia: Westminster Press, 1964), e.g., p. 145.

7. *The Resurrection*, trans. Rosemary Sheed (New York: Sheed and Ward, 1960), p. 225.

8. Ibid.

9. Ibid., p. 263.

10. "Evolutionary Humanism and the Faith," *Concilium*, XVI, *Is God Dead?* ed. Johannes Metz (New York: Paulist Press, 1966), 58.

11. *The Mystery of Time*, trans. John Drury (New York: Desclee Co., 1964), p. 191.

12. *Cf. Being and Nothingness*, trans. Hazel E. Barnes (New York: Citadel Press, 1966), p. 90.

13. *The Woman Who Was Poor*, trans. I. J. Collins (New York: Sheed and Ward, 1947), p. 356.

14. "Burnt Norton," *Complete Poems and Plays* (New York: Harcourt, Brace, 1952), p. 120.

15. See John of the Cross, *The Ascent of Mount Carmel*, bk. 2, ch. 14, nos. 10-11, in *The Collected Works of John of the Cross*, trans. Kieran Kavanaugh and Otilio Rodriguez (Washington, D.C.: Institute of Carmelite Studies, 1964), p. 146.

16. For an excellent discussion of this point, see Robert Johann's article cited in note 2.

Bibliography

Perhaps the most widely known and most frequently discussed work on the Christian notion of time is Oscar Cullmann's *Christ and Time,* trans. Floyd V. Filson (Philadelphia: Westminster Press, 1964). This work is a study in New Testament theology which examines the implications of the view of time characteristic of the early Christian Church. Another well-known work, which has a much broader scope than the book of Cullmann, is *The Mystery of Time,* trans. John Drury (New York: Desclee Co., 1964) by Jean Mouroux. This is an erudite but very readable theological investigation of the Christian implications of the problem of time, and especially of the relation between Christ and time. H. I. Marrou's *Time and Timeliness,* trans. Violet Neville (New York: Sheed and Ward, 1969), is also a very readable reflection on the question of time. Though the original edition in French was called a theology of history, this book does not attempt to give a systematic theological study of history and time; rather it is a series of brief essays—more popular than scientific—on various aspects of this question. Two articles by Karl Rahner deserve to be included in this bibliography: "The Comfort of Time," *Theological Investigations,* III, trans. Karl-H. and Boniface Kruger (Baltimore: Helicon Press, 1967), 141-157; and "Theological Observations on the Concept of Time," *Theological Investigations,* XI, trans. David Bourke (Seabury Press, 1974), 288-308. Many authors discuss the nature of time in connection with their discussion of history; for this reason the bibliography of the next chapter may be considered a continuation of this bibliography.

CHAPTER FOURTEEN

THE SACRAMENT OF HISTORY

THE EXTENSIVE AND CONSTANTLY GROWING LITERATURE on the theology and philosophy of history, which is one of the most striking signs of our times, explores many aspects of the meaning of human history and of salvation history. It would not be germane to the purposes of this book to consider all these various aspects. Rather, the intent of this chapter is to try to situate the spiritual life in the stream of salvation history, and in so doing to reflect upon the sacramentality of history, which, like most aspects of our contemporary life, has been thoroughly secularized.

All religions have a history. The Christian religion not only has a history; it *is* a history; it is history in its fullest and most sublime meaning. No religion is, by its very nature, called to take history so seriously as Christianity. Only the Christian, through faith, can grasp the true dimensions of all human history.

The term "sacramental," in its broad sense, can be applied not only to our tridimensional world, but also to the fourth dimension of history. Salvation history is a sacrament from several points of view. First of all, it is a profound mystery, and in its original meaning the term "sacrament" meant a mystery. Salvation history is the mystery of the eternal plan of the Father for the whole creation, the mystery to which St. Paul refers so often, the mystery "kept hidden for endless ages," and finally revealed in Christ Jesus (Rm 16:25; cf. 1 Co 2:7-10; Col 2:2-3; Ep 1:9-10). Secondly, salvation history is sacramental because, just as the sacraments in the strict sense are outward signs of a supernatural presence and activity, so the events of history are outward signs of God's presence and activity. History is not just an endless series of events, governed by chance, leading nowhere. These events are the manifestation of God's eternal wisdom and of the slow unfolding of his total plan for the cosmos and time centered in Jesus. Through historical events God reveals and communicates himself; through them he is continually saving and sanctifying the elect. The spiritual person constantly strives through the enlightenment and the discernment of the Spirit, to capture and be captured by God's self-communication in the events of history in general, and in the events of his or her own life in particular.

This sacramentality of history, however, must not be taken to mean some naively optimistic theory or theology of history, some unrealistic grand spiritual design, which ignores or fails to take sufficiently into account the many evils, and especially the immensity of human suffering that are often a part of history. In one sense existentialism, as a cultural phenomenon, is a revolt against universalizing explanations of historical necessity, whether Hegelian or other, that "justify" the misery and suffering of countless individuals, by an appeal to some grand design or process. And it seems that the brutality of our century, the two world wars, the holocaust, and all the rest have discredited all such appeals. This problem will be addressed in the following chapter in connection with the question of hope (pp. 217-219).

Salvation history may also be said to be sacramental because, just as the sacraments in the strict sense are made up of both events and words, so the whole history of salvation is a story of God's continual intervention in the world of man through events and words which are so closely united that they often become, it seems, interchangeable. We recall that the Hebrew word *dabar* means both word and also thing, deed, or event. Frequently in Scripture events are referred to as words and vice versa. In the Old Testament we sometimes read of God speaking through the *hand* of one of his prophets.* All language is, in the last analysis, "body language," and the bodily organs which can best communicate thought are the tongue and the hands. Hence, it is not surprising that these two kinds of expression are considered in Scripture to be interchangeable. We often use gestures, especially of the hands, not only to reinforce, but even to substitute for speech in the ordinary sense.

In the *Constitution on Divine Revelation,* the Council stressed the close relationship and unity between word and event in revelation: "The plan of revelation is realized by deeds and words having an inner unity: the deeds wrought by God in the history

---

*Modern versions of the Bible do not translate this phrase literally, but see the Douay and the original King James versions, e.g. 3 K 14:18; 2 Ch 10:15.

of salvation manifest and confirm the teaching and realities signified by the words, while the words proclaim the deeds and clarify the mystery contained in them" (2).

The self-revelation of God throughout salvation history has never been in the form of a body of abstract doctrine. It has sometimes taken place through words, as in the teachings of Jesus, but always in a historical context. Frequently it has taken place through particular events. Often these events were significant in themselves and could therefore be called words. Yet, they would not have had their full significance if they had not been enlightened by words in the strict sense. Often the words of the prophets were essential for capturing the true meaning of the events. Thus, for example, the escape of the Hebrews from Egypt might have seemed to be only one of many migrations of peoples which, over a period of several centuries, took place in the Fertile Crescent, were it not for the words which Yahweh communicated through Moses. These words brought home to the Hebrews the full meaning and the supernatural dimensions of the historical event. Later the prophets continued to bring home to God's people the profound and supernatural meaning of many historical events, which, without their words, might have seemed to be simply events of secular history (cf. e.g., Is 10:5-16; 42:9; 45:1-6; Jr 27:6-7; Am 3:7). For centuries the prophets were the interpreters of history. Basing themselves on the past, they spoke to the present about what was to come in the future.

Just as in the sacraments the word enlightens and specifies the event, so the word throughout salvation history has enlightened and specified the historical event, and in doing so has brought out its full supernatural significance as a saving event. As human communication is most effective when both word and gesture are combined and mutually enlighten and reinforce each other, so God speaks to us most forcefully when he combines his word with an historical event. In this perspective we can appreciate more fully the relationship of word and event in both the sacramentality of salvation history and in the whole sacramentality of the Church.

Throughout the Old Testament God spoke through historical events and in a sense made these events "words," until in the fullness of time he spoke through his divine Word; and here it was not so much a case of a historical event becoming a word as it was of the Word becoming a historical event. As St. Augustine has put it so succinctly, all the actions of the Word became eloquent words for us: *"facta Verbi verba."* The most precious and the most powerful combination of words and events in salvation history are the words and actions of Christ. It might be said that the Word incarnate was both a word and a gesture of God.

The original creedal formulas of both the first people of God and the primitive Christians follow the same pattern. First there is a brief summary of the saving acts of God in history; then, as a response to these saving events, a commitment is made to this God of history. We see this pattern in the great assembly which Joshua convoked at Sechem, in which the original covenant was renewed (Jos 24). Similarily, the kerygma of the early Christian Church consisted of two elements. First, there was a brief recital of a series of events, such as: Jesus, the Son of God, lived; he died to bring redemption; he is risen now, and he sends His Spirit. Secondly, a response to these events was called for in the form of a commitment consisting of concrete actions: believe, repent, be converted, and be baptized. The first creedal formulas found in the New Testament follow this pattern (cf. Rm 10:9-11; I Tm 3:16; Ac 2:23-36; 3:12-26; 10:34-43). In short, the first preaching in the early Church was not so much a communication of a body of doctrine as the proclamation of certain historical events which constituted the Good News. The early Christians did not die for their belief in a body of revealed truths but for their belief in a person, who became incarnate in history and whose saving actions in history called for total love.

Two conclusions can be drawn from these remarks regarding salvation history. The first is that the history of salvation is something far more profound that a simple bible history, which would be merely an account of the important episodes in the history of Israel and of Christianity. Nor does salvation history merely mean a process whereby we are saved and sanctified throughout the course of history. It means that God has made historical events themselves saving and sanctifying. This is something quite different from, and much more profound than, a concept of the Providence of God watching over his chosen people and guiding their development.

The second conclusion is that the reading of Scripture is important, indeed indispensable, in our lives, not only because it is the word of God, and therefore God himself speaking to us, not only because it is, together with the sacraments, the most fruitful source of spiritual nourishment, but also because it situates our spiritual life in the history of salvation. Without it we cannot understand the relationship between Scripture and our spiritual life, nor can we understand what real liturgical spirituality is, nor indeed the full scope of the Christian life itself. Without a constant reading of the Bible we run the risk of missing the real meaning of God's action in history and in our own personal lives. We run the risk of being like the two disciples on the road to Emmaus, who had missed completely the meaning of Calvary until their fellow traveller, "starting with Moses and going through all the prophets . . . explained to them the passages throughout the scriptures that were about himself" (Lk 24:27). Often events in our own lives will be made sacramental and diaphanous by reading the word of God in Scripture. We shall sometimes see, for example, why God allows chance events to play havoc with our best laid plans and our purest intentions.

The reading of Scripture in the assembly of the faithful is especially powerful in relating the events of salvation history to our own lives. The proclamation of the word of God in the liturgy calls for a response of faith. Thus faith does not consist merely in believing in certain historical events of the past, but in a lively realization that we ourselves are personally involved in the whole process of the history of salvation, both in the distant past and also in the present moment of our lives. Implicit in the proclamation of the word and in every authentic homily is Christ's statement in the synagogue of his home village: "This text is being fulfilled today even as you listen" (Lk 4:21).

The liturgy aims to immerse us in the living stream of saving historical events, especially through the sacraments. The sacraments are causal signs. Unfortunately theologians have often become so preoccupied with their causal aspect that they have neglected to develop sufficiently their sign aspect. In exploring this aspect, we must beware of taking a view that is too restricted and limtied. If, for example, we are to understand the sacrament of baptism adequately, we have to go beyond the mere pouring of water and the recitation of the formula that accompanies it. We must study all the ceremonies of the baptismal rite. Further, we have to see all these signs in the context of the liturgy of the Easter Vigil, which is in a very special way the feast of baptism. But since the Easter Vigil is the climax and the culmination of the whole Lenten liturgy, we have to go further and see baptism in the light of the liturgy of Lent, which was designed originally to prepare catechumens for baptism. All these things constitute, in a sense, the total "sign" of baptism. And once we have this total "sign" spread out before us, with all the rich texts from both the New and the Old Testaments, we can begin to appreciate how this sacrament situates us in the stream of the saving events of history.

*   *   *

When did our spiritual life begin? One might be tempted to answer: at the moment of baptism when the very inner life of God took possession of our whole being. But have we actually reached the ultimate source here? Would not the rite of baptism be empty symbolism if the saving act of Christ had not given it supernatural power? Our spiritual life, then, really springs from the life, death, resurrection and ascension of the Lord Jesus. But this saving act of Christ was, in turn, rooted in a long history; hence if we wish to continue to search for the ultimate origins of our spiritual life it becomes necessary to go back into this history. Indeed, it becomes necessary to go back to the very foundations of the world.

On Holy Saturday night, in the service of the word which immediately precedes the baptismal service, there are several Scripture readings which recount various episodes in salvation history. The one reading which can never be omitted is the account of the passage of the Hebrews through the waters of the Sea of Reeds, as they began their long pilgrimage to the promised land. These waters have always been considered an eloquent symbol of the waters of baptism. But among the other readings, the first is the story of the formation of the universe from the chaotic primeval waters over which hovered the spirit of God. This would seem to suggest that in the mind of the Church there is some connection between the historical event of the emergence of the universe in all its newness, freshness and crystalline beauty, and the emergence from the baptismal waters of the "new creation" (cf. 2 Co 5:17; Ga 6:15) in all the freshness, purity and beauty of the divine life. Baptism is indeed a liberation which is symbolized by the Exodus, but it is also a new creation which has reference to the old creation. The blessing of the baptismal water both during the Easter Vigil and in the ordinary rite of baptism also establishes a relation between the baptismal waters and the waters of creation: "At the very dawn of creation your Spirit breathed on the waters, making them the wellspring of all holiness."

It is certain that God created the universe not only in the Word, but also for the Word made flesh (Col 1:15-16), that is, for the total Christ, with his Body, of which we are members. Consequently, when he brought forth the universe, what he had in mind principally was the eventual emergence of us as members of Christ's Body from the waters of baptism. And this he had in mind in all the other saving events of history which prepared for the coming of Christ and the final saving act of his beloved Son. "Before the world was made, he chose us, chose us in Christ, to be holy and spotless, and to live through love in his presence, determining that we should become his adopted sons, through Jesus Christ ..." (Ep 1:4-5). "Come, you whom my Father has blessed, take for your heritage the kingdom prepared for you since the foundation of the world (Mt 25:34; cf. 1 P 1:19-20; Rv 13:8).

Some years ago one of the most popular theories of those who held that man came into the universe by a long process of evolution was expressed in the phrase: "ontogeny is the recapitulation of philogeny." This means that in the embryonic development of the individual human person there are various successive stages which strongly resemble the development of life from its lowest to its highest forms. Whatever truth there may or may not be in this theory, perhaps we can say by analogy that every Christian recapitulates that long evolutionary process which we call the history of salvation, and that, as a consequence, he cannot attempt to live his spiritual life without seeing it in the perspective of this history.

The Christian life should be one long, uninterrupted *anamnesis*. This Greek term is applied to that part of the eucharistic prayer in the Mass which immediately follows the consecration, when the Church recalls the blessed passion, death, resurrection, and ascension of the Lord Jesus. But the word in general means "remembrance," and in the Christian life it has an application which ranges far beyond this particular point in the eucharistic prayer. We have seen that one of the most salient characteristics of the biblical person was that he lived in a constant state of remembrance of the great actions of Yahweh in the history of his people. This *anamnesis* of the biblical person was for him a serious obligation. To neglect it would mean an abandonment of his people, who had been fashioned as God's people by the divine actions of the past, as well as an abandonment of the God who had performed them.

Christ was in the very act of remembering, in the act of commemorating the Exodus in the traditional paschal meal, when he commanded his disciples to commemorate what he had done at that meal in instituting the eucharist. At that point the obligation of remembering took on startling new dimensions. The Christian life must consist not simply in continually calling to mind the great acts of God performed in Christ Jesus, his saving mysteries, but in commemorating them in such a way that they can, in that special kind of reality which is sacramental, be truly made present. Thus, the continual *anamnesis* of the Christian consists essentially in bringing back from the past into the present the great saving mysteries of the life of Christ through the continual celebration of the liturgy.

Love creates a continual habit of remembrance. A lover stores in her memory every incident related to her beloved since the first moment when love was born. Israel, the spouse of Yahweh through the covenant, had a prodigious memory. But the Bride of Christ has a far more prodigious memory than Virgin Israel. The Church is a kind of living *anamnesis*. Every event which took place in the long history that prepared the way for the first covenant espousals, which were, in turn, a preparation for the espousals of the Church with Christ, and all the actions of the Beloved, have been carefully stored up in memory and are continually being recalled, pondered, and cherished.

The liturgy is the active expression of the memory of the Church. Every day she lovingly does in commemoration of the Bridegroom what he asked her to do. Every "today" is related to the mysteries of the Bridegroom, and in turn these call out of memory the various incidents of the history which prepared for him; they are reviewed and meditated on with love. The liturgy of each day is a perpetual *anamnesis*: it situates each day and the hours of the day in liturgical texts which recall not only the mysteries of Christ from the New Testament, but also the various saving events of that long love story of the Old Testament, all the way back to the foundations of the world. These biblical texts are recalled, not only to be meditated on, but to be given actuality and a contemporary meaning. It is the duty of the homilist to make sure that they achieve this purpose. If we are going to share fully in the life of the Church, we must participate in this constant and loving *anamnesis*. Only through the remembrance of the past can Christ become fully present in our present time. But we cannot share fully in the loving *anamnesis* of the Church without sharing fully in the liturgy, and without having a rich biblical background to draw from. The contemporary person living in a future-oriented culture, which all too easily turns its back upon the past, runs the risk of being characterized by amnesia rather than by *anamnesis*.

Constant *anamnesis* will engender in us many virtues, but perhaps the most characteristic will be gratitude. The greatest act of remembering is called the eucharist, a word which originally meant a thanksgiving. The dominant theme of vespers, the evening prayer of the Church, is thanksgiving, just as the dominant note of morning prayer, lauds, is praise. If our gratitude is truly Christian it will not be limited to the gracious actions of God each day or during the short span of our own personal lives; rather, with the Church, it will embrace all the acts of love of the Bridegroom throughout history. We would not be living the life of the Church to the full if our thanksgiving did not in some way, even though not always consciously and explicitly, embrace the whole history of God's love, which is really inseparable from his personal love for us. At times the radiant sacramentality of salvation history, the unspeakable beauty of God's wisdom and love manifesting themselves ever more fully through the unfolding of time, will lead our gratitude to soar far beyond God's benefits and to thank him, not only for his gifts, but simply for being who he is: "We give you thanks, we praise you for your glory."

Having asked when our spiritual life originated, we must now ask when it will reach its ultimate goal. Many would be tempted to answer: when our souls enter the beatific vision. But is this really the full and adequate answer? Enough has already been said to show that it is not. I have pointed out that the subject of the spiritual life is not the soul but the human person. It follows that our spiritual life will reach its ultimate goal only on the last day of all history, at the moment of the resurrection of the dead, when the soul will be reunited with the body. Then we shall finally be beatified as total human persons. Because our bodies are members of the Body of Christ, which is a community, each individual human body does not have its own time of resurrection. All the bodies of the members of the Church will rise simultaneously, communally, to form the one glorified Body of Christ. At that same moment the whole physical universe, which we are striving to draw with us towards the glorification of the resurrection, will be transformed. (cf. Ph 3:20-21). Our Christian life should continually look forward across what is left of salvation history to its final culmination in the Parousia and should share in the expectancy of the Church as it awaits with eagerness and intense desire the joyful coming of the Bridegroom in glory and majesty. The last lines of the whole Bible should be a dominant theme of our spiritual life: "The Spirit and the Bride say, 'Come'. Let every-one who listens answer, 'Come' . . . Amen; come, Lord Jesus" (Rv 22:17, 20).

Just as loving remembrance of the past generates thanksgiv-ing, loving expectancy generates hope (cf. 1 Th 4:13). This ex-pectant hope is based not only on the promises of the Lord, which in themselves constitute a rich biblical theme (cf. e.g., Ep 1:13-14; 2 P 3:8-15; Heb 9:15), but even more on the living and loving presence of the risen Jesus in his Church and in the life of every true Christian. Through his Spirit, Jesus gives the Chris-tian an anticipation of his future coming (cf. e.g., 2 Co 1:22; Ep 1:14; Rm 8:11) so that the dynamism of the Parousia is al-ready at work in his or her life (cf. e.g., Ph 3:11-13; Col 1:9-12). Authentic Christian spirituality fills the soul with loving remem-brance and ardent eschatological expectancy that enable the Chris-tian to live constantly in a spirit of thanksgiving and of hope. In other words, the Christian is called to be, all the days of his or her life, at once a living *anamnesis* and a living *maranatha*. The Chris-tian spiritual life is at every moment related to both the first and the last lines of the Bible. Its every day is related to the Genesis account of the origin of the days on the one hand, and to "the day of our Lord Jesus Christ" (cf. 1 Co 1:8) on the other. Indeed, not only does it, in its remembrance, go all the way back to the begin-ning of time, and, in its expectancy look forward to the end of time, it irresistibly breaks through the barriers of time on both ends and finds itself in eternity: on the one hand, in the eternal loving plan of the Father conceived from all eternity, and on the other, in the society of the blessed, in the bosom of the Father, in the splendors of the saints.

*   *   *

Christ is the center of history. Everything before him gets its whole meaning from the fact that it is a preparation for him. Everything after gets its whole meaning from the fact that it is a prolongation of him, and a bringing of him to fulfillment. The whole of salvation history can be capsulized by viewing all that led up to this focal point of history as a process of the many gradually converging toward the One, and all that came after as a process of the One expanding out to the many. This whole movement across all the centuries takes place by a continuous series of elections whose sole motivation is the mysterious pre-dilection of God, which is at the heart of the whole eternal plan of the Father. Before Christ, out of the many peoples inhabiting the earth, God elected one nation, the Israelites, as his chosen people. And he made it plain to them that the sole reason for his choice was his utterly gratuitous love of predilection: "If Yahweh set his heart on you and chose you, it was not because you outnumbered other peoples: you were the least of all peoples. It was for love of you . . ." (Dt 7:7-8).

Throughout the history of this chosen people we find a great variety of historical events and persons prefiguring and converging toward the One in whom all of them have their intelligibility and their fulfillment. All the long history of Israel, all the words of the prophets, all the actions of her great historical figures, gradually converge in a narrowing process of election to the one final, intense point of concentration: Christ the Lord. It is fascinating to trace the gradual selection on the part of God in this long converging historical series of elections of predilection, which really began long before he chose as his very own, not the greatest and most powerful nation on earth, but the very least. From all the sons of Adam he chose Seth (Gn 5:1-5), then Shem (Gn 9:26), the father of the Semites; then Terah, the father of Abraham (Gn 11:26) with whom God made a covenant which constituted him the father of the chosen people (Gn 15). After Abraham began a continuous process of gratuitous selections. God even departed from the usual hereditary rights of the first born, and Jacob was elected instead of Esau to carry forward the promise made to Abraham. Later among his twelve sons Judah was gratuitously chosen (Gn 49:8-12), and after him the messianic promise came to rest in one family, the family of David. Eventually the chosen people were reduced to a faithful remnant, among whom Mary appeared as the special object of God's mysterious love of predilection, and from her came the One towards whom the whole long process had been converging over the centuries.

After the birth of Christ, we see the One reaching out progressively farther and farther to draw the many to himself and to make them one in him: first Mary and Joseph, then the apostles, then the larger group of disciples, then the first three thousand converted on Pentecost, and so on as the movement reaches out to the whole of humankind through the Church which mediates Christ's redemption to the whole of creation. This progressive movement, this reaching out of the One to the many, is, of course, the source of all missionary and pastoral effort. Indeed, it goes far beyond. It involves the radical transformation of the whole of reality, spiritual and moral reality first, but also all cosmic reality. All the efforts of human society, all the strivings of human beings to realize more and more fully their own potentialities, all the expansion of human knowledge, all the reaching of human science and technology toward further points of outer and inner space—all these things are destined to be a part of that progressive and expansive movement through history in which the eternal plan of God gradually achieves its fulfillment.

The convergence of the many toward the One was a process that evolved in the old people of God; the reaching out of the One toward the many is a process now going on in the new people of God in the time-in-between; at the center of these two processes is Christ the Lord. Thus the whole of salvation history can be summed up in a triad, which may be expressed in these three terms: symbol or type, natural reality, and sacramental reality.[1]

The old people of God possessed a number of characteristics which distinguished them from all other peoples on earth: they were the chosen people (cf. e.g., Dt 7:6; Ex 19:5; Is 41:8), sons of God in a unique sense (cf. e.g., Ex 4:22; Dt 14:1-2), a consecrated and holy people (cf. e.g., Dt 26:19; Is 62:12), an anointed, priestly, prophetic and kingly people (cf. e.g., Ex 19:6; Ps 105:14-15). These qualities enabled Israel to fulfill its providential role in salvation history as a prefiguration of Christ Jesus, as already giving a kind of preview through symbolism and metaphor of the One in whom these qualities finally came to realization in all their literalness and fullness: Jesus, the chosen One, the Son of God, the holy One par excellence, the Priest, Prophet, and King in the fullest possible sense, the anointed One, the Messiah. Only by seeing Christ as the new Israel can we understand how profound is the statement that the many of the Old Testament all converged toward the One. In Jesus all that Israel under the Old Law had been, and had been doing symbolically, figuratively, and in metaphor became real, became absolutely literal, and reached its total fulfillment.

The reason why the whole history and the whole destiny of Israel were recapitulated and fulfilled in the One Man is that he was destined to be the source of a new people of God and to recapitulate the whole future as he did the past. And here we begin to see the reaching out of the One to the many. The founding of the Church was not just an arbitrary decision on the part of Christ. The new people of God issued from Christ as naturally, so to speak, and as inevitably as he issued from the old people of God.

Thus, the images, titles, and attributes which characterized that community which was Israel, and which subsequently found concrete, literal realization and fulfillment in the One Man can now be extended once again to a whole community, the new people of God.

But in each of these three members of the triad, the way in which the titles and attributes are applied is different. The things that are said of Israel metaphorically, symbolically, by way of prefigurement, type, or shadow, as St. Paul puts it, are said of Christ literally, in full, absolute, concrete reality; and they are said of the new people God sacramentally. The events that took place in the history of Israel and that gave it the distinctive characteristics we mentioned were, of course, real; but they derived their deepest meaning from the fact that they were types of what was to come. "These were only pale reflections of what was coming: the reality is Christ" (Col 2:17).

The ritual sacrifices of the Hebrews were literally real religious acts in themselves, and they had their own intrinsic value; but their deepest value and significance derived from the fact that they prefigured the one, once-and-for-all sacrifice of the Lord Jesus. The actions of Christ, on the contrary, have their value in themselves. The acts of the Church have their value in that they sacramentally re-present what Christ did. Thus, the sacrifice of the paschal lamb in the religious ceremony of the Hebrews, while having a limited special meaning for the Hebrews themselves, was a figure and a foreshadowing of the redemption and reconciliation that was to come; the crucifixion, resurrection and ascension of Christ were in literal reality the redemption of the world; the celebration of the eucharist is the sacramental reenactment of this eternal redeeming action of Christ.

Through the sacraments we are inserted into Christ, assimilated by him, and made one with him. Through the sacraments we become one with the chosen One. Our vocation is an election of predilection on the part of the Father to be one with the Son of his love. "Before the world was made, he chose us, chose us in Christ, to be holy and spotless, and to live through love in his presence, determining that we should become his adopted sons, through Jesus Christ . . ." (Ep 1:4-5). Through baptism we become children of God, sharing in the profound mystery of Christ's filiation. Through the sacraments we share in the messianic anointing of Christ. This is one of the reasons why anointing occurs in several of the sacraments. By the consecration received in baptism we are made holy, given a share in the very holiness of Christ and therefore of God himself.

Through the sacraments we share in the prophetic, kingly, and priestly role of Christ. (cf. e.g., C 11a; 12a; 34a-b; 35a) Having received the common priesthood of the faithful in baptism and confirmation, a child is a priest in a fuller sense than Aaron or any of the great high priests of the Old Testament because he shares sacramentally in the very priesthood of the one high priest who is Christ. When Peter tells the early Christians that they are "a royal priesthood, a consecrated nation" (1 P 2:9) he is quoting directly from Exodus (19:6), but in the context these words take on a whole new meaning, for the context speaks of "the holy priesthood that offers the spiritual sacrifices which Jesus Christ has made acceptable to God" (2:5). In baptism we are made one with Christ the King, and thus made to share in his unique kingdom in which all are kings (cf. Col 1:13-14). We are also sacramentally made one with him as the greatest of prophets. In its original meaning, the term "prophet" did not necessarily mean one who foretold the future, but a herald of the truth of God. Christ is the supreme prophet because he is that infinite truth in all its fullness. Sacramentally, all Christians share in his role of prophecy.

Because the sacraments are essentially causal signs, they are able to break through the limitations of ordinary signification and go to the reality signified. So great and so real is their power, so actually does the sacramental sign go beyond and transcend the limits of pure signification that Thomas Aquinas can write: "to everyone who is baptized the passion of Christ is communicated as a healing power, *as if he himself had suffered and died.*"[2] This sacramental power makes it possible for us to realize in our own life the prayer of St. Paul: "All I want is to know Christ and the power of his resurrection and to share his sufferings by reproducing the pattern of his death. That is the way I can hope to take my place in the resurrection of the dead" (Ph 3:10-11).

The sacramental world of the third part of the triad is something absolutely unique. In some ways it has something in common with the prefigurement of the first part, and in other ways with the reality of the second part; yet it is essentially different from both. Because it is a sign, it has something in common with the figures, symbols, and types of the first part; yet it differs radically from them because they could only signify something without having the power to cause it. It has something in common with the second part because it is a reality and not just a symbol. On the other hand, it is not ordinary reality, but sacramental reality, which is a kind of world of its own. It is something in between mere symbol and ordinary reality, without being just a mixture or a juxtapopsition of the two. Church-time is essentially sacrament-time, and here we have the deepest reason why Church existence is essentially an in-between and intermediate existence.

Another reason why the third part of the triad is similar to the first is that it not only looks back to the fullness of reality of the first advent of Christ but, like the prefigurement of the Old Testament, it also looks forward to the even more absolute reality of the second advent. Yet, unlike the first part of the triad, it does not simply prefigure the future. Because it is made up of causal signs, it can somehow make the future already present. The Church may be defined as a community which sacramentally prefigures and already anticipates the future life which Christ has destined for those who love him.

We can grasp the absolutely unique nature of the sacramental world and its essential relation to time and history only by seeing it in terms of the multidimensional character of the sacraments. The sacraments are triple signs: demonstrative signs of something happening in the present (a communication of grace), commemorative signs of something that happened in the past (the death and resurrection of the Lord), and prognostic signs of something that will happen in the future (eternal glory). This all-embracing view of the sacraments has to a large extent been lost sight of, principally because the traditional catechism, which necessarily must simplify things, has given only a one dimensional definition of the sacraments: "outward signs instituted by Christ to give grace." In this definition the sacraments are seen only as demonstrative signs; there is no reference to their commemorative and prognostic dimensions.

Because Church-time is essentially sacrament-time, Christians can continually relive the entire history of the redemptive process and share in its fruits. The Christian experience is an existential encounter with the past which speaks to them and witnesses to them in the present. At the same time, the sacraments bring about an intimate union between everyday life and the life to come. Christ is always "he who comes." He is the Christian future, the one who is continually "making the whole of creation new" (Rv 21:5). Christians are those who have been "brought into the light, and tasted the gift from heaven, and received a share of the Holy Spirit, and appreciated the good message of God and the powers of the world to come . . ." (Heb 6:4-5).

Through the sacraments, we can indeed taste the gift from heaven, but we can attain this gift in its fullness only after a long pilgrimage. Because the Christian life is immersed in the flow of time and history, it is essentially a pilgrimage. The temporal and sacramental character of the Christian life invites us to reflect upon the Christian as a wayfarer making his way through time and history, with every moment of time being transformed into saving history through the sacraments, until at last all time and history, all signs, symbols, and sacraments fade away in the presence of ultimate Reality.

Notes

1. For this point I wish to acknowledge my indebtedness to Herbert McCabe's book, *The People of God* (New York: Sheed and Ward, 1964), pp. 23-33.

2. *Summa Theologiae*, pt. 3, q. 69, art. 2.

Bibliography

Because the literature on this topic is so extensive, our selection of works is limited to a few which seem especially relevant to the contents of this chapter. Oscar Cullmann's scholarly book, *Salvation in History*, trans. Sidney G. Sowers (New York: Harper and Row, 1967) is a larger and more far-reaching work than his *Christ and Time*. Hans Urs von Balthasar's *A Theology of History* (New York: Sheed and Ward, 1963) is a small but thought-provoking book, rich with many profound insights. Asmund Lewry in *The Theology of History* (Notre Dame, In.: Fides Publishers, 1969) has succeeded admirably in condensing the major problems of the theology of history into a volume of only 96 pages. He also provides a helpful bibliography. Jean Danielou's *The Lord of History* trans. Nigel Abercrombie (Chicago: Henry Regnery, 1958) has as its subtitle "Reflections on the Inner Meaning of History." Though not a systematic study of the theology of history, Danielou's reflections make rich and rewarding reading. Another valuable work is *Christ the Meaning of History* by Hendricus Berkhof, trans. Lambertus Buurman (Richmond,

Va.: John Knox Press, 1966). James Connolly's *Human History and the Word of God* (New York: Macmillan, 1965) has a subtitle which reveals the nature of the work: "The Christian Meaning of History in Contemporary Thought." Karl Rahner discusses the multiple relations between profane history and the history of salvation in his article, "History of the World and Salvation History," *Theological Investigations*, V, trans. Karl-H. Kruger (Baltimore: Helicon Press, 1966), 97-114.

CHAPTER FIFTEEN

THE PILGRIM

THE CHRISTIAN is an exodus person because, first of all, Christ was an exodus person. From all eternity, before his exodus on the foreign mission of the incarnation, his life had been a procession from the Father, as light coming forth from light. He was born on a journey, and his birth brought a group of astrologers on a long pilgrimage from distant lands to visit him (Mt 2:1-12)—a pilgrimage which would serve as a proto-type of the countless pilgrimages which, over the centuries, would be made in his name. Shortly thereafter he had to go into exile in Egypt (Mt 2:13-15). From there he came back again to Nazareth (Mt 2:19-23). From the age of twelve he made a pilgrimage to Jerusalem every year for the Passover (Lk 2:41). His years at Nazareth no doubt seem to present the image of a very sedentary life. Yet, he must have felt more than any other person could that he had here no lasting city (Heb 13:14), and no one can read St. John without realizing that spiritually he was always going to the Father.

Then came the time when his mission called for an exodus from his home and his family at Nazareth. Thereafter, he was an itinerant Rabbi, wandering from place to place, with nowhere to lay his head (Mt 8:20). He was expelled from his own home town (Lk 4:29-30). When the time came for him to begin to organize his Church, his invitation to those who were called to be its foundation was not to become members of an organi-zation, or only to be disciples of his teaching, but to be followers. Again and again his voice rang out like an echo of the voice of God that called Abraham to leave his home and his friends and to go he knew not where (Gn 12:1-5): "Come, follow me." His call was for them to take the splendid risk their father Abraham had taken centuries before. Not one of these men knew where he was going; not one of them could suspect that eventually his call would bring them to the ends of the earth and to martyrdom.

Sometimes there was a kind of divine "ruthlessness" in his call. To the rich young man, upon whom he looked with love, he said: "Go and sell everything you own and give the money to the poor...; then come, follow me" (Mk 10:21; cf. Mt 10:35-39; Lk 14:26). In spite of the love in the eyes of Jesus which revealed how splendid the risk would be, the young man could not bring himself to take that risk. To the man who wanted to follow him, but only after having the opportunity to say good-bye to his people at home, Jesus said: "No one who looks back is fit for the kingdom of heaven" (Lk 9:62). Clearly, his followers would have to be future oriented. To another prospective follower who wanted first to bury his father, he declared: "Leave the dead to bury their dead; your duty is to go and spread the news of the kingdom of God" (Lk 9:60). The fundamental duty of all his followers would be to go, and to keep on going. There was never any promise of security; what he promised them was the cross: "If anyone wants to be a follower of mine, let him renounce himself and take up his cross every day and follow me" (Lk 9:23). They would have to risk everything. And ever after, Christian discipleship would consist essentially in a willingness, which for many would become a hunger, to risk all, even life itself.

Luke tells us that on the occasion of his transfiguration just before his last pilgrimage to Jerusalem, Moses and Elijah were seen talking to him about the exodus he was to accomplish in that city (9:31). He accomplished that exodus by passing from life to death and back to life again. And before the final exodus of his ascension he gave his apostles the mission of going into the whole world to preach the Good News (Mt 28:19). He had come into the world to call his own people to an exodus that would be greater and more dramatic than their exodus from Egypt, the exodus from the old covenant into the new. That mission had not been a success; but, working through his apostles, he would bring about a mass exodus among all the peoples of the world from the darkness of paganism into his kingdom of light. Baptism into the faith would not be the end of that exodus; it would be only the beginning. In the life of each Christian there would be a constant pilgrimage through time and history toward the final fulfillment of the Christian life. Moreover, every Christian, like Saints Peter and Paul, would have to be a tent-dweller until the folding up of his or her tent in the final exodus of death: "For we know that when the tent that we live in on earth is folded up, there is a house built by God for us, an everlasting home not made by human hands, in the heavens" (2 Co 5:1). "I am sure it is my duty, as long as I am in this tent, to keep stirring you up with reminders, since I know the time for taking off the tent is coming soon . . ." (2 P 1:13-14).

When Jesus told the Apostles that, going into the whole world, they should preach the Good News, the "going" was a present participle. It still is. The vocation of Christians is a "calling" which remains a present participle until the time comes for them to fold up their tents. Only after the final exodus will it become a past participle; only then will they have been called. Meanwhile, Jesus never stops calling his followers to keep on going. And just as Yahweh was a wandering God for the nomadic Israelites, who remained with them wherever they might go, so Jesus assured his followers that he would always be with them wherever they might go: "Know that I am with you always; yes, to the end of time" (Mt 28:20). He would be with them always in a great variety of ways. He would be with them in a special sense wherever there would be an assembly, even if only an assembly or two or three: "Where two or three meet in my name, I shall be there with them" (Mt 18:20). And wherever his followers would bring his name and his love in any part of the world he would be there in his eucharistic presence, dwelling in their midst in the tent of a tabernacle.*

Almost from the beginning the Christian life became known as the Way (cf. e.g., Ac 9:2; 18:25,26; 19:9). Moreover, Jesus told his followers: "I am the way" (Jn 14:6). Jesus is not just the goal of the Christian life; he is also the Way to the goal. During all the time that we Christian wayfarers are on the way, Jesus, the Way, is with us. Thus, we are at one and the same time in exile and at home. And if we ever get the feeling of being lost, we should recall the words of Dag Hammarskjöld in *Markings*: "It is not we who seek the Way, but the Way which seeks us."[1]

* * *

---

*The word "tabernacle" in its basic meaning signifies a tent, and it is used in the Bible to designate the sacred cultic tent in which the wandering God of Israel dwelt.

Pilgrim spirituality is a paradox. It is at once immanent in the world and transcendant to it, at once both incarnational and eschatological. Pilgrims can never be alien to this world; yet they must keep travelling through it towards something beyond, the heavenly Jerusalem, where alone they will find their lasting city (cf. Heb 13:14). Because the present world is our natural habitat, we must be interested in it; we must recognize the intrinsic value and worth of temporal realities; we must feel called, according to our particular vocations in life, to develop our potentialities and to bring them to fulfillment. At the same time, we are passing through and beyond these realities, while striving to draw this world with us to the final glorification. The great art of Christian spirituality is to know how to combine in creative tension the two aspects of this paradox. It was said of the early Christians: "Every foreign land is their home, and every home is a foreign land."

To say that Christian spirituality is essentially a pilgrim spirituality is to say that however incarnational it might become, it must always remain profoundly eschatological, for salvation and sanctification are always transcendent to everything purely human. They are not the fruit of any particular culture. They do not come about merely by a development of the inherent potentialities of people and their world, but by a dramatic intervention of the future world in the present world. As pilgrims, we are called to be living witnesses of this intervention and of the transcendent meaning of the Christian life, which must indeed become incarnate in every stage of history and in every culture, but which can never become definitively identified with any particular cultural world view. We cannot be faithful to our evangelical vocation as pilgrims if we resist change, if we remain unwilling to transcend historical and cultural forms which are already dated, if we cannot detach ourselves from sociological structures that are no longer relevant.

Present in every Christian spirituality, even the most incarnational, including that of the lay person most completely immersed in temporalities and in the promotion of secular values, is a constant tension, a constant pull into the future. Without this tension, a spirituality is not a pilgrim spirituality, and to that extent not Christian. The more deeply we become involved in temporal affairs and penetrate into the heart of secular realities, the more irresistibly should we feel the gravitational attraction of the risen Jesus, which keeps us moving on. Someone has said: "By the very way a bird walks on the earth, you can tell it has wings to fly."

* * *

In a sense, hope is the most characteristic virtue of the Christian pilgrim, for it is hope which gives to the Christian life its eschatological orientation. It may be called an exodus virtue, for it is found only where there is a movement from the present into the future. As I mentioned earlier, the Christian pilgrimage has always had as its model the exodus of the Israelites from Egypt and their forty years' pilgrimage across the Sinai desert to the promised land. Many aspects of the Christian pilgrimage make it a desert experience which has a special relationship with the virtue of hope. Precisely because the desert easily breeds a feeling of insecurity, and sometimes even a feeling of hopelessness, it provides the optimum conditions for the development of the virtue of hope.

Yahweh encouraged his people to have hope by recalling what happened during their desert insecurity: "For forty years I led you in the wilderness; the clothes on your back did not wear out and your sandals did not wear off your feet" (Dt 29:4-5). "In the wilderness, too, you saw him: how Yahweh carried you, as a man carries his child, all along the road you travelled on the way to this place" (Dt 1:31). In his great canticle, Moses sang eloquently of the tender care of Yahweh for his people during their desert pilgrimage: "In the waste lands he adopts him, in the howling desert of the wilderness. He protects him, rears, guards him as the pupil of his eye. Like an eagle watching its nest, hovering over its young, he spreads out his wings to hold him, he supports him on his pinions" (Dt 32:10-11; cf. Ex 19:4).

Christian hope is, in a sense, the most existential of all the virtues, for it involves the three major elements which make up the warp and woof of concrete human existence. It involves a hyphenation with others, as Gabriel Marcel has strongly emphasized.[2] We cannot hope for ourselves alone; it is of the essence of Christian commitment to hope for others also, since we cannot love our neighbor as we love ourselves unless we hope for him as we hope for ourselves. Hope also involves a hyphenation with the world, for the world has a Christian destiny and the Christian must hope for this Christian fulfillment of the world, without which the fullness of Christ cannot be achieved (cf. Ep 1:23). Finally, hope involves a hyphenation with history and time, for, as I mentioned above, it involves an exodus from the present to the future.[3]

But Christian hope is also essentially related to the past, for the anchor which represents hope is sunk deeply into God's promises in the past; it is attached especially to the Cross, which is often called "our only hope"; but it is sunk most deeply into the resurrection, which is the ultimate source of all Christian hope and the one reason why the Cross is our only hope. In other words, Christian hope is rooted profoundly in the total paschal mystery celebrated in the life of Christ in the past, but always awaiting fulfillment in the life of every Christian in the future. (cf. 1 P 1:3; Ep 1:18). Because Christian hope is related to both past and future, it is founded on both a memory and a dream. In a word, hope is based on the process character of the human person and his world; it is based on the realization that both are unfinished and continually calling for fulfillment. Hope is characteristic of one who is seeking fulfillment. Hence, though always related to the past, it is even more profoundly related to the future.

Hope is so much a Christian virtue that St. Paul frequently seems to imply that Christians might be defined as those who have hope (cf., e.g., 1 Th 4:13; Ep 4:4; 2 Co 3:12). Yet in spite of its importance, hope received in past centuries only scant treatment by theologians in comparison with the other two theological virtues of faith and charity, so much so that Charles Peguy could write some years ago that among the theological virtues hope was like a poor little sister left out in the cold.

Perhaps the principal reason for this is that, prior to Vatican II, the mentality of the Church was, generally speaking, more retrospective than futuristic. In contrast to the primitive Church, which looked forward with eagerness and vigilance to the Parousia, we were not a very strongly future-oriented people. Teilhard de Chardin once remarked: "The whole future of the earth, as of religion, sems to me to depend on the awakening of our faith in the future." And in *The Divine Milieu* he writes:

> . . . how many of us are genuinely moved to the depths of their heart by the wild hope that *our* earth will be recast? Who is there who sets a course in the midst of our darkness towards the first glimmer of a *real* dawn? Where is the Christian in whom the impatient long-

ing for Christ succeeds, not in submerging (as it should) the cares of human love and human interests, but even in counter-balancing them? Where is the Catholic as passionately vowed (by *conviction* and not by *convention*) to spreading the hopes of the Incarnation as are many humanitarians to spreading the dream of the new city? We persist in saying that we keep vigil in expectation of the Master. But in reality we should have to admit, if we were sincere, *that we no longer expect anything.* The flame must be revived at all costs. At all costs we must renew in ourselves the desire and the hope of the great Coming.[4]

In relation to Teilhard's reference to the humanitarians and their dream of the new city, it is interesting to note that the one who, more than anyone else, sparked the contemporary interest in the question of hope was a Marxist, Ernst Bloch, in his book, *The Hope Principle.*

In recent times, hope, the poor little sister of faith and charity, has been brought in from the cold, and has become the center of attention for many theologians and philosophers. One of the main reasons for this is that our contemporary view of reality has a profound orientation to the future. Indeed, we are caught up in a future-thrust unlike anything that has ever before occurred in history. The impact of the shock waves produced by this phenomenon has been felt most strongly where there has been a deep-set commitment to an established tradition.

The growing realization that the world is in a constant process of evolution, together with the growing power of science, technology, and social engineering to manipulate and mold the ongoing change of the world and human society, and thus in some sense to program the future, has oriented the contemporary understanding of the world fundamentally toward the future. In the measure in which people have become attracted by the future, the significance of the past and of tradition has declined. The contemporary mind seeks to leave behind anything that gives the impression of being an "establishment."

We human beings have been defined as transcendence in history, and both the historical and the transcendent or meta-historical aspects of our existence necessarily call for the virtue of hope. We are the only beings living in history with self-awareness, and consequently we alone are conscious of never being completely present to ourselves, of never possessing ourselves fully. In the depths of our being is a profound aspira-

tion to be wholly ourselves which makes us strive continually
to go beyond ourselves, to project ourselves into the future
in dreams and hopes. We look to the future in the hope that
in the historical process we can become more and more completely ourselves. Human existence is a continual going beyond
what one is at any given moment. Sartre defines man as "the
being who hurls himself toward a future and who is conscious
of imagining himself as being in the future."[5]

But because we are transcendent to history, our future, and
consequently our hope, are likewise transcendent to history.
As the existentialists keep reminding us, we are beings-toward-
death. The reality of death reveals to us the non-being that
is at the heart of our being, and it is precisely this negative
aspect of our nature that enables us to discover the deepest
level of our existence, namely its transcendence. The final instant in the flow of time known as death will find us still
not fully possessing ourselves, not completely fulfilled, and still
aspiring to fulfillment. If history's future did not eventually
lead to something metahistorical, all human hopes would fundamentally and ultimately be hopeless. Our history never achieves
its fulfillment in history itself.

Hence by both aspects of our human nature, its historicity
and its transcendence to history, we are destined to live an
exodus existence. Our history is a continual exodus as we leave
behind each instant and go forward to meet its successor. But
the great exodus will come when it is finally necessary for
us to leave behind, not only each instant of time, but time
as a whole, and go beyond it into a metahistorical future.
Our hope must go before us into this new future where there will
never again be future.

*   *   *

The principles for the solution of the problem of hope must
be sought in the Bible, which has sometimes been called "the
book of hope." Because the Bible is not a book of abstract
doctrine but primarily a story of the salvation of God's people
as they move forward through history toward an eschatological
fulfillment, it may be said that hope is its central theme. From
the very beginning, God's people are a futuristic people, an
exodus people, precisely because they are a pilgrim people.

In the Old Testament, Yahweh is not only the one who gives

hope; he is, as Jeremiah states on more than one occasion, "the hope of Israel" (Jr 14:8; 17:13). We have seen in an earlier chapter that Israel derived its notion of God, not from nature as other primitive peoples did, but from history. He revealed himself through his interventions in history as the God who controls all history. He manifested himself time and time again, not as one who insisted on the preservation of a permanently established order, but as one who was continually calling his people into the future, continually giving them a future to hope in. "I know the plans I have in mind for you—it is Yahweh who speaks—plans for peace and not disaster, reserving a future full of hope for you" (Jr 29:11; cf. 31:17). One might sum up the whole history of Israel by describing it as a constant straining forward in hope toward the fulfillment of the promises of Yahweh, all of which centered around the messianic promise. This hope was founded on the fidelity of Yahweh to his word, as evidenced by the great works he wrought for his people in the past. In a very special way, the desert covenant with Yahweh was the source of hope for the future. This covenant had made the Israelites a people peculiarly his own, and they knew that they could count infallibly on the fidelity of their covenant partner. "Let us keep firm in the hope we profess, because the one who made this promise is faithful" (Heb 10:23).

The Lord Jesus is the fulfillment of the messianic promise; and this fulfillment goes beyond the dreams and hopes that had buoyed up the hearts of his people over the many long centuries. In Jesus, the salvation so long awaited in hope is now present and dwelling in our midst. As Paul wrote to the Corinthians, "however many promises God made, the Yes to them all is in him" (2 Co 1:20). Because he was a man as existentially as any one of us, Christ was a being-towards-death, but a unique kind of death, a death that would conquer death and open the way to eternal life. In other words, he was not only a being-towards-death, he was also a being-towards-resurrection. "If our hope in Christ has been for this life only we are the most unfortunate of all people" (1 Co 15:19). Death remains; but it is precisely in and through death that hope finds its greatest fulfillment.

Biblical hope is essentially communal. It is something with far broader horizons than the attainment of beatitude by the individual soul. It is the social hope of a whole people. Because the human person's social dimension is just as essential to him as his strictly individual dimension, because the Christian

life is something communal, and because, on both the natural
and the supernatural levels, we move into the future, not simply
as individuals, but as members of God's people and of humankind, and at the same time as a part of the world, Christian
hope must reflect all this. If the corporate personality of the
Hebrews made their hope communal, how much more communal
should be the hope of those who are one in Christ? Indeed,
St. Paul seems to suggest that it is through hope that this
oneness is brought about: "There is one Body, one Spirit, just
as you were all called into one and the same hope when you
were called" (Ep 4:4). The Church is a community of hope,
and Christian hope is the hope of a whole people for a whole
people. All Christians are called to take part in the transformation of the world and the creation of history. The future
of humanity and of the cosmos is their future also.

As a theological virtue, hope has God as its primary object
and the eternal possession of him as its ultimate goal; it also
has God, his goodness, power, and wisdom, as its principal
motive. This must be kept in mind since so much of the recent
literature on hope concentrates heavily on historical hope and
on purely human hopes shared by secular humanists and Marxists, who are without a God to hope in. Purely human hopes
are not in themselves the theological virtue of hope. And yet,
the subject of this virtue is not a pure spirit, unrelated to
world, time, and human society. He or she is a human person immersed in all these and going to God in and through them by the
grace of the Lord Jesus who himself entered into them and
gave them the capacity for being related to the ultimate future
in God.

The hope of the individual Christian must be one with that
universal hope burning constantly in the heart of the Church,
which has cosmic, historical, social, and eschatological dimensions. Christian hope looks forward to the final coming of the
universal kingdom of glory, when Christ's fullness will finally
be complete. The whole Christian life is a perpetual advent.

Camus has remarked, "hope in the future is treason to the
present." There is some justification for thinking that a purely
ultramundane hope can indeed result in treason to the present
and also to the historical future of the world and of society.
This ultrafuturistic concept of hope has been the object of criticism and even scorn on the part of Marxists and secular humanists, who see in it a kind of escapism, a turning away
from one's responsibilities to the world and human society.

They see in it the cause of a passive acquiescence in social injustices because of the promise of "pie in the sky by and by."

In response to these charges, we can say that the authentic dynamic thrust of Christianity is towards a this-worldly, as well as towards an other-worldly future (cf. CW e.g., 21c; 38b-c; 39b-d; 45b; 57). The vocation of the Christian does not consist in waiting passively for his or her "rewards" after death. The "abandonment to divine Providence" recommended so strongly by de Caussade and other spiritual writers does not mean simply allowing oneself to be swept into the future by the flow of time in a spirit of resignation for whatever might come. Christians must go forward courageously to welcome the future with all its splendid risks. In union with the Providence of God, we must try to plan the future, and even in some sense to make it happen. We must continually strive to bring about the kind of future which will make the paschal power of Jesus and the mission of his Spirit more operative and more fruitful in the world. We as Christians can agree with the Marxists that the human person must seek fulfillment by striving to "create history" and by transforming the world. But our hope goes beyond theirs. Because of the resurrection, we know with the absolute certitude of faith that human existence will find its fulfillment in a transfigured cosmos. The Marxist has no such assurance. Only by having an ultraterrestrial hope can we really have a profound hope for this world.

*　　*　　*

A failure to see clearly and balance properly both the continuity and the discontinuity of the historical and the transhistorical future will profoundly affect the concept of hope. If discontinuity is overstressed, there will tend to be an excessive pessimism with regard to the historical future of humankind, and thus a lack of historical hope. On the other hand, if the continuity is overstressed, there could easily develop an excessive and naive optimism with regard to the future and human progress. As a matter of fact, in the continual exodus which is human existence in time and history, there are two evolutions going on which will never be separated until history has reached its end: the progress of the kingdom of God towards its final realization, but simultaneously the progress of evil towards the kingdom of Satan.[6] We shall always have in the historical future an ongoing realization of the parable of the wheat and the cockle, both of which are allowed to grow together in the field of human history until the end.

Even on the purely natural level, there is no law of human progress which provides assurance that the future will always be better than the present, and when natural progress seems to make the future better in certain ways, it often makes it worse in other ways. As all the contemporary discussion about ecology has brought home to us, scientific, technological, and industrial progress has brought about a pollution of the world and a waste and dissipation of natural resources which threaten to make the earth uninhabitable. The effects of original sin in the human person will never be eliminated in the historical future, which means that even the achievements of human progress can be used by the forces of evil to bring about disastrous results. However great human progress may be in "remaking" the world and controlling the future, the fact is that history is so dominated by chance and by human liberty, and so profoundly affected by sin, that throughout all the duration of the historical future the human person will continue to be at the mercy of chance events and free decisions.

Nor, on the supernatural level, is there any reason for naive optimism. The new aeon spoken of in apocalyptic literature, the aeon of justice and truth, has indeed come into the world in Christ, but the old aeon of sin and evil, the aeon dominated by the powers and principalities of darkness (cf. Ep 6:12) has not yet completely passed away. The two remain in conflict, even after the resurrection of Christ, until the end of time. Christian hope does not mean a naive acceptance of all that the world offers and promises. In fact, it calls for radical renunciation, since it is only through such renunciation that one can be free to move into the future.

The Cross will always remain central in the life of the Christian, precisely because it is central in the life of Christ. Sometimes enthusiastic proponents of incarnational spirituality give the impression that the world was lifted up, transformed, and committed to an even better future simply because Christ was born into history—as though all of this were accomplished independently of the Cross. But the Cross is no problem for Christian hope. Indeed, for centuries Christians have been repeating: "The Cross our only hope."

The expansion of the kingdom of God is brought about precisely by the Cross, and with the resurrection of Christ all the forces of evil have already, in principle, been vanquished, even though the final victory has not yet been made manifest. Unlike the Manichaean, "the Christian knows that God has no opposite Absolute; there is no opposite prime principle."[7] The Prince of darkness, no matter how great his power, must always be subservient to Christ, who has vanquished him through the resurrection. The redemption itself was brought about by the evil religious and civil authorities and by the executioners who crucified Christ. "We know that by turning everything to their good God co-operates with all those who love him, and all those that he called according to his purpose" (Rm 8:28). Suffering will always be present in the lives of Christians; how else could they renew the paschal mystery in their own lives? But this does not constitute any threat to hope, since these sufferings serve the same purpose as the sufferings in the life of Christ: they are the way to glory. Indeed, Jesus has taught us in the Beatitudes that in suffering we already possess and continue to develop eschatological blessedness.

In this perspective, Christians can have a view of history which is at once optimistic and realistic, for we know that all evil has already been vanquished in Christ and thus the evolution of the world is directed, not towards an ultimate catastrophe, but rather towards a share in the victory of Christ in which a transfigured universe will be forever an expression of this victory. The fact that all history, and therefore the historical future, is made up of the contingency of chance events and the free acts of human agents will continue to leave things in suspense, but Christians can still look forward to the historical future with the certitude of hope, for we know that a loving and benign Providence directs all chance events and free acts toward its own glorious purpose.

No one should be more interested in the future, and more open to it than we Christians. We must indeed maintain our interest in, and our commitment to the past, but the past as a continual summons to the future. If the Church is going to have any relevance for the contemporary person, it must avoid anything that might give the impression of being an "establishment," in the pejorative sense of the term, which implies the lack of a confident, welcoming attitude toward the future, an excessive desire to make the future conform to the past, a continual rearguard action so that the acceptance of the inrushing future will be as slow and as minimal as possible. Because the Church is essentially a pilgrim people, it would be a contradiction for it to become an establishment in this sense. And to every establishment of this kind Christians must be non-conformists. We must be ever ready to exercise a prophetic critique as regards the present condition of the world. As Karl Rahner has pointed out, "to subject the structures of this world ... to constant reappraisal and criticism is one of the concrete forms of Christian hope. ..."[8]

True Christians are the ones in whom is realized the prayer of Paul for the members of the Church in Rome: "May the God of hope bring you such joy and peace in your faith that the Holy Spirit will remove all bounds to hope" (Rm 15:13). Their prayer should be: "Maranatha—Yes, come Lord Jesus (cf. Rv 22:20). But in the meantime, before we finish our pilgrimage, may we prepare a better world to receive you when you come."

*   *   *

When the movement of the spiritual pilgrim through time and history finally brings him or her to the promised land where all hopes and dreams will find complete fulfillment, will life thenceforth and forever be a sedentary existence? For many this prospect would not be attractive. For many nothing seems so fulfilling as constantly moving into the unknown. The excitement of the chase is far more appealing than the eventual capture; the adventure of seeking is more stimulating than the eventual finding. Life becomes stale without new discovery; fulfillment is seen as an ever greater capacity for fulfillment. Actually, what awaits the pilgrim is far from being a static and sedentary existence. Arrival will mean the beginning of a never-ending advance into God.

Catholic theology has traditionally taught that in the homeland the pilgrim will see God *totum sed non totaliter*: he or she will see the whole God, but will never see him or possess him wholly. No finite person, no finite capacity, even when elevated far beyond its native limitations by the special supernatural gift known as the "light of glory," will ever be able to see and possess him totally and all at once, for this would require an infinite capacity. From the moment of arrival in the homeland, the pilgrim will be perfectly beatified by being completely caught up in an ecstasy of ineffable intensity as he or she beholds and possesses the ravishing beauty of God's truth and goodness. But finite capacities will never completely exhaust all the infinite riches of God. There will be a continual advance into God in the sense of a continual and never-ending discovery of new heights and depths of God's infinite love and beauty, a constantly deeper penetration into his inexhaustible riches. God is the one who is known as ever ancient and ever new, and his newness, which can never be exhausted, will for all eternity provide an excitement of new discovery that goes beyond all human powers to understand. The vocation of the Christian to be caught up in a "new creation" (cf. 2 Co 5:17; Ga 6:15) will lead to an eternal discovery of the absolute newness that is God.

Notes

1. Trans. Leif Sjöberg and W. H. Auden (New York: Alfred A. Knopf, 1965).
2. Cf. *Homo Viator*, trans. Emma Crauford (New York: Harper Torchbooks, 1962), p. 66.
3. Jean Mouroux tells us in the foreword to his book which explores the problem of time that this book grew out of an attempt to examine the meaning of hope, because, as he says, "I found myself running into the problem of time at every turn." Cf. *The Mystery of Time*, trans. John Drury (New York: Desclee Co., 1964), p. 1. See also Gabriel Marcel, *Homo Viator*, p. 53.
4. Trans. Bernard Wall (New York: Harper and Brothers, 1960), pp. 135-136.
5. *Existentialism*, trans. Bernard Frechtman (New York: Philosophical Library, 1957), p. 19.
6. Cf. Jacques Maritain, *On the Philosophy of History*, ed. Joseph W. Evans (New York: Charles Scribner's Sons, 1957), pp. 43-59, 132-140.
7. Maritain, ibid., p. 55.
8. "On the Theology of Hope," *Theological Investigations*, X, trans. David Bourke (London: Darton, Longman & Todd, 1973), 258.

Bibliography

Chapter 7 of the *Constitution on the Church* is the primary source for reflection on the pilgrim character of the Christian life. The riches of this chapter are brought out in commentaries already mentioned in the bibliographies of chapters 2 and 9.

In Germany, following the spark struck by the Marxist, Ernst Bloch, a Protestant theologian, Jürgen Moltmann produced a major work on Christian hope: *The Theology of Hope*, trans. James W. Leitch (New York: Harper and Row, 1967). Catholic theologians have also done significant work in this field. See, for example, the second part of *Theology of the World*, trans. William Glen-Doepel (New York: Herder and Herder, 1969) by Johannes Metz.

The literature on the philosophy and the theology of hope which has appeared in recent times is immense, and it is difficult to be selective. For an existential view of this question we recommend Gabriel Marcel's *Homo Viator*, trans. Emma Craufurd (New York: Harper Torchbooks, 1962). Of special interest is the second essay entitled "Sketch of a Phenomenology and a Metaphysic of Hope." The work of Gerald O'Collins, *Man and His New Hopes* (New York: Herder and Herder, 1969) is a relatively small and a very readable book, and it is of special interest because of its comparison of Christian hope with Marxist hope. Volume 59 of *Concilium* is completely devoted to articles on various aspects of the problem of hope: *Dimensions of Spirituality*, ed. Christian Duquoc (New York: Herder and Herder, 1970). Several journals have dedicated special issues to this question, e.g. *Cross Currents*, XVIII (Summer 1968), and *The Way*, VIII (October 1968).

Part VI

FULFILLMENT

CHAPTER SIXTEEN

THE MYSTERY OF CHRIST

THE GOAL OF PILGRIMAGE is Christian fulfillment. Two questions may be raised concerning the fulfillment of the Christian life. One is: what is it that brings the individual Christian to full stature; in what specifically and essentially does his fulfillment consist? The second is: how is the total Christ brought to full stature; in what sense can we speak of the fullness not only of the individual Christian, but of Christ himself? These two questions are distinct, but the first cannot be adequately answered except in relation to the second. St. Paul suggests this when he writes to the Church at Ephesus: "In this way we are all to come to unity in our faith and in our knowledge of the Son of God, until we become the perfect Man, fully mature with the fullness of Christ himself" (4:13).

The first question is related to what has traditionally been considered the central problem in spiritual theology: in what essentially does Christian perfection consist? It is interesting to note in this connection that words and phrases like "perfection" and "striving for perfection," which were for centuries the most commonly used terms in spiritual writings, have suffered a sharp decline in popularity since the Council and are now encountered only rarely. There are no good objective reasons for this. For, besides the fact that the Council employed these terms in a number of texts, (cf. e.g., C 11f; 39b; 40a,c; 42b,h), they have good scriptural warrants. The Bible speaks at least forty-two times of "perfection" and "the perfect" (cf. e.g., Mt 5:48; 19:21; 1 Co 13:10; Col. 1:28). Even though the most direct and most literal translation of Matthew 5:48 is: "You must be perfect as your heavenly Father is perfect," the *New English Bible* seems to go out of its way to avoid using the term "perfect"; its rendering of this text is: "There must be no limit to your goodness, as your heavenly Father's goodness knows no bounds."

We are faced here with a problem frequently encountered in spiritual ecology: the waxing and waning of the popularity of certain words and phrases, the subtle change that take place in their connotations and resonances. The term "devotion," from the Latin word "*devotio*," had a long and highly respected history in Christian spirituality; it was one of those "classical" terms that stood strong and firm for many centuries. Today it has, generally speaking, lost respect. The term "merit" was for a long time frequently used in spiritual literature; today it is practically never mentioned. When words like these walk onto the stage of our minds, there are Greek choruses singing offstage of all the associations, all the subtle nuances of meaning these words have picked up along the way of their use over a period of time. Something like this has been happening to the term "perfection." It would be tangential to our main line of thought to try to diagnose this phenomenon. I propose, rather, to summarize briefly traditional doctrine on the nature of Christian perfection or fulfillment, and then show how this doctrine fits into the larger question of the fullness of Christ.

In the first question we are dealing with Christian perfection and fulfillment in this life. In asking this question we have to keep two things in mind: first, absolute perfection and fulfillment are found only in Christ; and second, though all Christians are called to achieve perfection, in this life there is no one univocal and definitive degree of perfection to which all are called and which all must attain in order to achieve holiness. Up to the moment of death, sanctity always remains progressive and therefore relative. The question is therefore: what is the measure, the norm, the criterion according to which the life of a Christian is to be judged more or less holy, and therefore more or less fulfilled?

The constant teaching of the Church and of theologians has been that the supernatural love of God and neighbor constitutes the essence of holiness and of Christian fulfillment (cf. C 42a). This love is the principal and formal element of sanctity from which must spring all the other elements which go to make up the fullness of the Christian life. The perfectly fulfilled Christian is a great lover who loves with that unique and absolutely selfless kind of love which is proper to God, the love that springs from the inner life of the Trinity and that is communicated to the Christian by Jesus through the Spirit.

Scripture leaves little doubt on this point. After stating the

commandments of love, Jesus tells us: "On these two commandments hang the whole Law, and the Prophets also" (Mt 22:40).
St. Paul, writing to the Colossians, declares: "You are God's
chosen race, his saints; he loves you, and you should be clothed
in sincere compassion, in kindness and humility, gentleness
and patience. . . . Over all these clothes, to keep them together
and complete them, put on love" (3:12-14). Paul tells the Romans
that love is "the answer to every one of the commandments"
(13:10). Chapter thirteen of the first letter to the Corinthians
is an almost ecstatic hymn to the primacy of love in Christian
holiness. In reading this chapter St. Theresa of the Child Jesus
discovered her vocation to be love at the heart of the Church.
St. John in particular teaches that Christian fulfillment consists
in love. In his first letter he writes: "God is love and anyone
who lives in love lives in God, and God lives in him" (4:16).
Love means an affective union between the lover and the person
loved, in such a way that the beloved is in the lover and is
transformed into him or her, to become "another self." This
transforming union depends, of course, upon the nature and
intensity of the love. When it is a question of divine love,
the transforming power is beyond all limits. "Anyone who
is joined to the Lord is one spirit with him" (1 Co 6:17).

Although supernatural love is the essential element in holiness, it is not the only virtue required for Christian fulfillment.
For sanctity to be whole and complete all the other virtues
must also be present as integral parts of holiness (cf. C 40b).
But all the other virtues are Christian only in the measure
in which they are inspired, motivated, and directed by love;
only then are they integral parts of Christian fulfillment.

The various counsels may be considered accessory and instru-
mental elements in Christian holiness. Some of these, such
as fasting, are mentioned in Scripture; others come to us from
direct inspiration of the Holy Spirit. In the Council there was
much discussion in connection with chapters 5 and 6 of the
Church Constitution, concerning the ambiguities found in the
expression "the evangelical counsels." For centuries this expression has been taken to mean the counsels of poverty, chastity, and obedience, to which religious bind themselves by
vows. On the one hand, a number of other counsels are found
in the gospels, such as almsgiving, and are therefore evangelical. Indeed, some of these other counsels, are found more
explicitly than some of the so-called "evangelical counsels."
On the other hand, most theologians teach that of the three

so-called "evangelical counsels" only celibacy is explicitly stated in Scripture. There is no clear textual statement regarding obedience, and most scholars take the text (Mt 19:21) in which Christ invites the rich young man to sell all he has for the benefit of the poor, as only an invitation to join Christ's immediate disciples. For counsels to exist in Scripture, however, it is not necessary that there be explicit texts. That is why, at the beginning of the chapter on religious in the *Church Constitution,* there is the general statement that the three evangelical counsels "are *based* upon the words and example of the Lord" (43a).

Another complication which caused difficulty in the Council's discussions is that the so-called evangelical counsels, which have been considered to characterize the religious life, are really an invitation to all Christians and not merely to those who have been given the special charism of a religious vocation, at least if we do not restrict chastity to that particular form synonymous with virginity or celibacy. Moreover, there is a sense in which chastity, poverty, and obedience are not simply counsels but precepts, since all Christians are in some way bound to be chaste, poor, and obedient according to their state in life.

Christian perfection consists in the fulfillment of the precepts and not essentially in the fulfillment of the counsels. We have precepts from Scripture telling us that we have to be perfect as our heavenly Father is perfect, and that we must love the Lord our God with our whole heart. Theoretically, therefore, the counsels do not have to be followed in order to attain sanctity. In practice, however, the counsels, whether they are recommended by Scripture or by special promptings of the Holy Spirit, are a particular invitation of the Lord and a concrete manifestation of God's will, and they cannot be ignored if there is to be continued progress toward fulfillment.

Since holiness is a matter of precept, there is a real obligation on the part of everyone, and not just religious, to tend constantly toward Christian perfection (cf. C 42h). The Christian may not freely choose not to be fulfilled. Fulfillment is a Christian imperative. Christ was speaking to everyone when he said: "You must therefore be perfect just as your heavenly Father is perfect" (Mt 5:48). St. Paul tells us that we have been chosen before the world began to be holy and spotless (Ep 1:4); and Peter instructs us: "Be holy in all you do, since it is the Holy One who has called you, and scripture says: Be holy, for I am holy" (1 P 1:15).

The Greek word used in Scripture for the term "perfect" is *teleios*, which is derived from the word for end, *telos*. *Teleios* means being brought to full development and full maturity through the achievement of one's purpose or goal in life. Actually, *telos* has a double meaning: it means both an end in the sense of a terminus, and also a goal and a fulfillment. The Christian is not only invited but obliged to make the two coincide in his or her life, so that when death comes he or she will have fully achieved the Christian goal, which is perfection, the fullness of love. To reach the *telos*, the end, without being *teleios*, perfect, is the great Christian tragedy.

One of the possible reasons why the term "perfection" has fallen out of favor is that it seems to suggest a self-regarding and individualistic kind of spirituality. Actually, it signifies just the opposite; it stands for a great capacity for altruistic love and therefore a great capacity for self-giving. Christian maturity, which is another word for perfection or fulfillment, is similar to personal maturity on the natural level. The best measure of personal maturity is likewise a great capacity for selfless love. The ideal fulfillment in the Christian life is that both kinds of maturity be found together, so that the Christian person is brought to fulfillment both as a person and as a Christian.

The source of holiness in Christian life and action is the very holiness of God, infused into us principally through baptism, confirmation, and the other sacraments. In baptism we are given a real share in the inner life of the all holy God, through sanctifying grace, the infusion of the theological and moral virtues, and the gifts of the Holy Spirit. We grow in holiness and in Christian fulfillment in the measure in which the divine life within us takes fuller possession of us through growth in charity principally, and in the other virtues secondarily. Speaking of Jesus, St. Paul writes to the Colossians that "God wanted all perfection to be found in him," that "in his body lives the fulness of divinity, and in him you too find your own fulfillment" (1:19; 2:9). In other words, Christian fulfillment consists in participating in what St. Paul calls the fullness of Christ, *pleroma Christi*. (cf. e.g., Ep. 1:9-10; 20-23; Col 1:15-20; 2:9-10). But before attempting to explore the implications of Christ's *pleroma** for Christian fulfill-

---

*The Greek word *pleroma* meaning fullness has been taken over into the vernacular by some authors, especially Teilhard de Chardin, in whose writings it plays an important role.

ment, we must reflect on a closely related theme in St. Paul: the Mystery of Christ.

*   *   *

This theme is so central in the whole of Pauline theology that it has sometimes been called the gospel of St. Paul. He speaks of it in a few texts in his early letters (Rm 16:25; 1 Co 2:7-10), but it is especially in the captivity letters that it emerges into full light. (cf. Ep 1:3-14; 3:3-10; Col 1:24-28; 2:2-3). St. Paul sometimes uses the plural term "mysteries" (cf. e.g. 1 Co 4:1), but the Mystery of Christ is the all-embracing mystery which includes the others.

In ancient times the term "mystery," when used in relation to religious experience, had two meanings: either some sort of secret rite in which only the initiated could participate, or some kind of gnosis or esoteric doctrine whose meaning was unveiled only for an elite. But, as Louis Bouyer has pointed out, the Mystery of Christ of which St. Paul speaks is something essentially different.

> ... the Christian mystery, when it makes its first appearance, is not at all a secret rite. Nor is it an idea unveiled for an elite, but a design of God inaccessible to any creature as long as God Himself has not revealed it to the world and its powers. It is a fact, an historical event, in which human history reaches its summit. It is a unique fact in which God himself takes that history back into His hands while He himself descends into it.[1]

A mystery, Gabriel Marcel tells us, is not the same as a problem.[2] In a problem there is something hidden, as in a mathematical problem, for example—but once the solution has been reached, the hiddenness vanishes; once solved the problem disappears. A mystery, in the sense in which it is used by St. Paul, is something that will always remain unfathomable to the human mind. It can to a certain extent be revealed, but the more one succeeds in penetrating its meaning, the more mysterious it becomes, because the revelation opens up further reaches of hiddenness beyond. A mystery, unlike a problem, can never be fully solved by the human mind; involving the infinite, it goes beyond what the human mind can ever fully grasp. A mystery is unfathomable because it involves a light, an intelligibility which is too bright for the limited gaze of the human mind, and which will therefore ever remain incapable of being fully grasped or expressed. Even in the beatific vision the Mystery of Christ will never be fully fathomed.

This Mystery is the eternal plan of the Father to reveal and communicate himself and his divine love through the incarnation of Jesus in human flesh and history, and through his death and resurrection, and thus to draw all people, all reality, and all history to himself, by recapitulating all things in Christ. It is the mystery of God's gratuitous and unfathomable love revealed in Christ Jesus, the whole loving plan surrounding this self-gift of God to us, and the gradual and progressive unfolding of this plan in history.

At the heart of the Mystery of Christ is the mystery of the Church, the Body of the Lord, in and through which the eternal plan continues to unfold in time (cf. Col 1:24-27). In and through the Church the mystery kept hidden since the foundation of the world continues to be revealed to people of all times and all cultures. Through the Church the great events of the incarnation and the redemption are prolonged across time and space. In the Church Christ continues the self-revelation and self-communication of the Father. The Church makes it possible for people of every age and culture to become one "in Christ Jesus" by being fashioned into a community which is an anticipation of the community of love in heaven.

We have said that the Pauline mystery differs essentially from the pagan mystery religions because for the latter "what was mysterious about them and what had to remain so, was their rites,"[3] whereas the Mystery of Christ is the whole plan of God's loving design to save and sanctify all humankind in Christ Jesus. Yet, in its sacramental dimension, the Mystery of Christ finds expression in rite, without, however, becoming identified with it. For all sacramental existence and expression is bound up with rite, though not limited merely to it. In this connection, it is important to note that the basic insight which led to the liturgical renewal was, among other things, that the liturgical rites had taken on something of the false mysteriousness of the mystery religions, in the sense that their fundamental intelligibility had become obscured by opaque historical layers of archaic forms and expressions, which did, indeed, create for many an aura of mystery, but a false kind of mystery. At times this tended to create for many something which, to a degree at least, approached the kind of magic mentality found in the mystery religions. The great effort of the liturgical movement has been to strip away these layers of opaqueness, of hiddenness, of "mysteriousness," in order to allow the fundamental Mystery of Christ reflected and lived in the liturgy to shine forth in all its beauty. On the other hand, much of the freewheeling that has taken place in the liturgy since the Council (and contrary to its directives) has been inspired by a loss of the sense of mystery, and a false identification of mystery with irrelevance. The great Mystery of Christ can never be adequately realized in a "liturgy" whose forms and expressions are immediately intelligible and "relevant" simply because they are shallow and superficial.

Among the many mysteries that go to make up the all-embracing Mystery of Christ, the most important is the paschal mystery. Indeed, it may be truly said that the paschal mystery is the only mystery and that all others are expressions of it. Durrwell is quite correct in saying that "there is only one Christian feast, round which all the other feasts cluster—Easter. . . ."[4] The *Constitution on the Liturgy* emphasizes the same theme when it suggests that all the mysteries of the liturgy are paschal mysteries (cf. e.g., 10b; 61).

St. Paul constantly places the Cross at the center of the Mystery of Christ (cf. e.g., Col 1:19-20; 2:14; Ep 2:13-15). That is why he can say: "As for me, the only thing I can boast about is the cross of our Lord Jesus Christ, through whom the world is crucified to me, and I to the world" (Ga 6:14). The love which brings the Christian to his fulfillment must be what has been traditionally called *caritas crucifixa*, a crucified love.

In a number of texts, St. Paul identifies the Mystery of Christ as a mystery of wisdom. "It is all to bind you together in love and to stir your minds, so that your understanding may come to full development, until you really know God's secret in which all the jewels of wisdom and knowledge are hidden (Col 2:3; cf. 3:8-11). Because the Mystery finds its focal point, its fullest realization and expression, its highest point of intense concentration in the Cross, it is a mystery of wisdom which is folly to minds unenlightened by the blinding light of the secret (cf. 1 Co 1:21-25; 2:6-10).

Michel Quoist, in a prayer which he explicitly bases on St. Paul's text on the Mystery of Christ in the first chapter of Ephesians, combines the historical, the cosmic, the ecclesial, and the sapiential aspects of the Mystery:

I would like to rise very high, Lord;
Above my city,

Above the world,
Above time.
I would like to purify my glance and borrow your eyes.
I would then see the universe, humanity, history, as the Father sees
them.
I would see in the prodigious transformation of matter,
In the perpetual seething of life,
Your great Body that is born of the breath of the Spirit.
I would see the beautiful, the eternal thought of your Father's Love
taking form, step by step:
Everything summed up in you, things on earth and things in heaven.
And I would see that today, like yesterday, the most minute details
are part of it.
Every man in his place,
Every group
And every object.
I would see a factory, a theatre, a collective-bargaining session and
the construction of a fountain.
I would see a crowd of youngsters going to a dance,
A baby being born, and an old man dying.
I would see the tiniest particle of matter and the smallest throbbing
of life,
Love and hate,
Sin and grace.
Startled, I would understand that the great adventure of love, which
started at the beginning of the world, is unfolding before me,
The divine story which, according to your promise, will be completed
only in glory after the resurrection of the flesh,
When you will come before the Father, saying: All is accomplished.
I am Alpha and Omega, the Beginning and the End.
I would understand that everything is linked together,
That all is but a single movement of the whole of humanity and of
the whole universe toward the Trinity, in you, by you, Lord.
I would understand that nothing is secular, neither things, nor peo-
ple, nor events,
But that, on the contrary, everything has been made sacred in its
origin by God
And that everything must be consecrated by man, who has himself
been made divine.
I would understand that my life, an imperceptible breath in this
great whole,
Is an indispensable treasure in the Father's plan.
Then, falling on my knees, I would admire, Lord, the mystery of this
world
Which, in spite of the innumerable and hateful snags of sin,
Is a long throb of love towards Love eternal.

I would like to rise very high, Lord,
Above my city,
Above the world,
Above time.
I would like to purify my glance and borrow your eyes.[5]

Notes

1. *Rite and Man*, trans. M. Joseph Costelloe (Notre Dame, In.: Notre Dame University Press, 1963), pp. 139-140.

2. *Being and Having*, trans. Katherine Farrer (Westminster: Dacre Press, 1959), p. 100. See also *Creative Fidelity*, trans. Robert Rosthal (New York: Farrar, Straus and Co.), p. 152: "Here we observe something basic to my whole thought, namely, that mystery is not, as it is for the agnostic, construed as a lacuna in our knowledge, as a void to be filled, but rather as a certain plenitude. . . ."

3. Louis Bouyer, *The Meaning of Sacred Scripture*, trans. Mary Perkins Ryan (Notre Dame, In.: Notre Dame University Press, 1958), p. 175.

4. *In the Redeeming Christ*, trans. Rosemary Sheed (New York: Sheed and Ward, 1963), p. 257.

5. *Prayers*, trans. Agnes M. Forsyth and Anne Marie de Commaille (New York: Sheed and Ward, 1963), pp. 13-15.

Bibliography

Thomas Aquinas composed a special treatise on the question of Christian perfection just four years before he died: *De Perfectione Vitae Spiritualis*. The traditional works in spiritual theology usually give considerable attention to this problem. See, for example, Garrigou-Lagrange, *The Three Ages of the Interior Life*, trans. Sr. M. Timothea Doyle (St. Louis: B. Herder, 1948), chs. 8-13.

For the question of the Mystery of Christ, Claude Tresmontant's *St. Paul and the Mystery of Christ*, trans. Donald Attwater (New York: Harper Torchbooks, 1957) deserves favorable mention. Several books on the theology of St. Paul discuss his teaching on this topic: Lucien Cerfaux's *Christ in the Theology of St. Paul*, trans. Geoffrey Webb and Adrian Walker (New York: Herder and Herder, 1959) gives a competent analysis of Paul's doctrine in bk 3, "The Mystery of Christ." Fernand Prat in *The Theology of St. Paul*, trans. John L. Stoddard (Westminster: The Newman Bookshop, 1956) discusses this topic less extensively: cf. I, 308f., and II, 4 ff. and 383 ff. All commentaries on Ephesians and Colossians necessarily give an interpretation of the Mystery of Christ. A good example of a brief commentary can be found in *The Jerome Biblical Commentary* (Englewood Cliffs, N.J.: Prentice-Hall, 1968). A much fuller commentary is found in the two volume work on Ephesians by Markus Barth, XXXIV and XXXIVA in the *Anchor Bible* (Garden City, N.Y.: Doubleday, 1974). A scholarly treatment of this question is found in the article "Mystère dans la Bible" by K. Prümm in *Supplément au Dictionnaire de la Bible* (Paris: Librairie Letouzey & Ané, 1960), VI, especially 203-225.

CHAPTER SEVENTEEN

PLEROMA

IT IS IMPOSSIBLE TO GRASP the full scope and the deepest meaning of the Mystery of Christ without understanding what St. Paul calls the Pleroma, the fullness of Christ. The Pleroma has been called "the innermost depth of Paul's vision, the central statement of everything he wrote."[1] In its most complete and definitive form, the Pleroma is the final fulfillment of the Mystery of Christ. It is the total Christ totally fulfilled. Only in relation to the Pleroma of Christ can the individual Christian grasp the meaning and the full dimensions of his or her own personal fulfillment.

Because divinity in all its fullness dwelt in Jesus (cf. Col 2:9), he filled the whole of creation from the beginning. Since he was the Word of God, "all things in heaven and on earth . . . were created through him and for him" (Col 1:16). The entire cosmos from its first origins was filled with his creative presence, and he was the destiny of the whole cosmic process.

In the incarnation the fullness of divinity was united with the fullness of humanity, so that all fullness might reside in him. This fullness of humanity means several things. It means, first of all, that no one was ever so perfectly and so fully a man as he. The fullness of human life and its most perfect wholeness were present in him. No one was ever so perfectly whole as a human being; no one was ever so fully one with his environment. No one could ever achieve the full and intimate union of love with others which he achieved; no one was ever so fully one with the cosmic realities around him as he; no one ever entered so fully into the duration of time and realized in himself the meaning of its fullness. Moreover, his union with others was not limited to the relatively few persons who entered into the short span of his life on earth; it extended to the whole of humanity of all time, which he embraced in an intimate bond of love and sought to make of it his own Body. All of his actions flowed from this loving union, which inspired the act of universal redemption. He was intimately one not only with the cosmic realities which entered directly and immediately into his personal life on earth; from the beginning he laid claim to the fullness of the cosmos and planned a special transcendent destiny for it by making it the body of his Body. Similarly, not only the thirty-three years of time that measured his existence on earth were his; he made the whole of time and the fullness thereof his own.

Through his resurrection he achieved the fullness of his status as Son of God, and in achieving this fullness he communicated it to his environment. He became the head of a humanity destined to share his glorification. He drew this humanity more fully to himself, made it his own Body, and communicated his fullness to it, so that it could now become his fullness; through his Spirit, he already gave it the first fruits of the eventual sharing in his glorification. He became in a new and fuller sense the head of the universe. Drawing it definitively to himself as the body of his Body, he recapitulated the whole of creation in himself and made it a "new creation." (cf. 2 Co 5:17). By bringing about a cosmic rebirth, he already established the magnetic force which would eventually draw the whole universe to its ultimate transfiguration. He directed time and history to carry ineluctably all mankind and the whole universe to the fullness of the Parousia. "Thus Christian history is a channelling of human riches towards our Lord, who is yet also their source."[2] Having received his fullness, his Body and its body would forever be "the total Christ." They would forever be the fullness of him who had shared his fullness with them, "the fullness of him who fills the whole creation" (Ep 1:23). "And when everything is subjected to him, then the Son himself will be subject in his turn to the One who subjected all things to him, so that God may be all in all" (1 Co 15:28). Christ the One and the created many are brought together and united in a whole which, while it cannot contribute any greater fullness to Christ, since he is in himself the absolute Pleroma, can serve to reveal this Pleroma in all its radiant perfection.

"In this way we are all to come to unity in our faith and in our knowledge of the Son of God, until we become the perfect Man, fully mature with the fullness of Christ himself" (Ep 4:13). Christians must see their fulfillment as a share in this fullness. "From his fullness we have, all of us, received" (Jn 1:16). "In his body lives the fullness of divinity, and in him you too find your own fulfillment, in the one who is head of every Sovereignty and Power" (Col 2:9).

Christian fulfillment is not according to the pattern of the Greek gentleman, who disciplines himself to achieve a perfect balance of the moral virtues, according to the principle *nihil nimis*, "nothing too much." The moral virtues do indeed need a measure, but not the virtue of love in which Christian perfection essentially consists. It has often been said that the only measure for love is to love without measure. Moreover, Christian fulfillment is not something that can be attained simply by self-discipline. It is a sheer gift of the fullness of Christ (cf. Ep 1:3-10; 4:12, 15-16). Only through perfectly altruistic love, which consists in sheer self-gift, can Christians enter fully into the Church and the new cosmos, which they are called to build, "so that the saints together make a unity in the work of service, building up the body of Christ" (Ep 4:12). Only in this way can they attain the gratuitous gift of the fullness of Christ (cf. Ep 3:16-19).

* * *

Wholeness and fullness have been one of the major themes of this book. I have repeatedly insisted that the wholeness of human persons depends upon their oneness with their environment, and, for want of a better word, I have frequently used the term "hyphenation" to signify this oneness. At the same time I have suggested that this oneness is far more profound than simply a union brought about by having something tacked on from the outside. Looking back from the vantage point at which we have now arrived, we are in a better position to grasp both the intimacy and the depth of the human person's union with his environment on both the natural and the supernatural levels, and thus to understand the meaning of Christian Pleroma.

On the natural level our union with others is something that affects our whole personhood profoundly. If there is no "I" in the full sense of the word without a "Thou," our relationship with others must be more profound than mere external associations. On the supernatural level our relationships with others go much deeper, far deeper than we can hope to understand. For who can really grasp the meaning of the oneness of Christians in the love of Jesus? Who can explain the intimacy of a union that partakes of the ineffable intimacy of the union between the persons of the Trinity?

We have already reflected in a general way on the notion of the sacramental character of the Church as found in the *Church Constitution*. But there is one important aspect of this notion which must be brought into clear focus in this context. The *Constitution* speaks of the Church as "a kind of sacrament or sign of intimate union with God, and of the unity of all mankind," and also as a causal sign, as "an instrument for the achievement of such union and unity" (1b; cf. 9f; 48b). The Church as a sacrament not just in relation to Christ but also in relation to the world, a causal sign of the communion of all mankind in and through its union with Jesus, appears as something relatively novel in the official teaching of the Church. Schillebeeckx considers this notion of the Church as the sacrament of the world to be "one of the most charismatically inspired texts of the Council."[3] Upon this notion the Council based a great deal of what it had to say about the role of the Church in the world. Indeed, it considered this notion so important that it repeated it again in the *Pastoral Constitution* (42c-d).

The Church "is the momentous visible form or meaningful presence in this world of an already accomplished communion of men."[4] It is constantly at work to be a causal sign of intimate union not only for its members, but also for all humankind. Its work is not only to draw its own members into an ever more intimate union in Christ Jesus, but also to draw all humankind, by every means possible, into some degree of sharing in the communion which the Church itself signifies. Cosmic time is given to the Church by Christ so that it may gradually draw the whole of humankind into that state of union which has been predetermined in the eternal plan of the Father. Cosmic time will continue to be given to it until the last of the elect will have been prepared for the eternal communion which is the society of the blessed. Then God's loving purpose for the Church and the world will have been fully realized. The Pleroma of Christ will be finally complete. The Parousia will take place. The Church and the world will be definitively transfigured with the glory of the Son of God.

Teilhard de Chardin, fascinated by Paul's doctrine of the Mystery of Christ and the Pleroma, constantly dreamed of Christian fulfillment in terms of an eternal communion of love.

Across the immensity of time and the disconcerting multiplicity of individuals, one single operation is taking place: the annexation to Christ of His chosen .... To what power is it reserved to burst asunder the envelope in which our individual microcosms tend jealously to isolate themselves and vegetate? To what force is it given to merge and exalt our partial rays into the principal radiance of Christ? To charity, the beginning and the end of all spiritual relationships. Christian charity, which is preached so fervently by the Gospels, is nothing else than the more or less conscious cohesion of souls, engendered by their communal convergence *in Christo Jesu.* . . . *Jesus, Saviour of human activity to which you have given meaning, Saviour of human suffering to which You have given living value, be also the Saviour of human unity; compel us to discard our pettinesses, and to venture forth, resting upon You, into the uncharted ocean of charity.*[5]

*   *   *

In speaking of the Christian's oneness with the universe I have already pointed out that the continuity between the human person and his cosmic environment is such that it is impossible, even for science, to draw a clear line where one ends and the other begins. But, as Karl Rahner has pointed out, the union between the two is much more profound than this.

For the soul, as united to the body, must also have some relationship to the "whole" of which the body is a part, that is, to that wholeness which constitutes the unity of the material universe. . . . Yet it is impossible . . . to penetrate the problem of this real ontological unity of the universe. . . . that basic oneness of the world, so difficult to grasp, yet so very real, by which all things in the world are related and communicate anteriorly to any mutual influence upon each other.[6]

Even on the purely natural level we already have an intimation that the human person must have a supra-individual destiny, that "the extra-human world also takes part in the end-events," and "that man and the material world form a one-destiny community."[7]

Creation was never viewed in the Old Testament simply as a past event but rather as the beginning of God's powerful activity which would continue to lead his people and humankind towards their destiny. From the beginning, the destiny of the world was bound up with the destiny of the human person. The cosmos shared in his fall; the earth was cursed because of his sin (Gn 3:17). Having shared in his fall, the universe was destined to share also in his redemption. As Marcus Loane has pointed out, there is a striking parallel between the first three chapters of Genesis and the last three chapters of Revelation.[8] In the beginning is the garden of paradise (Gn 2:8-9) in which the trees, including the tree of life, are watered by the rivers that flow through it (Gn 2:9-14). Because of sin, Adam and Eve were banished from the garden and kept from returning to it by the angel's flaming sword. But because Christ sheathed that flaming sword in his own body,[9] the Bible can end with a vision of the "new creation" in the form of a garden city, where the trees of life, whose leaves are the healing of the nations, are watered by a crystal-clear river (Rv 22:1-2). Here the God who walked in the original garden in the cool of the evening, and from whose presence Adam and Eve hid their faces (Gn 3:8-9), is now seen face to face (Rv 22:4). The ban is lifted (Rv 22:3); never again will the earth be cursed. On the contrary, it will share in the redemption of sinful humanity; it will have a part in the ultimate glorification. Both humanity and the universe will constitute the "new creation" (cf. Rv 21:1-5). In the womb of the earth is the dust of the apostles, the martyrs, the virgins, the confessors—all the saints of the ages, except Mary. "From the beginning till now the entire creation, as we know, has been groaning in one great act of giving birth" (Rm 8:22). In that act of giving birth it will itself be reborn.

Karl Rahner writes:

> We Christians are . . . the most sublime of materialists. We neither can nor should conceive of any ultimate fullness of the spirit and of reality without thinking too of matter enduring as well in a state of final perfection. . . . We have so to love our own physicality and the worldly environment appropriate to it that we cannot reconcile ourselves as existing to all eternity otherwise than with the material side of our natures enduring too in a state of final perfection. . . . As materialists we are more crassly materialist than those who call themselves so. . . . We recognize and believe that this matter will last for ever, and be glorified for ever. . . . The Ascension is the festival of the true future of the world. . . . In this celebration we anticipate the festival of the universal and glorious transfiguration of the world which has already commenced, and which, since the Ascension, has been ripening and developing towards the point where it will become manifest.[10]

Only in the transfiguration of the world will the human person find the profound meaning of the headship of creation given to him in the beginning (Gn 1:28). This headship is so meaningful that the world must be made conformable to glorified humanity. Not only the hegemony of the human person over creation, but the hegemony of the Lord of the universe will be manifested in its fullest possible measure through the transfiguration of the cosmos. Only then will it be possible to understand fully the

meaning of Paul's statement that all things were created for him
(Col 1:16). Since Christ in the incarnation became fully conformed to the material universe, it is fitting that the material universe should become fully conformed to its glorified head. It is
fitting that he who "holds all things in unity" (Col 1:17) should
unite the multiplicity of creation, along with the whole of humanity, into that final Christian communion which is the Pleroma
of Christ. "Then will come the time of the restoration of all things"
(Acts 3:21). Then the human race as well as the entire world,
which is intimately related to man and achieves its purpose
through him, will be perfectly re-established in Christ (cf. Eph.
1:10; Col. 1:20; 2 Pet 3:10-13)" (C 48a). Only then will there be
the total Christ totally fulfilled. Only then will the Lord Jesus be
able to turn over to the Father a creation completely united and
fully perfected (cf. 1 Co 15:24), and creation will be elevated to a
participation in the triune life of God. The basic reason why
Christian spirituality cannot be genuinely other-worldly without
being this-worldly is that the ultimate Christian destiny is not
only other-worldly but also this-worldly—in such a way that the
two coincide.

Earlier I spoke of the interiority of God invading the exteriority and the materiality of the world through the liturgy. At the
end, the exteriority and the materiality of the world will invade
the interiority of God communicated to the society of the blessed.
In the beginning, the liturgy of heaven, though intimately united
with the liturgy of earth, differed radically from it because the
heavenly liturgy was purely spiritual. It began to change when
the body of the risen Lord and the body of Mary were drawn into
heaven to share in that liturgy, indeed to become a focal point of
it. The bodies of Jesus and Mary are the harbingers of the full
invasion of the bodies of the elect and the whole universe into the
liturgy of heaven. It is fitting that the human body and cosmic
reality which play such an important part in the liturgy of time
should also have a part in the liturgy of eternity. Then we shall
be able to grasp fully the implications in the phrase at the end of
the gospel of Mark about proclaiming the Good News to the *whole
of creation* (16:16).

Our vision of the Christian destiny of the world fulfilled in the
Pleroma of Christ should have an effect on the way we view and
relate to the material world in this life. The Christian who sees
the world in the perspective of the Pleroma can cry out with
Teilhard de Chardin:

Now the earth can certainly clasp me in her giant arms. She can swell me with her life, or draw me back into her dust. She can deck herself with every charm, with every horror, with every mystery. She can intoxicate me with her perfume of tangibility and unity. She can cast me to my knees in expectation of what is maturing in her breast.

But her enchantments can no longer do me harm since she has become for me, over and above herself, the body of Him who is and of Him who is coming.[11]

*   *   *

Finally, there is the question of time and history. Here again the term "hyphenation" fails to express the profound way in which they enter into the very depth of the being of the human person. They are not like some kind of external vehicle which carries him along ceaselessly. They enter profoundly into his very existence and make it so thoroughly fluid that he can continue in being only in a successive stream of instants. On the supernatural level the inadequacy of the term "hyphenation" is even greater. Salvation and sanctification depend essentially upon time, upon saving and sanctifying historical events. Moreover, the whole Christian meaning of life derives from being caught up in the Mystery of Christ, the plan of God that fullfills itself in time and history, the plan whose every instant of slow, successive unfolding coincides with the eternal moment of its conception, the plan for the whole evolution of the history of the world until it finally reaches its metahistorical goal in the Christ of the Parousia.

The evolution of the plan of the Father does not, of course, necessarily call for an evolutionary theory of the origin and development of the cosmos. Yet, the theory is now widely accepted that our world has gone through a long process of evolution, and there is no theological reason why the human person cannot be seen as having taken part in that evolution, provided allowance is made for a special intervention of God for the infusion of the spiritual soul in the emergence of the first human being, and also for the fact of original sin. Indeed, there is a certain attraction in seeing the lordship of Christ in terms of the whole process of the evolution of the world. This perspective gives a vast scope to the Mystery of Christ, who then becomes the point of convergence towards which all the movement of the universe has been tending as towards its final fulfillment right from the beginning.

In this vision we see the long period of millions of years of the maturation of the universe from the moment of its creation, from the first stirrings in matter, from the first amorphous and primitive beginnings, through the long tortuous upward movement to when it finally became capable of the first minimal spark of life. Then the further long process of maturation and slow upward movement during which this life evolved and gradually grew into higher and more perfect forms, until, after more millions of years, it was finally ready for the last preparation and the infusion of the spiritual soul by God. It would seem as though this process had reached its "omega point" in the human person, the king of the universe, the first Adam. But no; he was to have all his meaning, as we can see now, from the fact that he was only the *first* Adam, and thus just the beginning of another process, another long and arduous upward movement which finally came to the fine point of concentration when the second Adam issued from the chosen people. But this was still not the end. The incarnation was only in view of the redemption, the paschal mystery, in which Christ issued from his unglorified flesh into his glorified state, and the Church issued from Christ and started on its pilgrimage towards glorification. Then came the long process of centuries during which the glorified Christ, through the missionary, apostolic, and sacramental action of the Church, through the scientific, technical, and sociological achievements of human endeavor, and especially through charity in the world, has been gradually preparing souls, bodies, and the universe for their final glorification.

The most eloquent spokesman for this sweeping view of the Mystery of Christ is Teilhard de Chardin, for whom the whole long process of cosmogenesis eventually became a process of Christogenesis by which the evolution of the world converged ever more fully toward Christ, its Omega point, to be finally and fully achieved in the Parousia. As the Omega point, Christ alone gives meaning and intelligibility to the cosmos and the whole long process of its history. This is not the place to attempt an assessment of the doctrine of Teilhard de Chardin. The fact that we have quoted him on several occasions does not necessarily mean that we espouse everything in his writings. Nor is it necessary to subscribe to everything in his teachings to have a vision of the cosmic dimensions of the Mystery of Christ.[12]

Even apart from the doctrine of cosmic evolution the following lines of Teilhard may, with a few adjustments, be made appropriately descriptive of the evolution of the plan of the Father, in the sense of its gradual growth and unfolding throughout the centvries:

> From the commencement of things an Advent of ploughing and harvesting began, in the course of which, gently and lovingly, the determinisms reached out and moved towards the growing of a Fruit that was beyond hope and yet awaited. So harmoniously adapted and arranged that the Supreme Transcendent might seem to be engendered wholly of their immanence, the energies and substances of the world concentrated and purified themselves in the stem of Jesse, composing of their distilled and accumulated riches the sparkling jewel of Matter, the pearl of the Cosmos and its link with the personal, incarnate Absolute: the blessed Virgin Mary, Queen and Mother of all things, the true Demeter. . . .
>
> And since the time when Jesus was born, when He finished growing and died and rose again, *everything has continued to move because Christ has not yet completed His own forming.* He has not yet gathered into Himself the last folds of the Garment of flesh and love which His disciples are making for him. *The mystical Christ has not yet attained His full growth.* In the pursuance of this engendering is situated the ultimate spring of all created activity . . . Christ is the Fulfillment even of the natural evolution of beings. . . .
>
> Like a vast tide the Being will have dominated the trembling of all beings. The extraordinary adventure of the World will have ended in the bosom of a tranquil ocean, of which, however, each drop will still be conscious of being itself. The dream of every mystic will have found its full and proper fulfillment. *Erit in omnibus omnia Deus.*[13]

The risk which is the Christian life on earth will have come to an end. The splendor will go on forever.

Notes

1. "Introduction to the Letters of St. Paul," *The Jerusalem Bible*, ed. Alexander Jones et al. (Garden City, N.Y.: Doubleday, 1966), p. 262.

2. F. X. Durrwell, *The Resurrection*, trans. Rosemary Sheed (New York: Sheed and Ward, 1960), p. 227.

3. *World and Church*, trans. N. D. Smith (New York: Sheed and Ward, 1971), p. 91.

4. Ibid., p. 92.

5. *The Divine Milieu*, trans. Bernard Wall (New York: Harper and Brothers, 1960), pp. 124, 125, 128.

6. *On the Theology of Death*, trans. Charles H. Henky (New York: Herder and Herder, 1961), pp. 26-27. See also F. X. Durrwell, *The Resurrection*, pp. 272-273.

7. Leo Scheffczk, "The Meaning of Christ's Parousia for the Salvation of Man and the Cosmos," in *The Christian and the World* (New York: Kenedy, 1965), p. 135.

8. *The Hope of Glory* (London: Hodder and Stoughton, 1968), pp. 84-85.

9. *Cf.* ibid., p. 85.

10. "The Festival of the Future of the World," *Theological Investigations*, VII, trans. David Bourke (New York: Herder and Herder, 1971), 183-184.

11. *The Divine Milieu*, p. 138.

12. *Cf.* Karl Rahner, "Current Problems in Christology," *Theological Investigations*, I, trans. Cornelius Ernst (Baltimore: The Helicon Press, 1961), 165.

13. *The Future of* Man, trans. Norman Denny (New York: Harper and Row, 1964), pp. 305, 308. The Latin quotation of Teilhard (who made it a habit to quote Latin phrases without translating) refers to 1 Co 15:28: "God will be all in all."

Bibliography

Karl Rahner has a number of articles in *Theological Investigations* which are pertinent to the topic of this chapter. The following deserve particular mention: "The Resurrection of the Body," II, trans. Karl-H. Kruger (Baltimore: Helicon Press, 1963), 203-216; "The Festival of the Future of the World," VII, trans. David Bourke (New York: Herder and Herder, 1971) 181-185; "The Theological Problems entailed in the Idea of the 'New Earth'," X, trans. David Bourke (London: Darton, Longman and Todd, 1973) 260-272; and "Immanent and Transcendent Consummation of the World," ibid., 273-289. I have found the article of Leo Scheffczk, "The Meaning of Christ's Parousia for the Salvation of Man and the Cosmos," quite insightful. It is part of an anthology of contemporary theological writings entitled *The Christian and the World* (New York: Kenedy, 1965), pp. 130-157. Perhaps the best work on Teilhard de Chardin's ideas concerning the Mystery of Christ and the Pleroma is Christopher Mooney's *Teilhard de Chardin and the Mystery of Christ* (New York: Harper and Row, 1966).

For a discussion of the Pleroma of St. Paul, the sources, generally speaking, are the same as those indicated in the bibliography of the last chapter for the Pauline Mystery of Christ. The most erudite treatment I have come across is an article entitled "Plérome" by A. Feuillet in *Supplément au Dictionnaire de la Bible* (Paris: Letouzey & Ané, 1972), VIII, 18-39. Lucien Cerfaux has a briefer treatment in *Christ in the Theology of St. Paul*, trans. Geoffrey Webb and Adrian Walker (New York: Herder and Herder, 1962), "The Body of Christ and the Pleroma," pp. 462 ff. There is a good treatment of the question in an article entitled "Fulfilment," by J. Schildenberger in *Sacramentum Verbi*, ed. Johannes Bauer, (New York: Herder and Herder, 1970), I, 289-295.